General Methods of Effective Teaching

A PRACTICAL APPROACH

Crowell Series in American Education

James C. Stone, Advisory Editor for Education

General Methods of Effective Teaching

A PRACTICAL APPROACH

Joan M. Leonard

*Principal, Bay Ridge High School;
Former Instructor in Methods of Teaching
Science, St. Joseph's College.*

John J. Fallon

*Assistant Principal, Administration, New York City
Public Schools; Former Adjunct Lecturer in Education,
St. John's University and Instructor in Psychology,
Fordham University.*

Harold von Arx

*Adjunct Assistant Professor, Supervision of Student
Teachers, Pace College; Assistant Principal, Supervision
of English, New York City Public Schools.*

Thomas Y. Crowell Company

New York · Established 1834

Artwork by Vantage Art Inc.

L. C. Card 77-187601
ISBM 0-690-32283-6

Manufactured in the United States of America

I-QU-RK

Preface

This book is a practical text intended for use by students learning to be teachers; those enrolled in student–teaching programs and courses in education and methods; beginning teachers; and more experienced teachers who want to improve their techniques through professional institutes, workshops, and in-service and on-the-job training programs. It is predicated on the belief that teaching is an art involving certain learned skills and that, with knowledge of these skills, creative imagination, and talent, an individual can motivate others to learn.

The major thrust of the book, then, is the identification and illustration of the techniques and procedures that a teacher can use to increase his effectiveness and to help make the learning experience dynamic, meaningful, and relevant to today's student. The practical—the "how to"—approach is always used; real, workable methods are provided for actual classroom situations. Because each learning experience—based, as it is, on the interaction of individuals—is unique, teaching techniques must be modified to fit each situation and guidelines for such modification are provided. While the classroom concerns of the teacher receive major emphasis, his responsibility for activities such as homeroom and administrative assignments is also given full consideration. Because students are bombarded with dramatic and exciting learning experiences through the communications media, we have reached out beyond the school itself into the community to show teachers and prospective teachers how to use its resources. The scope of this involvement with the school and the community cannot be overlooked when discussing the total environment of today's teacher.

The material is divided into four parts: Part I defines teaching–learning interactions, analyzes the interrelated variables at work in an interaction, and describes how to plan for effective units and lessons; Part II provides practical procedures for identifying and organizing the components of a learning experience into a dynamic teaching–learning interaction; Part III explores types of lessons that will increase the degree of student involvement in learning; Part IV looks at the important non-teaching assignments which teachers are given, investigates the rapidly expanding role of auxiliary personnel, and examines the need for continuous professional development.

The chapters in each part have been organized around questions a teacher might ask about a technique or activity: What? Why? When? Where? Who? How? Some chapters deal with things—the things a teacher should learn to handle skillfully: models, charts, specimens, projectors, tapes, and the chalkboard. Many chapters deal with the techniques of teaching: motivating, questioning, planning, using audio-visual aids, and evaluating both the students' performance and the teacher's effectiveness. All chapters deal with people: the teacher, the students, and those people who can be drawn upon to expand and enrich teaching–learning interactions. The problems and activities presented at the end of each chapter are concerned with challenging the student or teacher using this book to bring his special insights to bear on real situations that he will encounter.

The authors hope that this book will aid the prospective, the new, and the growing teacher in learning to plan so that he can teach with confidence both the well motivated, adjusted student and the disenchanted, disaffected students who are all-too-frequently found in today's classrooms. The techniques, methods, and procedures described here will open the door to the adventure of working with young people, and the experiences, ingenuity, sensitivity, and scholarship of each individual will carry him on.

We wish to thank James Bergin, Herman Makler, and Catherine Wilson, of the Thomas Y. Crowell Company, not only for their encouragement and assistance, but also for their recognition of the value of the practical approach in teaching.

Contents

PART ONE

INTERACTION: KEY TO EFFECTIVE TEACHING

PART TWO

THE DAILY LESSON: A MODERN PERSPECTIVE

ix

PART THREE

THE EXPANDED CLASSROOM: INCREASING STUDENT INVOLVEMENT

List of Figures

Interaction: Key to Effective Teaching

1
Lessons as Teaching–Learning Interactions

WHAT IS A LESSON?

A lesson, in the traditional or classical sense of the word, has been defined as an activity in which a teacher actively dispensed, and students passively received, information. The student was most often seen but not heard. This methodology may have been valid in the days when a teacher was the only—or one of the very few—sources of information available to students, but as communications methods have improved, they have found that they can secure more information themselves. Today's student has come to rely less on his instructor, for with the mushrooming of radio, movies, and television, he can hear and see historic, scientific, and artistic events as they occur.

> He has seen men step out of the lunar excursion module "Tranquility Base" and walk on the moon.
>
> He has witnessed the inauguration of a president and the coronation of a queen.
>
> He has traveled to the Antarctic, the Olympic games, and even to the environs of the planet Mars.

Students are literally drowning in this sea of information. Daily they receive more varied data than any teacher can ever hope to provide in the same time period.

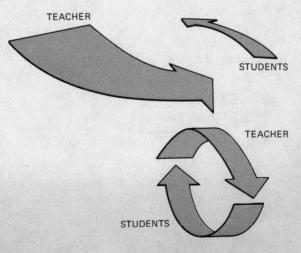

TEACHER

STUDENTS

FIGURE 1.1
Teacher domination

TEACHER

STUDENTS

FIGURE 1.2
Interaction

3

The role of the teacher then has changed from that of an information dispenser to that of one who develops the skills and techniques of learning. The character of the lesson has also changed from a unidirectional activity (teacher to students) to a dynamic interaction in which both teacher and students play active roles. The teacher can no longer merely furnish facts; he must:

Teacher roles

Focus attention on problems for investigation

Introduce the skills required in investigations

Help develop and sharpen the student's abilities in critical thinking, reasoning capability, and creative expression

Encourage a spirit of self-motivation in the student that will help him continue the learning process throughout his life

Good teachers—effective teachers—have always had these as their major objectives. Their techniques and approaches depended on the exigencies of their day, but the best have always been alert, adaptable, and aware of their students as individuals. Awareness and adaptability are still needed today.

The student's role has changed too. In contrast to his predecessors, today's student brings to each class session not only more information, but also a broader experiential background than ever before. Because of this broader spectrum of experience, the student needs, more than ever before, programs which will help him learn the techniques of learning—the skills of listening, reading, and critically evaluating all he has experienced. Students and the teacher together must devote their energies to learning how to:

Techniques of learning

Investigate causes and interrelationships of variables in a problem or question

Apply reasoning and creative ability to former knowledge and new situations

Organize the multiplicity of experience into some coherent unity

Within this framework of new student and teacher roles, a lesson can become a learning experience where ideas are exchanged and explored, data critically examined and correlated, and generalizations developed and validated. Such a lesson can significantly be termed a *teaching–learning interaction*—a give and take activity in which all participants are actively involved.

FIGURE 1.3
Lessons are interactions

Today in an atmosphere of computerized, compartmentalized learning involving sophisticated hardware, texts, and learning aids, it is more important than ever before that teachers clearly understand

their role in a teaching–learning interaction and accept the need for vitalized, dynamic, and relevant lessons.

WHAT ARE THE VARIABLES IN A TEACHING–LEARNING INTERACTION?

Every lesson should be examined in terms of the variables at work in it including:

You, the teacher, and the students	The Who Variables	*Interaction variables*
The purpose of the lesson	The Why Variable	
The subject matter or content	The What Variable	
The setting and atmosphere	The When and Where Variables	
The procedures and techniques	The How Variable	

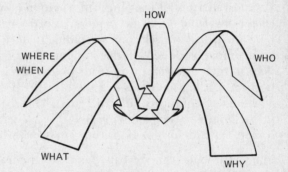

HOW

WHERE
WHEN

WHO

WHAT

WHY

FIGURE 1.4
Dynamics of interactions

Although each of these variables can be examined as separate factors, they are all irrevocably and dynamically bound together in any complete lesson and each has a significant impact on all of the others. The way in which you, the teacher, facilitate the interaction by recognizing and using all the different variables is a key factor in helping to make a lesson a productive, meaningful experience.

The Who Variables

Your students and you, the teacher, are the two major "who" inputs in teaching–learning interactions, and you must all be active participants—both givers and takers—to make a lesson an interaction. *The who variables*

The first who variable. To make full use of all the resources available, and to help insure maximum student involvement you should consider the following factors.

1. *All of the students in any one of your classes do not have the same general characteristics.* There is no one "typical" student. Each student brings to an interaction experiences and skills unique to him as an individual. He may have had some content exposure in previous classes in your subject area. Some students are better prepared or more interested in your subject than are others. Each student has had many learning experiences through mass media, job situations, and roles in his family and community. Some may have hobbies or other school experiences related to a particular area in your field. Some may have done extensive reading in your subject. These are resources of experience and skills that cannot be ignored or minimized.

The who variables

Other students in the same class may be equally uninformed, unskilled, or uninterested in your subject. To them everything is new, not always comprehensible or relevant. Your job will be to motivate, interest, and actively involve both of these extremes of the experience spectrum, as well as those whose interests and abilities lie between these extremes.

2. *Each student when he reaches your class has attained some definable reading level.* Lack of ability in reading will hamper his progress in virtually all areas of learning. Information about a student's reading level is available on his permanent record, or it can be secured from his counselor. Your selection of reading materials and assignments for a class must be done with the student's reading level in mind. A student in the tenth year, who reads on the seventh year level, and who is given reading materials designed for the twelfth year, will be overwhelmed, discouraged, and frustrated. This reaction will be expressed in his limited participation in class work, general lack of interest, and sometimes rude or emotional outbursts in the classroom.

Many students can verbally express themselves fairly well, can respond to your questions with ease, and yet have a reading problem. They may do poorly on written exams and papers where the emphasis is on reading and following written instructions.

Use the technique of supervised study to help your students with reading difficulties. Discuss individual problems with guidance counselors and reading specialists for remedial help.

You may have little to say about the text you use in a class and it may be the only one currently available to you. If this is the case, keep on the alert for some substitute but more readable materials, but don't use new materials before you have really explored them. Read new materials yourself to see if they fit the needs of your program.

When you find materials that are really tailored to the abilities of your students and the needs of your program, bring them to the attention of your department chairman or assistant principal. You might suggest that a portion of a department conference or a workshop session be devoted to a discussion of the merits of this material.

Above all, be realistic. Get to know the reading levels of your students as quickly as possible; work with the materials you have available; and search for more appropriate materials.

3. *A student may have a hearing deficiency, vision problem, or other physical handicap which can hamper his participation in class work, discussions, or laboratory work.* You can check the health record of any student who appears to have hearing or vision problems. Grade advisors, guidance counselors, or the school nurse can give you additional insight. Sight and hearing deficiencies can have far-reaching effects on the student's achievement. Some students may have to be referred for medical assistance or financial aid in getting hearing aids, or glasses. Seat these students in the front of the room, or in some central location. If during the semester you think a change in seating is advisable, make the change simply and quietly. Speak to the students involved before or after a class, and let the new seating arrangement take effect the next school day.

The who variables

Ask your chairman or assistant principal what method is followed in alerting teachers to those students who suffer from epileptic seizures or who might require any special assistance in an emergency. This information is always kept strictly confidential, but is of great value in helping you meet situations with tact and confidence.

4. *There are other medical and psychological problems which you must face; a student may be drinking, smoking pot, or taking "pills."* This is a problem that you should not undertake to solve alone, thereby depriving you and your students of more specialized assistance. If you notice changes in behavior, drowsiness, general lack of interest, or unusual behavior in a student, you can discuss the current status of his work with him, and try to get some insight into the reasons for his behavior. Talk to the school nurse, the attendance coordinator, and his other teachers to obtain a broader picture of the student; define the problem not only in terms of your subject area, but also keep the *whole* student in mind. What is happening to him and how can he be helped?

Conferences with him and with the other resource personnel including a drug coordinator might be in order. This is not designed to cross-question the student, intimidate him, or alienate him. Your role may be only to bring the student and the best resource people together, and then offer realistic support and encouragement. Using appropriate personnel is not "passing the buck," but rather constructively helping the student.

5. *The specific time of day and the number of class periods preceding the one for your class can directly affect a student's level of participation and performance.* As a day unfolds, students tire. You do too. Even after a lunch break, both you and they may need some time to regain maximum efficiency. If this is the fourth or fifth class of your day, or if it is the seventh or eighth period of a student's day, the fatigue factor is a real one to face. A lesson that went well during Period 2 may not be workable Period 7. Your plans must be flexible and realistic. As a day moves on, you must reexamine your proposed lesson in terms of sharpening questions and reevaluating the progression of ideas for introduction in order to add variety and increase the clarity of your presentation.

The who variables Some degree of this period-to-period modification will always be necessary. No two classes are the same and questions that stimulate and challenge one group may fall flat with another. Remember, too, that you will be hearing the same material several times in one day, but the students are hearing it for the first time each period.

6. *Students may have after-school jobs or specific responsibilities at home that affect the time they devote to homework or independent study.* Jobs may be necessary for some students as they look forward to college — or simply to the senior prom. In real terms, something's got to give and sometimes it's the school work. You can usually obtain this information in an informal chat with the student. However, if outside work is seriously affecting the student's school work, you should discuss it with him on a more formal basis and help him establish a realistic time schedule in which he can do his work. Be sure to alert the grade advisors to these problems.

7. *Your students will have particular talents, abilities, and interest.* Some are gifted in sketching — they might design and prepare interesting charts and displays for use in class. These charts may not have all the professional touches of those you purchase, but they represent a real time and talent investment by a student. A contribution of this nature can't be purchased from any supply house; it is the kind of valuable resource you should try to add to your program.

However, do not permit a student's talents in one area to deprive him of learning the specific skills in another. A student's talent in sketching, for example, must not be allowed to compensate or substitute for a lack of ability to add or spell.

8. *Some students come to your subject voluntarily, others because they are required to do so.* Most students are in the latter category in the elementary grades and the beginning years of high school. This makes for quite a spectrum of interest range in your class. Some students come to a class with preconceived ideas about your subject. They are predisposed to like it or not to like it. You may occasionally find yourself dealing with the unsuccessful achievement, not of that student, but of his brother or sister in another class the previous year.

Not all students will want to major in your field. Some will want to. Your job is to provide meaningful learning experiences for both groups of students, so that each will come away with a feeling of accomplishment, and the knowledge that they have added to their intellectual development.

9. *Sometimes an event which precedes your class may have a significant impact on your students.* You should recognize this impact and be prepared to capitalize on these ready-made motivations. For example, after an Afro-American assembly program, the English teacher might incorporate into that day's lesson some of the themes and content of that assembly. He might use some of the works of the black poets featured in the program. This, of course, calls for a high degree of awareness, flexibility, and scholarship.

The who variables

There may be other school events which upset the students and prevent them from focusing on the work of a class. Perhaps a fire drill had to be repeated because student response was poor. A field trip in another class may have been canceled. Students may enter your class frustrated and angry because they have been disappointed or feel their time was wasted.

These events do affect students and, consequently, your lessons. If the matter seems serious, then you might have to discuss it with the entire class. If the matter is simply one of clarification and definition, then try to provide them. Do not, however, fall into the trap of just socializing or commiserating about a problem. Constructively discuss problems, but don't share ignorance. You may feel that a question should be thoroughly discussed after a period of fact-finding and research.

You should be aware of all these real but sometimes intangible factors affecting a student's achievement level in your class. Students in their various environments — their school, their work, their home, and their community — must be considered as independent, important "who" variables in each teaching–learning interaction.

The second who variable. You, the teacher, are the other "who" variable in a teaching–learning interaction. To meet the challenges of new curricula and programs, you should provide yourself with the broadest possible background in subject matter in your particular area. Admittedly, no one can be an expert in all areas of social studies, science, or any other discipline.

You may have concentrated on a particular field in college or graduate school but, on the elementary, intermediate, junior, and senior high school levels, the need today is not so much for specialists as for teachers who are well informed in a number of areas. They are then equipped to help students understand the interrelationships between the disciplines at work in a problem and to challenge and stimulate them to think.

You will find that there is a continual need for updating your skills and information resources. Courses can give you new perspectives, and can add fresh ideas to your program. In-service programs and summer workshops can be invaluable in helping you keep up with the latest developments in your field.

You will also find that other teachers in your school possess many different skills with audio-visual aids, classroom management, or the use of questioning technique that you can learn and adapt for use in your own classes. Your chairman or assistant principal is a most

The who variables

valuable resource person on skills and techniques. Teachers frequently "inter-visit"—they observe one another's lessons to get first-hand information on the introduction of a topic, or the use of a demonstration, or to watch a workshop session in progress. We can all learn from one another, and the first step is the sharing of a common learning experience.

Read professional journals, magazines, and other relevant publications for articles, description of techniques, and announcements of new teaching materials. A technique used in one part of the country may often be just as useful in your school; another may not be workable at all because of the differences in locations or available materials.

Do not ignore or neglect to use your school and immediate community personnel and resources in your program. One of your first jobs in a new school is to identify the resources available and determine how they can be most effectively used. You are not the only information or experience source available—try to use all those at your disposal.

There is *no* "best" kind of teacher; there *are* effective teachers and, varied as they are, they have in common three essential characteristics: good, diverse content and skills background; flexibility; and awareness. Your flexibility should include:

Teacher flexibility

☐ Learning new skills yourself

☐ Experimenting with and using different techniques, approaches, and types of lessons

☐ Meeting the questions of your students and admitting when you do not know the answers

☐ Adapting to the limitations of the available materials and then improvising

☐ Adapting your lessons to the developments of a day

☐ Seeking out and accepting constructive criticism

This spirit of flexibility in approach and outlook is essential for the teacher who reaches his students, but it must be accompanied by keen awareness. You should constantly be aware of:

Teacher awareness

☐ A lesson as an instrument of interaction rather than an exposition of your own knowledge

☐ The students as young individuals with unique capabilities, interests, and problems

☐ The resources available for use in your programs

☐ Your strengths and weaknesses; your likes and dislikes

☐ Your attitudes toward learning which will have a marked effect on your students

☐ The variety of avenues through which learning can take place

☐ What you are saying—do you mean what you say; do you say what you mean

It is essential that you be yourself. Don't try to "be" another teacher that you admire. You can learn from others, but you must develop your own style. Students are very quick to spot a "phoney." They don't want a "know it all," or someone who tries to give the impression that he has all the answers. No one has. When you don't know something, admit it. Try to establish an open atmosphere in your classes where students can learn to try, to ask questions, and to admit with dignity when they don't understand.

The who variables

Students don't want to be patronized, humored, or tolerated; they want to be recognized and treated as individuals. Students should be familiar with the goals of the program; they should help to formulate and define them. They should understand what your expectations for them are, and where you are going in the course of study. To accomplish this you, the teacher, must be aware of your goals and how you intend to reach them.

FIGURE 1.5
Keystone for teaching

These three characteristics then—flexibility, awareness, and preparation—are essentials for the effective teacher, and *effective* is the key word:

In reaching the students where they are and helping them to broaden the base of their experience

Effective is the key word

In helping them move from "seeing" to "looking"; from "hearing" to "listening"

The What Variable

This facet of an interaction reflects the content or subject matter in that lesson or unit. In some subject areas, teachers have broad latitude in developing a course of study which has a high degree of individualization and relevance to a particular class. In other subjects, the teacher may be somewhat more restricted because of the specificity and structure of the course of study provided or mandated. However, no matter what the degree of specificity associated with a course, you must organize and adapt it as much as possible to the needs of your students, the materials available, and the operating conditions you find present. Your skill in recognizing these variables and your flexibility in relating what you have done to what you want to do will increase with experience. During your first year of teaching,

The what variable

you will probably follow established courses of study, and depend heavily on more experienced supervisors and teachers for direction. As you grow in experience and confidence, you will modify the programs to reflect your own teaching style and the needs of your specific program.

The what variable

In most instances, there is an established course of study provided by either the state or local department of education or curriculum study. This must be a starting point for you. This general outline provides you with the major goals and concepts that are to be included in the program. It gives you a framework within which you can start to work. In many departments, one or two experienced teachers working with the chairman modify this general outline in light of the specific time schedule, and the number of periods, class levels, and students in their particular school situation. This adaptation helps the individual teachers organize their work by adding more detail to their operating framework. Lessons — effective lessons — cannot be planned in a vacuum, and this preliminary modification of the course of study serves to give you a more concrete, realistic starting point for developing a program tailored to the needs of your classes.

FIGURE 1.6
Course of study in transition

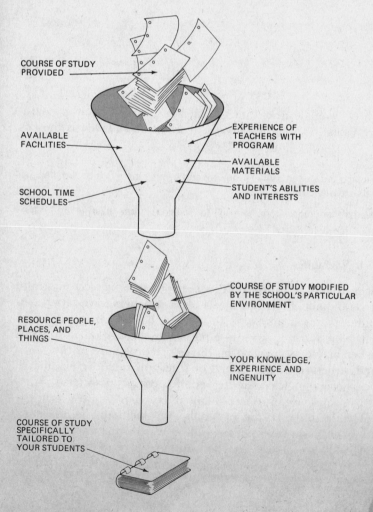

COURSE OF STUDY PROVIDED

AVAILABLE FACILITIES

EXPERIENCE OF TEACHERS WITH PROGRAM

AVAILABLE MATERIALS

SCHOOL TIME SCHEDULES

STUDENT'S ABILITIES AND INTERESTS

COURSE OF STUDY MODIFIED BY THE SCHOOL'S PARTICULAR ENVIRONMENT

RESOURCE PEOPLE, PLACES, AND THINGS

YOUR KNOWLEDGE, EXPERIENCE AND INGENUITY

COURSE OF STUDY SPECIFICALLY TAILORED TO YOUR STUDENTS

In developing the plan for a semester's work, you will get a picture not only of the specific units involved, but also where the course of study is leading you—what basic concepts are being emphasized, what major themes recur and tie together all the different units presented. Before you can effectively introduce any of this course content, you must have a clear picture of precisely what it is you are expected to teach. Anyone can recite a list of facts or definitions for the students to memorize. However, this is not teaching, and to avoid it you must have a clear understanding of the major themes of the course, as well as those specifics you want to introduce. You must relate the current work to the past work, and to the investigations still ahead. Without this concrete, overall plan of the semester, you will find yourself teaching isolated facts and concepts that have limited or no meaning to your students.

The what variable

Students who are asked only to memorize and never taught to relate see no reason for what they are doing and become frustrated and bored—in short, they "turn off" in your subject.

In approaching the "what" component of an interaction as an effective teacher, you must:

☐ Be familiar with both the content of each unit and the sequence of units

Using the what variables

☐ Be aware of the general goals of the entire course of study, and the concepts and skills that are emphasized throughout it

☐ Provide learning experiences throughout each unit that will help students relate the present work to that before and after it, develop an understanding and appreciation for major themes

☐ Be well read on current events in your field so that you can always relate the "what" you are teaching to the "now" in the real world

☐ Be realistic in adapting the "what" you are teaching to the real setting in which you are working

☐ Discuss the content and procedures with your supervisor and colleagues to find out how they have adapted the course of study to the requirements of their programs and time allotments

The When and Where Variables

The setting in which the teaching–learning interactions are going to take place—the particular classroom, school, and community—is another variable. Get to know what is available in all those resource areas that can add to the activities that you plan.

The when and where variables

In a specific classroom
1. *Is this classroom the best one available for the activity planned?* Do you need a laboratory, workshop area, typing room, or some room with specific hardware? What procedures are followed in your school for temporarily using a room different from the one to which you are regularly assigned?

2. *What bulletin boards and display areas are available in your room?* These display areas can be used by you or your students for setting up exhibits or displaying projects and models. These additions furnish a personal touch to a classroom, help the students to identify with the room and with the work done in that area. They also provide a means for complementing the study underway, and give the students further opportunity to participate actively in the work of the class. For instance:

The when and where variables

Using display areas

☐ Use a series of maps to illustrate the changes in territorial boundaries of a country

☐ Mount a collection of pictures of different types of plants to illustrate the variety of species in the plant kingdom

☐ Display collages, block prints, or linoleum cut prints made by students

☐ Display labeled mineral specimens from a student's or the school's collection

☐ Set up a bulletin board on current events about a certain geographical area, or some environmental problem

☐ Mount photographs taken on a field trip

☐ Post a graph relating the maximum daily temperature to the number of degrees of daylight so that data can be added to the graph daily

☐ Arrange a collection of plants to illustrate a desert environment, or a woodland area

3. *What shades, lighting fixtures, and electrical equipment and outlets are present?* How are requests for repairs of any of these facilities handled? Is a projection screen mounted on the wall, or will you have to order one each time you want to show a film? Can a white, opaque window shade be used as a projection surface in the event that a regular projection screen is not available?

4. *Are you in the same room the period preceding the one you are now considering?* Do you teach all of your classes in one room? Do you share the room with another teacher? Do you have to move from room to room as the students do? What storage and closet space is available in the room? Can you leave materials in the room, set up and ready for use each period, or do you have to have them brought to the room each time they are needed?

Your ability to have access to and to use all the facilities of a room is an important and real consideration for you. If you can leave materials out, ready for use, you will find that you save considerable time each period. You will not have to distribute and then collect equipment every forty or fifty minutes, and the students will arrive in a classroom where things are waiting for them, and will not have to wait for material to arrive before work can start. This makes a difference in their approach to any activity. Work can start virtually immediately, and the interest and momentum generated in the motivation and preliminary discussion will not be lost.

5. *Can the seating arrangement in the room be varied and adapted to different situations?* You may have a standard pattern in the classroom you use. This may be the only one possible for your program of class meetings. If you are demonstrating something at your work area, you can, if safety permits, have the students gather around your desk to closely observe what you are doing. However, if the class is large this procedure may not be the most satisfying.

The when and where variables

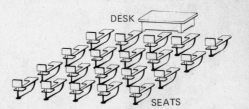

FIGURE 1.7
Standard seating arrangement

If you have more flexible seating, you can experiment with the best seating pattern for each type of activity introduced. For example, a pattern such as the one in Figure 1.8 might be best for a discussion or some workshop sessions. You can even try this seating pattern for demonstration work if you put the demonstration table in the center of the pattern. You might arrange the tables or chairs in the pattern shown in Figure 1.9 to facilitate small group discussions, laboratory work, or workshop experiences. You might even adapt this seating pattern for use in a supervised study session if you provided some means of screening off the work area of each student from that of the others near him. A screen such as the one in Figure 1.10 might pro-

FIGURE 1.8
Circular seating pattern

FIGURE 1.9
Small group seating pattern

vide that additional degree of flexibility for this work area. An arrangement for viewing films or transparencies might be the one shown in Figure 1.11.

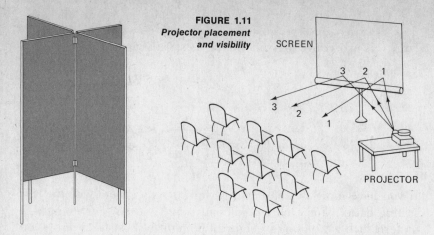

FIGURE 1.10
Study space divider

FIGURE 1.11
Projector placement and visibility

SCREEN

PROJECTOR

The particular arrangements you utilize will depend on the physical set-up of the room, the specific activity, and the number of students involved. If you can, try these arrangements in your program and then create your own best seating patterns.

6. *What provisions can be made for your lateness and absence?* There may be times when you are unavoidably absent or delayed. A substitute teacher in your field may not know precisely where you are in a unit, so, to avoid wasting part of a period or an entire period, institute some procedure for checking homework, or have a set of challenging supervised study or workshop assignments prepared. These materials should be readily available for the substitute and thus for the class, and the procedures for introducing them and using them should be written out clearly. The directions and instructions on where they are located should be on file with your immediate supervisor or in your attendance recording book. In the case of your late arrival, you might initiate a procedure in which a student teacher puts homework questions or problems on the chalkboard for consideration and correction by students. This is another technique for using every moment available for meaningful, constructive activities related to the major themes of the course. It also encourages a spirit of involvement and purposeful activity.

In the school. In addition to your analysis of the resource materials and physical set-up of your classroom(s), you should explore those resources open to you in your school. These resources can be grouped under headings: people, places, and things.

1. *Resource people.* Your immediate supervisor is your most available and valuable source of information concerning teaching techniques, procedures, materials, and classroom management. You can work with him on testing, developing demonstrations, workshop experiences, new homework assignments, and specifics of questioning and summarizing.

The when and where variables

Other teachers in your department may be skilled in a particular presentation technique, the art of motivating, the use of audio-visual aids, or conducting workshops. You might with their permission observe them in action and learn some of the "tricks of the trade" from them. Teachers in other subject areas are resource people for you too; they may be using techniques or materials which you can adapt to the needs of your program.

Grade advisors, guidance counselors, the school nurse, and the attendance teacher are among the other valuable resource people in your school. They can furnish you with background information on students who are particularly talented or particularly limited in your subject area. Your discussions with these resource people will help you to acquire greater insight into the problems of your students so that you can meet their specific problems with more tact and understanding.

The librarian in your school is a resource person. She may conduct library lessons for your class to introduce them to the facilities of the library, and to help them explore some topic for a project or report.

Students in your classes are also resource people. They have particular hobbies and talents which can provide meaningful inputs in any interaction. Hobbies and talents are not restricted to the scholastically gifted students alone; some of the less academically inclined students have mechanical and manual skills or have interests that can add variety and depth to lessons. As you get to know your students through laboratory, workshop, or supervised study sessions, and informal chats, you can ascertain this kind of information. Keep such data handy so that at an appropriate time you can call on one of the students to tell about a hobby, or a trip, or some skill he has mastered. Students are very interested in hearing about what other students are doing. In addition, these personal touches give the quieter, more reserved, or less confident student a chance to shine.

The audio-visual aids coordinator in the school can offer useful suggestions for the incorporation of new or more traditional audio-visual aids into your programs. He may have an established training program in progress so that you can learn to use all the facilities and equipment available when you wish to do so. If no such program is underway at present, explore the materials he has available during your preparation periods or at some convenient time during the week. You might like to use one new piece of equipment each week and thus build up knowledge of their uses.

2. *Resource places.* Familiarize yourself with the different types of facilities available in your school. Locate the:

Resource places

- ☐ Laboratories
- ☐ Workshops
- ☐ Audio-visual center
- ☐ Library
- ☐ Auditorium
- ☐ Gardens or greenhouses
- ☐ Music center
- ☐ Gymnasium and swimming pool

Some of these facilities are used more frequently by one department than by another. You can explore what is available and then determine when each one is scheduled for use. Learn the procedure used in your school for changing classrooms or scheduling classes for a particular work area. The program chairman or assistant principal can best help you with this. For example, you might want to have a series of library lessons followed by a workshop session. You might want to move from your usual classroom to the surrounding school grounds or gardens, and then to a laboratory for more individualized work on specimens collected or data gathered. Your utilization of the facilities available will depend on the specific kind of program and your ingenuity in using everything in your environment to make your lessons more interesting and challenging.

During your first few months in a school, you should set up your own program of exploratory activities. You might like to do this in cooperation with several other new teachers and a more experienced teacher who can show you around. Usually teachers new to a school participate in orientation sessions at the start of the school year, but these do not give you the opportunity to do more than scratch the surface. To get to know the school you have to be in it a while and work with its facilities. You can prepare a checklist such as the one in Table 1.1 to help you organize the information about your specific school.

TABLE 1.1

Personnel or facility	Location	Special feature
Library		
Gymnasium		
Auditorium		separate lighting and film center
Audio-visual center		
School Nurse		office hours
Attendance Coordinator	Room . . .	

Keep up to date on materials in your school library so that you can use them in your lessons. The librarian may issue a monthly or bi-monthly listing of new arrivals. Introduce some of the newer books as homework assignment sources, or enrichments in your lessons. Borrow the books for the day and show them to your students. Indicate the title and author. Then have the librarian place them on reserve for use by your students. Be sure that you try to select a variety of books to accommodate the variety in reading and interest levels you will find in your classes.

The when and where variables

Explore the auditorium and its stage in terms of using them as inter-action sites. Perhaps you might want to have a lesson on the stage itself illustrating staging techniques, or you might want to investigate acoustical problems specific to your school. You might have the class meet daily on the stage to prepare a backdrop for a play or a "sing." The school orchestra might move from its rehearsal studio or room to the auditorium for a practice session in order to judge the sound effects in the large hall or to become familiar with their seating arrangements in preparation for a concert.

3. *Resource things.* In addition to the resource people and places in your school, there are many resource things. The equipment used in your own field is the most obvious example of these resource "things." In science the amount of equipment kept on hand is quite extensive. In some schools, all science supplies are kept in one supply area. In others, however, materials for biological science and for physical science are kept in separate areas. If science is your field, be sure to explore both supply areas. Equipment usually considered in the realm of one area can be adapted for use in another, thus adding variety and clarity to presentations. Each subject area has a reservoir of equipment, reference materials, and audio-visual aids which are usually inventoried. Some departments prepare annual inventory lists of the materials on hand and distribute them at the start of the school year. Consult these inventory lists to acquaint yourself with current stock, and provide yourself with a ready reference to use in your planning. Remember that other departments in the school have a wealth of resource materials too. Don't neglect these either.

Displays of student art work, awards for athletic teams and competitions, articles written for the school newspaper or literary magazine are other resource things. Search out the materials available in your school. Determine the reserves of experience, talent, and equipment that can assist you in providing a richer variety of learning experiences for your students.

Your ability to use what is available; seek out the less obvious but most worthwhile resources; use a variety of resource people, places, and things; and be flexible, innovative, and inventive in your approach to teaching–learning interactions is one of the measures of your potential for teaching effectiveness.

In the community. The community outside your school is an area which must not be excluded, if you are to help students understand and relate to their environment. Each community has a variety of resources waiting for you. These include:

Community resources

- ☐ Museums
- ☐ Art galleries
- ☐ Newspapers
- ☐ Hospitals
- ☐ Department stores
- ☐ Banks
- ☐ Zoos
- ☐ Botanical gardens
- ☐ Publishing houses
- ☐ Food stores
- ☐ Libraries
- ☐ Manufacturing firms

These should be used in your programs through field trips, assignments, and visits. Students can survey all the detergents on sale in a local grocery market to determine the variety in size of box, quantity of detergent per box, price per box, and price per ounce. This kind of data can be used to illustrate the need for clear and accurate labeling, the variety of products in an area, and the use of advertising and packaging techniques.

Museums, art galleries, concert halls, and libraries can provide your students with reading resources and audio-visual experiences far beyond those possible in a classroom. Learning cannot be confined to a classroom. It is a twenty-four-hour-a-day process that happens in a variety of ways. Do not limit the effectiveness of any teaching–learning interaction by ignoring any of the resources of your community or the experts in that community. Doctors, nurses, writers, painters, musicians, business men, merchants, and engineers can be guest speakers in your classes to share their experiences with the students. If you want to use resource people from outside the school, discuss these plans with your supervisor or assistant principal. They can frequently suggest experts who are willing to participate in such discussions and programs.

The yellow pages of your telephone directory will help you locate the museums, galleries, and other resource places. These institutions usually have prepared trail guides or guide sheets for use by students who are touring exhibits or collections.

Watch the newspaper for art shows, movies, concerts, and department store special exhibits. And don't forget the television "special" as a teaching tool.

Be sure to collect articles and pictures pertinent to your subject area. These can be sources of homework assignments, projects, and reports. Establish a display board featuring current happenings in your community or topics in the news which relate to your subject area or to some specific problem you are considering. Students can bring in the items that they gather from reading materials and thus keep the display board up to date.

The when and where variables

Keep posted on the student activities in your school. Find out what trips are scheduled, what the teams are doing, or what competitions or fairs are currently being held. Use what the students are doing as motivations, illustrations, applications, or enrichments in your lessons.

Your alertness and ingenuity are critical in helping you to effectively use your classroom, school, and community setting to make teaching–learning interactions dynamic, meaningful, and stimulating.

The Why Variable

The aim or purpose of any lesson is usually regarded as the "why" variable. It may be that a lesson on the causes of the War of 1812 is what you plan for a particular day. This lesson will help students explore the factors contributing to that conflict and may also help them to recognize the sources of conflict in another era or areas. The content "why" in a lesson, then, can have more far-reaching implications in the growth of the student than is initially evident.

The why variable

Each lesson usually has several purposes aside from the principal, obvious one, labeled the aim. These include development of critical thinking, awareness of the interrelationships of variables, and provision for some aesthetic or creative experience. These less obvious but associated aims become more apparent as the students acquire factual background information and gain experience in its application and use. Learning facts is relatively easy, but real learning can only start here. Working from an ever broadening fact and experience base, a student should be learning to question, critically evaluate, and organize his knowledge. In short, he should be learning to think and to creatively express his ideas and feelings. This is the real function of all teaching–learning interactions.

Students in your classes must recognize that each lesson is a step toward some goal. These goals, aims, or "whys" must be realistic, and appropriate to the age and scholastic level of the students. Students must have an idea of where they are going and feel involved in helping to establish and achieve these goals. All too often students do not feel this sense of involvement and do not actively participate in the work. The teacher often feels that the material to be "covered" is vital and that his subject is the most important one for the student to have. However, remember that each teacher usually feels this way about his subject area, while the students are not majors in any field; they are just exploring and sampling. Later when their experience is wider, they will make their own choice of a specialty field. There are too many students sitting in today's classrooms feeling completely overwhelmed by the content being poured down their throats. Such students have probably turned against the subject and, in the worst cases, against formal education in general.

The why variable

Helping your students establish and recognize realistic goals for a lesson or a unit is always a challenge. Success hinges on your own recognition of what you want to accomplish in an area, your possession of a broad experience background in the subject, and your belief that what you are doing is important and relevant to your students. You must keep in mind in this regard that all students are not in your class for the same reason: some may need the course for graduation, some may like the subject, some are really curious about it. Therefore, you cannot count on any uniform degree of interest. However, children and young people are not taught *for* subject matter but *through* it. A student may not understand the function of a lesson, or the relationship of one lesson to another; he may not see the relevancy of a lesson to himself. Your job is to accept the student where he is and then try to relate what you are doing to him and to what he does. If a student sees you as one of the few adults who take an interest in him or recognize him as an individual you have made a big step toward establishing a rewarding teaching–learning interaction. Get to know the community and its problems; they comprise your students' environment. Tie their problems and experiences into your program as motivations, problems for study, or discussions whenever you can. At the same time, by your interest in what you are doing and your respect for the individual encourage them to join in the adventure of learning.

The How Variable

The how variable

This variable in the interaction deals with the practical, realistic implementation of ideas and plans in terms of real students and real situations. One may know what to teach and when and where to teach it, but the "how" of teaching it is the crux of the matter. Without a knowledge of how to introduce ideas, how to motivate, and how to encourage your students the value of your work is greatly diminished. There is a limitless variety of techniques and aids a teacher can use in a classroom to engage interest, stimulate thinking, and develop the potential of the students. However, no teaching device or aid can be, of itself, the key to creative thinking. In fact, any one technique or aid used repeatedly with no variation loses its impact. Your effectiveness as a teacher in a teaching–learning interaction rests, in large measure, on your abilities in this area and your potential for growth in learning new teaching skills and techniques.

PROBLEMS, QUESTIONS, AND ACTIVITIES

1.1 What aspects of the cultural and ethnic backgrounds of your students will influence your lesson planning?

1.2 What factors in the physical environment of your students, such as housing and transportation, will affect your lesson planning?

1.3 PRELIMINARY SELF-EVALUATION

Appearance

1. What can I do to capitalize on the positive factors of my appearance to make myself a more effective teacher?

2. To what factors in my grooming should I pay particular attention?

Voice

1. In what ways have I analyzed and evaluated my own voice quality?

2. What measures could I take to make any necessary improvement in the projection of my voice, so that what I say can be heard by my students?

Scholarship

1. To what extent could I perfect my preparation for today's lesson, by reading, research, and other investigations?

2. How am I keeping up to date on current developments in my academic, commercial, or vocational specialty?

Avocational Interests

1. To what extent do I develop avocational interests that might conceivably be of help in relating to my students?

2. To what extent am I developing leisure time interests that will tend to make me a more mature and interesting person?

1.4 List ten specific resources (community level) that you might realistically use in your program.

1.5 Critically evaluate the following aims for a forty-minute period.

1. To appreciate poetry.

2. To investigate some of the properties of chlorine.

3. To plan a balanced meal for a family of four.

4. To evaluate the culture of France in the eighteenth century.

5. To learn the components of the sonata form as exemplified in Mozart's *G-Minor Symphony*.

Rewrite those that you find unsatisfactory.

Select any one of the aims. Devise a motivation for that lesson that will involve the students in the attainment of this aim.

NOTES

NOTES

2
Types of Teaching–Learning Interactions

WHAT ARE INTERACTIONS?

The major vehicle for teaching–learning interactions is the regular meeting of the class—the daily lesson, which should be structured, yet not be rigid or inflexible. Each lesson must reflect your preparation, planning, and the understanding of its importance and relevancy. Traditionally, labels or titles have been assigned to lessons in order to classify them as different types of learning experiences. The titles serve no other function.

In a *lecture,* the teacher is obviously at work, directly providing information or introducing concepts. The students are involved, directly but perhaps less obviously. They are listening, taking notes, and thinking. Sometimes one phrase "triggers" off a train of thought in a student that truly makes this an interaction for him.

In a *laboratory* or *workshop,* the student is more directly and obviously involved in doing the work and investigating the problem.

The extensive preliminary preparation the teacher invests helps make the lesson workable and meaningful, but may not be obvious to the unskilled eye.

In *supervised study,* the teacher's preliminary work in preparing programs for individual students is crucial in making the interaction worthwhile. The student is at work on a project or assignment designed for him, enlisting assistance only when he requires it.

In a *discussion* the teacher may have no recognizable role except that of a member of the audience, an active listener evaluating what he hears.

A *review lesson* is a teaching–learning interaction which permits both you and your students to look at a topic again with new, different, and greater insight.

WHERE DO TEACHING–LEARNING INTERACTIONS DIFFER?

Interactions differ in the extent to which students and teacher are directly and obviously involved.

However, the percentage of teacher involvement and percentage of student involvement that can be assigned to any type of traditionally labeled lesson is precisely what we do not want to delineate here. An interaction is that series of activities, tasks, and procedures that you will use to create a lesson that challenges, and stimulates your students.

Another difference lies in the development and activities used in the interaction. In developing the aim of a specific lesson, you must also consider the best means for achieving it. What specific activities will most effectively engage the students' interest and facilitate their progress toward accomplishing the aim?

> Is a laboratory or workshop experience the "best" way possible?   *Arousing interest*
>
> Is a discussion the technique to use?
>
> Is a supervised study period required?
>
> Is a review lesson in order?
>
> Is a field trip desirable?

Any specific lesson will probably be a hybrid of the traditionally labeled types. One lesson may be part review, part discussion, part workshop, and part supervised study. A review lesson might take the form of a field trip.

The classic labels ascribed to different lessons are meaningless in and of themselves. Each lesson, no matter what formal or informal label you choose to give it, presents you with the challenge of using the variety of procedures, activities, techniques, and materials at your disposal to:

> ☐ Create the most effective teaching–learning environment   *Teacher goals*
>
> ☐ Provide meaningful learning experiences for your students

Each interaction must provide the student:

> ☐ A reason for being there   *Interactions must provide*
>
> ☐ A direction to go
>
> ☐ A way of getting there
>
> ☐ A net effect or change

To insure that each interaction does provide these opportunities for individual growth and development, each lesson must be carefully planned and organized.

WHAT IS THE DEVELOPMENTAL APPROACH?

The best general framework for structuring most of the interactions you plan is the *developmental approach.* It incorporates the components common to all interactions, adds dimension or organization, and provides you with a frame of reference for your planning.

In this approach interaction components are structured as follows:

The developmental approach

Motivation

Aim

Development

Medial summary

Further development

Summary

Assignment

Enrichment

Within this framework a teaching–learning interaction is that program of activities that you and the students, working together, use to achieve the aim of the lesson.

Although each of these aspects of a lesson will be treated in depth in individual chapters, an overview of some of the essentials is in order here.

Motivation is that means by which you engage the interest of the students when you introduce a problem or focus attention on a question. It will help them to crystallize the specific problem to be solved or task to be performed.

The *aim* of the lesson is the "why" of the day or the unit. It concisely states the problem for investigation or the statement for examination or verification. It can be phrased as a question, or as a statement. Above all you should try to have the aim formulated by the students. They should clearly define the work of any day no matter what specific techniques or activities are involved. You have already designed an aim for the lesson and developed a set of activities which will help students achieve it. However, the first step toward their active involvement is *their* realization and formulation of the aim, even though they may not phrase it exactly as you have.

The *summary* too is common to all lessons. It is a concise statement of what has been accomplished, discovered, or done up to a given point. The summary statement may be reserved for the end of a class period, or it may be best to summarize salient or critical aspects of a lesson several times during a class meeting. No matter when the summarizing is done the students should be directly involved. They should recapitulate in their own words the key ideas of the lesson. The number and timing of the summaries will depend on the type of interaction involved. In a discussion a closing statement by the moderator will often be sufficient. Toward the end of a lab lesson the summary may involve sharing data or experimental results in an effort to explore the operation of some principle in a system. At the close of a supervised study lesson, each individual should be able to summarize his progress. The summary not only crystallizes what has been accomplished in the lesson but also provides for further activities or investigations. This can be expressed in the shaping of the work for the next class meeting, designing a specific homework assignment for that day, or indicating some enrichment areas for exploration.

The developmental approach

An *assignment* is an integral part of a teaching—learning interaction and should be the natural outgrowth of a day's lesson. It serves a variety of purposes and fills a number of needs for any student. The assignment should be a personal challenge for the student—a challenge to review his work, forge ahead in his reading, develop a skill, or explore an area previously unknown to him. Developing creative, challenging assignments as outgrowths of the class work is an often neglected area. The homework assignment is the student's individual extension of the work done with others in class.

Enrichment, another thread common to all lessons, consists of those topics or skills, not a usual part of a course of study, which expose the student to stimulating and thought-provoking associated areas. They include the latest developments in the field, the interplay of one topic with another in another subject area, or the work of a student on a project related to the one the class is considering.

These structural components of a developmental lesson provide you with the framework on which you and your students can create a dynamic, viable learning experience. The next step to explore is planning—the means by which you make maximum use of all resources available.

PROBLEMS, QUESTIONS, AND ACTIVITIES

2.1 You and some of the other teachers in your subject department use a laboratory—workshop orientation for your classes. Other teachers in the department have refrained from using this approach because they feel that labs let students play or "fool around" and thus waste time. At a departmental conference, this difference in approach is to be discussed. For a given unit of work in your subject area, indicate the exact number and nature of the lab or workshop experiences you would use. Show how one of these lab or workshop experiences can be used profitably in terms of:

   1. Covering material required

   2. Staying in the unit-time allotment

   3. Providing a worthwhile learning experience

2.2 Sometimes the pleasure and the excitement of a field trip are dampened by the fact that the student knows he will be required to make an oral report or a written report about it. Describe some methods by which you can evaluate the success of such a trip, and use the information and experiences learned, other than the report.

2.3 Your experience and your training have made you a great champion of the idea that demonstrations and field trips should be used frequently in your teaching. Several of your more experienced colleagues criticize your frequent departure from what they consider a pattern of daily lessons. How would you share your insights about these learning activities with your colleagues?

2.4 Describe an occasion where you might use the lecture method of teaching for all or part of a class period in the secondary school.

1. What modification of this technique would you employ to be sure that the students were being trained to listen attentively?

2. If you wished the students to take notes, what measures would you take to be sure such notetaking was well done?

2.5 One day, at lunch, a colleague says, "The developmental approach is okay in your subject area, but not for mine." How would you reply to this comment?

2.6 For the next department conference, you have been asked to describe a unit you are planning to teach. Include in your description:

1. The aim(s) of the unit

2. The aims of at least three different lessons in the unit

3. The different types of learning activities to be introduced

4. Types of assignments, projects, and enrichments

5. Provision for review

6. Type of evaluation to use

NOTES

NOTES

3
Different Types of Plans

WHAT IS A UNIT PLAN?

A course of study will be one of the starting points in your planning. These syllabi or course outlines are usually organized into units or major topics. Some outlines follow a sequential pattern with each topic depending directly on the one preceding it, as is illustrated by the following Chemistry unit.

CHEMISTRY

Major Theme of Unit—Structure of the Atom

First Atomic Theory of Matter
Robert Boyle
Dalton's Atomic Theory
Work of Avogadro and Guy-Lussac
Thomson Model of the Atom
Work of Becquerel—radioactivity
Rutherford atom
Bohr atomic model
Work of Max Planck
Quantum theory of atomic structure

FIGURE 3.1
Sequential unit plan

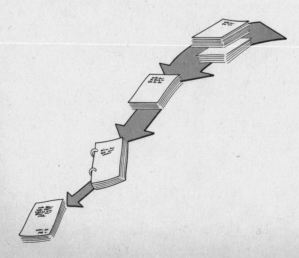

In other cases, many different, seemingly unrelated, topics are presented and later correlated, as is illustrated by the following English unit.

ENGLISH

Major Theme of Unit—Man vs. Society

Plays
   Antigone—Sophocles
   Death of a Salesman—Arthur Miller

Short Stories
   Under the Lion's Paw—Hamlin Garland
   The Pearl—John Steinbeck

Poems
   Prisoner of Chillon—Lord Byron
   Song of the Shirt—Thomas Hood
   Man with the Hoe—Edwin Markham

Novels
   The Jungle—Upton Sinclair
   To Kill a Mocking Bird—Harper Lee

Biographies and Autobiographies
   Native Son—Richard Wright
   Borstal Boy—Brendan Behan

FIGURE 3.2
Correlated unit plan

WHAT IS A RESOURCE FILE?

With a unit plan in mind, as you organize the unit content into a series of sequential learning experiences, you should also consider the materials and equipment you can use in these lessons:

Lesson enhancers

- ☐ Demonstration equipment
- ☐ Pictures
- ☐ Lab or workshop direction sheets
- ☐ Transparencies, films, filmstrips, film-loops
- ☐ Maps
- ☐ Charts
- ☐ Reference books and materials
- ☐ Field trip locations

In addition to these standard materials, available in your school and community, there are other sources for lesson enrichment. You often see articles in newspapers or pictures in magazines which relate to a unit that you teach; an idea for a homework assignment or project may come from a television program; an advertisement could suggest a transparency that would add interest and variety to a lesson. When you see these things or get these ideas, clip them out, write them down, and save them until you are ready to use them. Since you never seem to see an article when you are teaching the lesson to which it relates (it always appears three weeks after or six months before), where to keep the materials until you need them is a major consideration.

The best answer for this is a filing system—a *resource file,* which has a file folder for each unit. Every time you see an advertisement, picture, or article you think is relevant, clip it out and file it in the appropriate folder. Do the same with descriptions of demonstrations you find particularly interesting or challenging. Include in this file items such as:

A resource file should include

- ☐ Department inventory lists on charts, films, and other audio-visual materials
- ☐ Project ideas
- ☐ Field trip locations, and directions
- ☐ Discussion topics
- ☐ Laboratory experiments

The items should be incorporated into your planning and lessons at appropriate times, not merely filed away to look impressive or gather dust. They should be used, evaluated, and then kept or discarded periodically. One year you may use a demonstration in one lesson, and the next year you may try a variation of it in a different portion of the term's work. Pictures or articles you clip out this week may be stimulating motivational devices to use this year; by next year, however, some of the material may be out of date and should be discarded.

You should also keep a record in this file of the "disasters"—those activities that sounded right or looked good on paper but proved too difficult, not workable, or not worth the time investment.

After a period of time you may find that your resource files have grown quite large. You might, if space permits, invest in a filing cabinet to keep all the materials organized and ready for use. The function of these resource items is the same as the seasoning in cooking —adding spice and zest to a diet. Remember to cull out the poorer teaching resources and keep adding new ones. This will help promote a dynamic quality in your interactions. Write to the major publishing houses, equipment firms, and the United States Superintendent of Documents to have your name included on their mailing lists. Professional journals and magazines offer you additional sources of bulletins, pictures, and poster ideas.

WHAT IS A MATERIALS SUMMARY?

Once you have an idea of what major concepts are emphasized in a unit, and the types of teaching materials available to you, you are ready to plan a series of learning experiences. As you develop each lesson, you should prepare a specific plan containing the procedures and activities designed to accomplish the aim of that lesson. This is the lesson plan. As you prepare this plan you must constantly evaluate the available teaching aids and materials to select the most effective ones for use in class. To help in this part of your preliminary planning, you might use a scheme such as the *materials summary* shown in Figure 3.3.

FIGURE 3.3
Materials summary for three lessons

MATERIALS / LESSON	Microscope Slides	Film-strips	Charts	Films	Film-loops	Fresh Materials	Trans-parencies	Models
How is a seed formed?	pollen tubes stigma germination		flower and seed structure	seed germination		apples, marigolds, pea pods	pollination	
What is the structure of a seed?	corn embryo bean embryo		bean germination corn germination		seed dispersal	lima beans, bean seedlings	corn and bean cross-sections	flower model
What is a fruit?		development of fruits				walnuts, peach, apple, orange, cherry, pepper, coconut, beans	apple cross-section	flower model

Note the following about this summary:

The lessons are part of a unit in ninth grade science.

The specific categories of materials included are based on the particular character of the unit (e.g., microscope slides), and the materials known to be available in the inventory of the department of science.

All films, filmstrips, charts, etc. were previewed for suitability, clarity, and correctness.

Not all the materials indicated for any one lesson were used in that specific lesson.

The specific type of learning experience was determined after a consideration of the supplies at hand.

All dissections of fruits were performed before class to try technique and gain experience.

In your preliminary planning you have moved from a general course outline to a specific unit of work. The unit plan, the resource file, and the materials summary will help you to take the next step in this progression—the development of a working plan of action for the specific learning experiences which make up a unit. You are now ready to examine the daily lesson plan.

PROBLEMS, QUESTIONS, AND ACTIVITIES

3.1 What are the principal factors about the classes you are teaching that you must consider while planning a unit of instruction?

3.2 Investigate the resource materials available from the Superintendent of Documents, Washington, D.C.

3.3 Examine several issues of a professional journal in your subject area. Select a demonstration, an assignment, a workshop experience, and an enrichment that you could use in one of your classes.

3.4 Prepare a materials summary for one lesson in your subject area. Use materials readily available in your school and community.

Design a card index system for recording the location or source of each item or material included so that you can quickly locate them when you need them again.

NOTES

NOTES

4

The Lesson Plan—What It Is and What It Is Not

WHAT IS THE PLAN'S PERSPECTIVE?

The plan that you create for any specific lesson can be viewed from two perspectives.

Two views of the lesson plan

It is a plan for a one-time teaching–learning experience.

It is a plan for one of a series of lessons that, like a couplet at the end of a sonnet, can stand alone but is more meaningful if read in the context of the complete sonnet.

In each of these capacities the lesson requires careful planning. The subject content on which it is based will be part of a larger unit of instruction, like a bit of information that is fed into a computer to be used immediately, or later correlated with other information. No one lesson can encompass all the facts or concepts of the unit of which it is a part, but—although it is a fragment of the total content material —it must also be considered as a unique and complete learning experience. Any specific lesson happens only once; the next time you teach the same content the students are different, the classroom may be different, the time and the environment are different. Each lesson must be planned and structured so that it has a clear-cut attainable goal, and you must have provided types of learning activities to help your students achieve this goal.

Effective, productive learning experiences do not just happen. Those interactions that may appear least structured, open-ended, or extemporaneous, are usually the best planned. The teacher need not be overtly "directing the show" but he must establish a climate vital for an interaction. A student can learn only in an atmosphere in which he feels that his participation is satisfying to himself and meaningful to others.

WHAT ARE THE COMPONENTS OF A LESSON PLAN?

Motivation

☐ The developmental method—the discovery-inquiry approach to an interaction —begins with an activity or question that will arouse the student's interest in such a manner that he will be challenged to investigate a process, question, problem, or procedure.

☐ These activities help students to focus on a particular topic for investigation and to formulate a specific question or statement about it.   *Aim*

☐ Demonstrations, laboratory and workshop experiences, audio-visual aids, and discussions are among the techniques used to permit students to gather data, illustrate principles, and solve problems.   *Development*

☐ Frequently questions are used to help students crystallize ideas, detect difficulties, and move the interaction forward.   *Pivotal questions*

☐ Sometimes during and always at the end of an interaction, the results of the interaction are assessed and concisely stated.   *Summary*

☐ Specific work for the individual student to do as an outgrowth of the interaction is provided for the following meeting or for some definite time in the future.   *Assignment*

☐ Additional items such as current events, new research discoveries, or a student's project or report, can be added where appropriate and if time permits.   *Enrichment*

These are the structural components of a plan for any teaching–learning interaction. They are essential in your planning and vitally important in making a class session an interaction.

WHAT IS THE LIFE CYCLE OF A PLAN?

A lesson plan has three stages of development:

☐ The creation of the plan

☐ The use of the plan

☐ The future of the plan

The following guidelines are offered for establishing, carrying through, and maintaining your lesson plans.

The Creation of the Plan

Any lesson plan must be designed within the framework of the length of the class session, the subject content to be presented, and the specific type of learning activities to be used. Your plan for each lesson should:

☐ Capitalize on the most recent learning experience of that class by summarizing, reviewing, viewing film clips, pictures or models   *Establishing the lesson plan*

☐ Specify the content goals, the skills goals, and/or the appreciation goals for which you are designing the lesson

☐ Recognize the length of the period involved

☐ Outline in detail the types of learning activities you want to use: demonstration, audio-visual aid, discussion, field trip, library lesson, review

☐ Include a list of all materials you will need, copies of any diagrams or prepared sheets you will distribute during the class, and a list of any reference books you might want to use or make reference to.

☐ Specify the nature of any special facilities or personnel required such as a laboratory specialist, visiting speaker, or librarian

☐ Describe clearly the motivational activity or question to be used

Establishing the lesson plan

☐ Have ready a sketch of the chalkboard outline you will develop during the lesson

FIGURE 4.1
Plan for a chalkboard outline

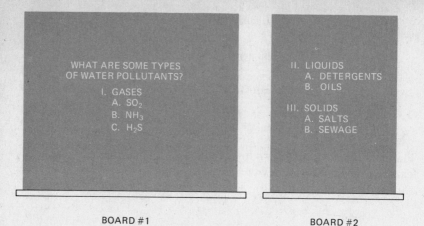

WHAT ARE SOME TYPES
OF WATER POLLUTANTS?

I. GASES
   A. SO_2
   B. NH_3
   C. H_2S

II. LIQUIDS
    A. DETERGENTS
    B. OILS

III. SOLIDS
    A. SALTS
    B. SEWAGE

BOARD #1   BOARD #2

☐ Include a list of the enrichment materials, trips, and activities for that lesson: current showings or exhibits, local field trip by individual students, books, records, magazines, business shows, museum collections, department store exhibits

☐ Specify some of the questions that you will use during the lesson to challenge, summarize, and engage the slower or quieter student

☐ Detail the specific types of summary activities or questions you will use

☐ Clearly define the homework assignment you have designed as an outgrowth of that specific lesson

It is not possible or even desirable to plan every second of every lesson. Student questions, snags in demonstrations, or the exploration of a student's answer may require that you deviate from this written outline. The plan at this stage is a guide to *what* you want to accomplish and your best thoughts on *how* you are going to do it.

The plan must be reasonable, not rigid, because the teaching–learning interplay, which requires flexibility, is the final determinant of what will be achieved.

Once you have written out the plan for a lesson, look it over critically. See if you have included all the necessary details. Try out the demonstrations and laboratory experiences before attempting them in class. You may have to drastically change your plan if some materials you need are not available, or some equipment is out for repair. One of the advantages of the materials summary list described earlier in the book is that you have listed all the alternative materials available in your school and, in the event that one item is out, you can readily secure a substitute with minimum effort.

Once you have done this preliminary surveying and planning and you have tested the equipment and tried the demonstrations, it is time to use the lesson in class.

The Use of the Plan

No lesson can be declared workable until it has been tried. Up to the point of its use the one vital ingredient that is missing is the students—their experiences, their reactions, their questions. You may have a growing awareness of the capabilities of your students, but you can never know them completely. Due to their reactions, a lesson may develop differently from the way you initially planned it. You will need some guidelines for using your prepared plan in class, but care must always be taken that such lines do not become rigid.

1. *Prepare a time schedule for your lesson.* Just before the start of the period set your watch to some convenient hour—say ten o'clock. Make a note of the hour in the margin of the plan. Then indicate in the margin the approximate time you think you should be reaching different activities. For example:

10:00 motivation

10:04 aim on board

10:25 medial summary

10:30 demonstration on ———

10:35 summary

Carrying out the lesson plan

This kind of time scale helps you keep to your schedule and not get bogged down in one section or in digressions that are merely interesting irrelevancies. This does not mean that you must rigidly, blindly adhere to the time schedule you plan. You may find that a student's question has uncovered a fundamental weakness or has opened up a new avenue for pertinent discussion. Adapt your plan to the real lesson situation. In view of what you find you might schedule a workshop session or a discussion period for the following class meeting and continue with the lesson you planned. Or you might modify the lesson you planned, to summarize or review a segment of work on which the new work directly depends.

2. *Use the plan as a guide during the lesson.* Do not read from the plan as though it were a road map with only one recognizable road. If you have your notes in a binder or folder open on your desk you can consult them briefly and unobtrusively during the lesson. If there is a passage which you want students to copy or consider verbatim, have it written out on a separate card and use this when you write or read it. Or you can prepare rexographed or mimeographed copies of the selection and distribute them to the students when needed. While they read materials like this you have a few moments to consult your plan or guide and check your time without appearing to be continually reading from a "prepared script."

At the start of your teaching career, your plans will be quite detailed, with statements on all activities and procedures you want to include. This will give you greater confidence. Later, your notes on these activities will be more concise—a phrase instead of two or three sentences—and yet will convey the same information to you.

3. *Keep your students in mind when planning a lesson.* You may have just come from a sophisticated teaching–learning environment where extensive use is made of the lecture technique, and work is quite independent in character. Remember that students on pre-college levels are less skilled at taking notes, outlining, and coordinating information from reading and classroom work than are you. Keep this difference in mind as you plan, and as you teach. You may find that you try to cram too much into each lesson. Many beginning teachers feel that they can teach a given syllabus in much less time than one semester or school year—the content material is "so simple and straightforward." It may seem simple to you with your additional four or six years of study after high school, but it is not so simple to your students; it is their first exposure to some of the concepts and principles so familiar to you. Do not be discouraged if your lesson plans at the start are too comprehensive, or "flop" because they are too crammed with material to be workable. You will soon know if this is happening: Students will ask questions that indicate they do not understand a fundamental concept; a quiz or exam will show that most of the students in a class have not mastered a skill; problems in workshop or laboratory sessions will tell you that they do not know how to proceed.

Be alert to this problem. As your lesson unfolds, be sure to provide time for students to ask questions and complete the work they are doing without a sense of rushing or being pushed, and for you to ask diagnostic questions, summarize, and review. This sense of timing can only come with experience. Observe your students in action, working in real classroom situations. If you are sensitive, alert, and observant, you will quickly develop an idea of how much can be done in a given time period.

4. *Make your plans realistic and flexible.* Do not completely plan five or ten lessons in advance. You can rough out the general sequence of activities you would like to schedule, and the scope of the content material you want to explore. But the specifics of any daily lesson can only be effectively and realistically planned on the foundation of the previous day's work. Lessons planned in detail far in advance generally require such extensive revision before you use them that the effort is in large part wasted. Your lessons must reflect the real nature, the real status, and the real atmosphere of each individual teaching–learning situation.

There may be unexpected changes in the class schedule or length of period as a result of some occurrence in the school or community. In the case where the session is abruptly cut short, make a note in the margin of your plan as to where to begin planning the next session. Medial summaries are of great assistance in this regard. These brief resumes of the major work done up to a given point help students in organizing information and crystallizing ideas. If you leave all the summarizing for the end of the lesson, and the period is curtailed, the students do not get the benefit of a summary or review. In the event the period is extended, you should have some materials available for use, or topics for discussion, for example, enrichments or drill exercises, to profitably use this additional but unexpected time. In both cases—the shortened and the lengthened periods—any plan you have designed must be modified "on the spot" to reflect the real classroom environment.

Carrying out the lesson plan

You may have several different classes in the same subject area during any given day. Therefore, a lesson plan can be used more than once during a day, and every time you use it you do so in a different context. Each usage gives you a wider experiential background—you have learned by trial and error what is *right* and what is *wrong* with your plan. Each plan has a more extended lifetime than you might at first expect.

The Future of the Plan

At the end of each class period, if time permits, make notes about the different aspects of the lesson including:

☐ Questions.

Which elicited salient facts or directed attention?

Maintaining the lesson plan

Which were unclear?

Which served to engage the less participative students?

☐ Activities.

Did you encounter any difficulties in using equipment?

Was the time too short for accomplishing the proposed work?

Did *you* do all the work? Were the students involved or just spectators?

Were the work instructions clear?

Were there any safety hazards you had not envisioned?

☐ Summaries.

Did you have time for a profitable summary?

Did *you* have to do the summarizing because of lack of time?

Was the medial summary too lengthy?

These are but a few of the many questions you should ask yourself directly after the class session. If you can make notes immediately about the more successful features of a lesson, all the better. Perhaps

*Maintaining the
lesson plan*

you will have to wait another period or two and teach the lesson again before you can do a thorough job of evaluating it; in this case, you still have the experience of the first class trial in mind as you use it a second time. Your experiences and feelings about the flow of the lesson, the responses of the students, and the progress you made with your original plan will condition your approach and progress the next time you teach the same lesson.

You evaluate the aspects of a lesson to reorganize and restructure activities for a more effective and efficient development—not to prepare *a perfect plan. There is no such thing!* Nor can any plan be kept unchanged and inflexible for ten or even three years. The immediate evaluation helps you identify those activities that once worked well in a given area of learning and those that do not appear to work well now. The next time you teach that topic or unit you may develop some more effective audio-visual aid or technique than the one you used this time, but this will be done on the basis of your experience with your students in a given time reference. Each lesson and the plan for it should be evaluated by you in this manner—what worked and what did not, and what modifications were made to improve the lesson.

Any lesson plan, therefore, does have a future. Usually segments of a lesson, rather than the total plan, have extended use. In the course of several applications of a specific plan you will also begin to identify those activities which were most successful with modified classes, or with honors classes. The experience you gain helps you develop more realistic, workable, and challenging lessons each time you teach. Your lesson plans and the notes you have made on specific activities and questions should be kept for future consultation, and at the end of each unit you should follow the same analytical procedure with your unit plan. You should ask questions such as:

*Analyzing the lesson
plan*

Was the sequence of topics you used effective or did you reorganize the plans?

What workshop, laboratory lessons, demonstrations were most challenging and interesting? Which did not accomplish their intended purpose? Can anything be salvaged?

Did you find that a specific film, chart, or transparency would have helped at a given point but that none was available? Did you suggest these to your supervisor for possible ordering? Were some homework assignments so involved that they did not sufficiently engage the student's interest?

Your professional growth is up to you. You can synthesize the experiences you gather daily, continue to improve your techniques, and explore new approaches. This calls for a continuous in-depth self-evaluation of your lessons in terms of their impact on your students. Ideas, procedures, and materials will be constantly discarded; others will be continuously fed into your planning.

This kind of approach is stimulating for you too. Teaching in this frame of reference will never be boring or dull either for you or your students. This continuous appraisal and evaluation requires time, but it is a most rewarding activity as you and your students are direct beneficiaries.

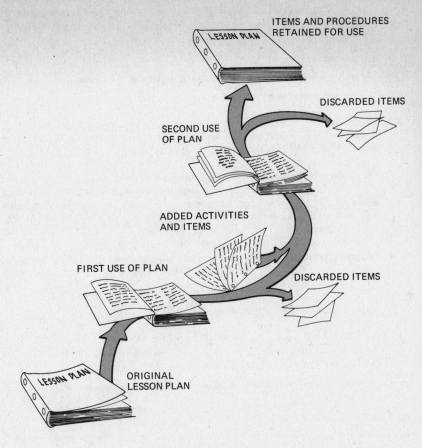

FIGURE 4.2
Life cycle of a lesson plan

ITEMS AND PROCEDURES
RETAINED FOR USE

LESSON PLAN

DISCARDED ITEMS

SECOND USE
OF PLAN

ADDED ACTIVITIES
AND ITEMS

FIRST USE OF PLAN

DISCARDED ITEMS

LESSON PLAN

ORIGINAL
LESSON PLAN

WHAT THE PLAN IS NOT!

Up to this point we have underscored what a lesson plan is. Now it is important to summarize what a lesson plan is not.

A lesson plan is not

- ☐ A rigid, inflexible "sacred" document

- ☐ An inhibitor

- ☐ A speech or manifesto

- ☐ A substitute for the real give and take of a real classroom interaction

- ☐ Designed in a vacuum apart from real students and a real teaching–learning environment

The plan for any lesson is at its simplest a guide. It outlines that which you want to accomplish and summarizes the ways in which you want to accomplish your objectives. Specific aspects of a lesson are examined in detail in the next section of this book. Each is discussed in terms of what the aspect is, what its functions are, and what are the realistic guidelines for using it in real teaching–learning interactions.

PROBLEMS, QUESTIONS, AND ACTIVITIES

4.1 Recently in the course of a review of a book dealing with current problems in education, the reviewer remarked, "Why must a teacher have a plan, anyway?" Answer this question succinctly. In your reply, give arguments based on your experiences

    1. As a student

    2. As one who has critically observed other teachers at work

    3. As a beginning teacher

4.2 What are three characteristics of bright students that must be considered when you are planning a lesson for an advanced class. Just how does each of these characteristics affect definite phases of your plan?

4.3 Prepare a brief questionnaire to be given to each member of your subject class that will give you some helpful information about his interests, hobbies, aspirations, and work experiences. Be sure to include your introductory comments and specific directions for the answering of each item, as well as a statement about the confidential nature of these responses.

4.4 Despite your careful planning you find that a lesson tends to "drag" a bit; there seems to be part of the period where little, if any, progress is made

    1. What might be some reasons for the occurrence of these "dead spots"?

    2. How might you go about eliminating them?

4.5 Select a topic in your area of specialization. Plan three different lessons, each of which you would use as an introductory lesson for a unit in this topic. Use the following guidelines in preparing the three plans.

    1. In plan I, use the question-answer developmental technique with no audio-visual aids.

    2. In plan II, use audio-visual aids extensively.

    3. In plan III, use a field trip or a guest speaker as the principal feature of your lesson.

4.6 Indicate what specific kinds of learning activities you would use to introduce a unit of work in a class where the average reading score was two years below grade level.

NOTES

NOTES

PART TWO

The Daily Lesson: A Modern Perspective

5
Aim and Motivation

WHAT IS AN *AIM*?

A college freshman decides he wants to become a dentist.

An archer takes a bead on a target in a competition.

A politician sets his sights on a high elective office.

In each case a goal is established; an aim is defined.

The aim of a lesson is also a statement—of a theory you want to prove, or a question you want to investigate. And as such it performs a very important function. As molecules of a gas in a container move about randomly, aimlessly bumping into each other, so students, or a class, can drift when they have no specific goal. This kind of random drift quickly generates confusion, apathy, and even hostility, not only toward one activity but toward learning in general. If, however, individual students or a class have together identified and delineated some area for study—some relevant, challenging question or problem to investigate—then their work will have meaning and value because they have an aim.

HOW DO YOU FORMULATE AN AIM?

Your very first consideration in planning any interaction, whether discussion, laboratory or workshop experience, or review, is establishing precisely:

☐ The question to be considered

☐ The statement to be examined

☐ The problem to be investigated

Components of the aim

In each unit of work in your subject, you must identify those essential ideas or concepts you believe most vital, since all the material included in a unit is not of equal importance. Many items are included to illustrate, supplement, or enrich the essentials. You must exercise your critical judgment in boiling down the unit of work into a workable number of basic ideas around which you will organize a series of lessons. For example, in investigating acids in a chemistry class, three major themes could be established for this unit:

Sample aims

How can you determine if a substance is an acid? (includes properties and tests for acids)

What makes a substance an acid? (includes theories of acids, pH, relative strengths of acids)

How do acids behave with other substances? (includes reactions of acids)

These three are the sequential aims around which you can organize a series of lessons for this unit on acids. Each of them will require more than one lesson; some may involve a lab session and/or demonstrations which continue for several days or a week. However, these three questions serve as the skeletal framework on which to plan and then build the series of classroom interactions.

The aim you design can be expressed in terms of a statement or a question. Both are useful forms for establishing the major concern of an interaction. Statements like:

Aim formulators

The role of the choreographer in a musical

Using a spirit duplicating machine

Comparison of the styles of Hemingway and Steinbeck

and questions such as:

What are some of the properties of chlorine?

What are the essentials of a time-payment contract?

What are the factors affecting a price-support system?

are practical and effective means of formulating the aim of a lesson. The choice is yours—you should try using both to see which form works best for you in any given situation.

In formulating an aim you must be realistic in terms of:

Be realistic about your aim

☐ The subject content treated

☐ The grade level of the students

☐ The time available

You can't realistically ask a ninth grade art class to discuss the impact of the work of Picasso on the Cubism school.

You can ask them, after extensive reading and discussion and workshop experience to distinguish works of Matisse from those of Goya or Manet.

You can't expect a sixth grade math class to derive the Schroedinger wave equation.

You can ask them to solve some rate or acceleration problems.

You can't realistically expect a class to learn to appreciate the works of William Shakespeare in forty minutes.

You can begin a comparison of the characters of Hamlet and Macbeth.

When you have designed an aim for a lesson or a series of lessons, ask yourself the following questions about it:

☐ Is the aim realistic in terms of the time available?   *Is your aim realistic?*

Will you need one day? Two days?

Will you have sufficient time to include all the learning activities required?

☐ Is the aim geared to the grade level of the students?

Are you asking the impossible and thus frustrating the students when you can't accomplish what you want to do?

☐ Is the aim too general or vague?

Are you asking students to study all aspects of a topic when there is time for only one or two considerations?

Is the aim too broad in scope so that the students don't know precisely where they are going?

☐ Is the aim too limited?

Will the aim you created be accomplished within the first five minutes of the class session?

☐ Is the aim feasible in terms of the equipment and materials available to you?

Can you develop a series of differentiated learning activities during which the students can gather sufficient information and experience to accomplish the aim?

☐ Can the aim be achieved?

Is the aim you devised one of those unsolvable problems that are largely a matter of opinion and that can never really be resolved?

Would the work involved in this investigation really take a lifetime, and not a few class periods?

☐ What is the value and importance of that aim?

Does it call for mastering a skill, conveying some information, providing vocational guidance, or developing maturity of judgment?

☐ Is the vocabulary used too sophisticated?

Can the aim be phrased in simple, more understandable terms?

☐ Does the aim express what you want to do?

Do you mean what you say?

Even after this preliminary work with the aim you have decided upon, your consideration of it has just begun. You can now begin to:

Design activities which will involve the students' interest in the problem you   *After the aim is* want to consider. This is called *motivation.*   *established*

Prepare the program of activities, audio-visual aids, and questions you will use to achieve this aim. This is called *development.*

Create opportunities for reexamining the aim against the new background which the learning experiences will have provided. This is called *summary*.

WHAT IS A MOTIVATION?

In the past decade unprecedented amounts of money and talent have been devoted to finding out why people buy products — what catches their fancy, what stimulates their interest in it, and what will make them buy it.

Once these factors are categorized and tabulated, the information is used in designing packages, advertising, or identifying some feature of the product that will satisfy these needs and thus sell the product. This work in stimulating interest and determining the "appeal-base" of a product falls under the heading of motivation.

A lesson with its specific aim needs motivation too. The motivation — that question you ask, news items you read, demonstration you perform, or transparency you show — must engage the student's interest in a topic and stimulate his curiosity about a problem so that he can:

Uses of the motivation

Focus on a specific topic

Formulate a question or a statement about it

Become directly involved in creating a meaningful learning experience

The motivation can determine, usually at the start of a class session, whether the student will respond to you, or turn you off. This is why motivation and aim must be considered together when you plan your lessons. Your aim may be an excellent one, but will get nowhere if only you are interested in it or see its importance. The motivation you design may appear effective, but if your aim is too vague the students will not be able to grasp it. In either case the class is frustrated. These two components of the lesson — aim and motivation — are so dynamically and critically interrelated in the planning and the development of a lesson that they must always be treated together.

WHAT ARE SOME TYPES OF MOTIVATIONS?

Motivations can be categorized and compared in two ways:

Types of motivations

Gimmicks vs. "real" motivations

Intrinsic vs. extrinsic motivations

Gimmicks vs. "Real" Motivations

The *gimmicks* are activities or objects which only catch the eye and the temporary attention of the students and are not an integral part of the lesson. Firing off a cap pistol, tossing paper planes around, or showing a picture of a pretty baby at the start of a lesson may elicit "Ooohs" and "Aahs" and some laughter, but usually little else.

Such activities *can* meaningfully relate to a lesson: Sailing a paper plane could illustrate a point of aerodynamics, or air pressure; firing a cap pistol would be pertinent to an investigation of noise levels and sound. So it is important to remember that whatever you use for motivation might be considered merely attention-getting in one frame of reference, and worthwhile and genuinely involving in another.

A *"real" motivation* is an activity, question, or object that really starts students thinking about a given topic. It is not just a contrivance, an eye-catcher, or a crowd pleaser.

Gimmicks are limited in the degree that they can be used in the interaction which follows their introduction. In a television commercial, a cartoon character, a talking bubble, or a chattering insect is "cute" — it's something you remember when you go shopping, but it usually does not represent any inherent, or outstanding characteristic of a product. It fulfills the advertiser's immediate purpose if the consumer buys the product. However, selling a product by using a gimmick can be as dangerous as using gimmicks to motivate lessons. Consumers do not want to be duped into buying, and students do not want to be tricked into learning. Products should be sold on the strength of what they contain and what they do, and lessons should be initiated by some activity that leads students to think about a real situation, problem, or question. No one — consumer or student — likes to be "conned," and discovery that they have been makes them resentful. So, if you use a gimmick, be sure *you* recognize that it is, and be sure to communicate that impression to *your students*.

Intrinsic vs. Extrinsic Motivation

Another way of categorizing and comparing motivations is by classifying them as *intrinsic* or *extrinsic*. An intrinsic motivation is an activity or object directly involved with the topic you are going to investigate. An extrinsic motivation stems from outside the subject matter area, but is in some way analogous to it. Two examples can best illustrate the difference between these classifications.

Example I. The aim you propose for this lesson is: *To examine some factors affecting a system at equilibrium.*

Before the start of the lesson, fill and then seal three glass tubes with nitrogen dioxide gas. At the start of the lesson present the following demonstration.

Intrinsic motivation

> Immerse one tube in a beaker of water at room temperature to demonstrate that the color of gas in the tube remains unchanged. Immerse a second tube in a beaker of hot water to demonstrate that the color of gas in the tube deepens to a dark brown. Immerse the third tube of gas in a beaker of ice water and show that the color of the gas in the tube fades, until the gas is almost colorless.

You ask:

What did you observe about these specimens of gas?

How can we explain these observations?

What should we investigate in order to verify your hypotheses?

Aim — stated by a student: What are (some) factors affecting a system at equilibrum? (You added the word some.)

This is an intrinsic motivation. You are using an equilibrum system to direct attention to some aspect of that type of system which is to be investigated. Your demonstration and series of questions were all designed to use the information already at the disposal of your students in further exploring that subject area.

Example II. The aim you propose for the lesson is: *To examine some factors affecting a system at equilibrium.*

Extrinsic motivation

At the start of the lesson, you describe a local movie theater, and set up a problem about it.

On a weekday, the theater will open at 1:00 P.M. and the show starts at 1:30 P.M. Its seating capacity is 500. The feature picture lasts $2\frac{1}{4}$ hours; the short subjects last $\frac{3}{4}$ of an hour. Total cycle of showing = 3 hours.

By 12:30 people are lined up outside the theater.

You ask:

What will happen as soon as the doors open?

In which direction will most of the people be moving at 1:15?

How does this flow of people compare to the one you would find at 4:30? At 5:00?

At 8:00 P.M. the ushers tell the ticket seller that there are no seats available.

You ask:

What generally happens when this situation occurs?

(number leaving = number entering)

The last show starts at 10:30.

You ask:

Describe the flow of people between 9:45 and 10:30. At 10:45.

At 11:00, the manager announces that the projection system has broken down and cannot be repaired. Rainchecks will be offered.

You ask:

What happens to the flow of people now?

What bearing does this example have on a system such as

$$N_2 + 3H_2 \rightarrow 2NH_3 + \Delta?$$

What should we investigate about equilibrium systems?

Aim—stated by student: What are factors affecting an equilibrium?

This is an extrinsic motivation which is analogous to the system to be studied further. It serves to start students thinking about a familiar problem or area, and then transfers the information in a known area to a less familiar but similar one.

Extrinsic motivation

The terms intrinsic and extrinsic also refer to their application to the state of mind of the student. Does he want to learn for the sake of the learning itself (intrinsic) or is he motivated by some outside stimulus (extrinsic)? The use of the terms in this context is more fully explored in the section dealing with review lessons.

WHAT CAN BE USED IN DEVELOPING MOTIVATIONS?

No matter what the classification or term you assign to the motivation you use, you must relate it to the specific aim you have formulated for a lesson. There is a limitless number of materials and techniques for use in motivating lessons:

Motivation developers

☐ Clippings or pictures from a newspaper

☐ Quotations from an old or a current source

☐ Film clips

☐ Transparencies you make or purchase

☐ Charts or maps

☐ Demonstrations

☐ Challenging questions or statements

☐ Live specimens

☐ Field trips

☐ Data tables

☐ School events or happenings

☐ Television programs

☐ Portions of a recording or taped speech

☐ Aspects of a recent assembly program

☐ Items in the school newspaper or magazine

☐ Newspaper or magazine advertisements

☐ Questions asked by students the previous day, or during a lab session

☐ Segments of the homework assignment

Your sources of motivating ideas and materials are limited only by your awareness of what is around you, and your own creative talents. You do not need "things" to motivate: you need ideas; you can create mental pictures; you can recreate events. The "things" you use—the materials, the specimens—are, however, valuable additions. The type of activity you use will depend on the aim you developed. The motivation activity should be brief—about three or four minutes. This gets the class to the aim of the lesson in perhaps an eighth or tenth of the class session time, and leaves a substantial block of time to develop the idea, or investigate the particular problem.

Motivation developers

Your appraisal of the resource materials available to you in your school and community is your first step in developing meaningful motivations. One of the major uses of your resource file is to permit you to collect just such items all during the year to be used at the right moment. An article you clipped out of the newspaper six weeks ago (be sure you labeled it by source and date), may be the item you want to create a challenging situation to start off tomorrow's lesson. A demonstration that failed last year, or last week, may be just the right activity to start off an investigation.

It is not always possible to look in the morning newspaper and find the item you need for the day's lesson, so keep looking for potential items. Periodically, go through your resource file to discard those items that are out of date or unworkable. Restructure or reorganize other items and reclassify those that can be used in several different settings.

There may be times when an event occurs that has so much built-in motivation that you may restructure your lesson for that day in order to make use of it. A presidential news conference, a medical breakthrough, an athletic achievement, the return of an explorer or astronaut are such examples. They call for immediate use to capitalize on their full value in a learning activity. This kind of last-minute change requires flexibility and a sense of awareness about your total environment.

Use materials that can be appreciated by your students. A passage from a very technical, dry research paper is usually much less effective than the headline or lead sentence in the newspaper article about it.

Do not speak in sixteenth-century English, when you can use twentieth-century speech. This does not mean that you should use all slang, or should refrain from using "long" or "big" words or poetic, lyrical sentences. It does mean that at first you have to meet students where you find them, and usually the simplest, most direct words are the best. As you develop a unit, you will introduce those terms, synonyms, antonyms, and homonyms that your students should learn to broaden and strengthen their vocabulary and language resources. Although you start by meeting the students where they are, you do not leave them there.

Be sure to use items which can be readily seen throughout the room. If you think it important, duplicate the article and distribute copies to students. Use the opaque projector to look at small objects or pictures. Get students together at your work area to look at demonstrations, if that can be done safely. Use the microprojector to look at a slide or a live specimen. Use the overhead projector to view diagrams or transparencies of flow charts, data tables, or diagrams.

Be alert to what is new in theater, recordings, sports, medicine, economics, politics — in short, to what people, both the young and the somewhat older are talking and thinking about. Motivation should always reach into the area of your students' interests. Once you engage the student, make him stop and look, then you can begin to help him listen and want to explore a topic which sometimes quite suddenly he sees in a whole new light. That's the job you have cut out for you when you establish the aim and then create a motivation tailored to it.

Motivation developers

WHAT ARE THE GUIDELINES FOR AIM AND MOTIVATION?

Integrating the Aim and Motivation

The sequence of aim and motivation depends on whether you are concerned with your planning or the development of the actual lesson.

Integrating aim and motivation

In your planning you will have to establish the specific aim of an interaction before you can create or select the questions, audio-visual aids, or demonstrations that you will use to motivate that topic.

During the lesson, however, the motivation will precede the statement of the aim — the motivational activity guides students to a recognition of the problem to be explored. From your point of view, motivation grows out of the aim; from the students' perspective, the opening activities or motivation leads to the aim.

Stating the Aim

If you walk into your class and write on the board:

Aim: The Causes of the American Revolution

You will be sure to provide an aim for that lesson

Stating the aim

You will be sure that it is in the terms that you want

but

You will not have involved your students in planning the teaching–learning interaction that day

An aim is not important unless it is understood and accepted by the students. You may formulate an aim for an interaction that you feel is relevant and most worthwhile, but unless students can determine that aim for themselves, the learning will be merely another exercise in rote memorization.

Students may phrase the aim differently from the way you have it in your plan. Use their words instead of your own, if their words are correct—both grammatically and in content orientation. Do not try to get a student to guess what your exact words are. Do not try to get a student to say "aspects" instead of "factors," to say "types" instead of "kinds." You can suggest some words or some modifications of a proposed aim to make the aim more viable. The inclusion of the word "some" permits a good deal of flexibility in a lesson. You will investigate some, and not all the causes, factors, or examples. The most viable, dynamic interactions will be those in which students feel most involved, in which they have helped to crystallize the problem to be studied that day.

Determining Your Role

You will, by your skillful demonstrations, or use of specimens or articles, arouse the students' interest in a topic. Then, using a series of carefully designed, and well-worded questions, help the students to "zero-in" on a specific aspect of it. You will guide, but not seem to direct.

The questions you ask will depend on the motivation you develop. For example, if you want to initiate a study of some of the factors at work in establishing the ecological balance in a lake, you can start with a graph.

FIGURE 5.1
Graphic motivation

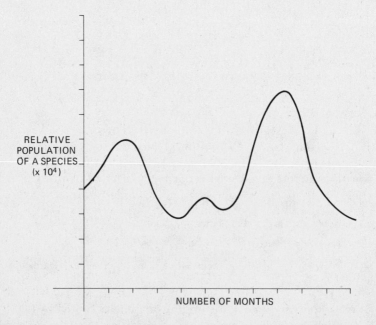

This graph (Figure 5.1), prepared as a transparency with accompanying paper copies for students, indicates the population of a species versus time. The questions you ask here are the important links to the aim, and might include:

What conclusions can be drawn from this graph?

How can you explain this sudden drop? (refer to some specific point on the graph)

What additional information should be secured in order to better understand the meaning of this graph?

Your role in this phase of the lesson is to provide the introductory activities and materials, and then use a series of questions which start students thinking and questioning until they crystallize the question or problem to be tackled. Specifically, you elicit the aim. You involve students in a problem that they recognize as both real and understandable, and then elicit from them the specific goal or aim they establish for that day's interaction. Once the aim has been set up by the students, write it on the board as either a question or a statement. Usually the aim can be written in the upper portion of the first board you will use. It should remain there all during the lesson. It helps latecomers move into the mainstream of activities, and provides you with a reference point for summarizing and assessing progress during the lesson. It is a concrete statement of what you all intend to do and it will be used again several times during that session. You minimize confusion by having the aim written out on the board for all to share and consult periodically.

Teacher's role in aim development

Using the Aim

Your next area of concern is the transition from the delineation of the aim to the area of the lesson where investigations are conducted, facts and data are gathered, and experiences are shared that will serve to accomplish that aim which you and the students have established.

Using the aim

Do not abruptly turn from the chalkboard and tell students that your first demonstration will answer _____ or show that _____. Have the students outline a series of investigations, discussions, or problems that would be valuable in determining the information they will need. Instead of your taking over and providing all the activities and procedures, let the students again have an active role in establishing a work schedule. The demonstrations, the specimens, and the problems you have prepared and pretested can then be introduced at appropriate moments. It may even appear that you just happened to have the materials handy. If students are discussing a scene in a play, you might have pictures of a stage production of it ready to use when the topic gets around to staging techniques used. If the lesson deals with learning to set up columns of figures in table form, then you can have ready the problems you designed. One transparency for you and paper copies for the students can be used at just the right moment.

If you are investigating the requirements for food production in a plant, let the students set up the procedures to be tested. If they have established this as the aim of a lesson, your question following the statement of the aim might be, "From your own experience, what materials do plants seem to require in order to survive?"

*Using
the aim*

Students will probably suggest light and water. You can then ask, "What types of experiments might we set up in order to show that a plant needs light for food manufacture?" Students, with some stumbling and hesitation, and some groping for words and ideas, will indicate how to screen off a plant, or one of its leaves, from the light. You can then do this to a plant, or have a student prepare the plant in the manner the other students have described.

If time is a factor, you may want to immediately evaluate the effect of depriving the plant of light. In this case you should set up the same demonstration several days before. Now you can bring it into action. Explain how this plant was prepared in the same way as the one the students have just done. You should also explain the reason for using this kind of demonstration. Students can then evaluate the results of their suggested work. They have had an active hand in designing the aim, and also in setting up the experiments and procedures for its accomplishment. Your preliminary work with materials and equipment facilitates the smooth transition and movement of the lesson. Be sure to develop a working chalkboard outline of the factors in your investigations, data tables, diagrams, and outcomes so that students can use this outline frequently as they progress through their established work schedule.

WHEN DO YOU USE THE AIM AGAIN?

Each activity in the interaction—the demonstrations, the discussions, the problems—must be tailored for one objective: providing the class, the students and you, with the means for accomplishing the task they set out to do. Periodically you should stop to evaluate what you've done and how it is helping you to attain your goal. This is the area of evaluation and summary. At one or two appropriate moments in the lesson, when you have completed one segment of work, you should stop and ask a question such as, "How has what we have just done helped to answer our question?" This type of question asks students to look over their work and apply it to a specific example. They are called upon to determine the relationship of an activity to the solution of a problem. They assess progress, crystallize ideas, and get ready for more work. The additional question you then ask might be, "What further investigations should we undertake to gather more information about this problem?" This type of question uses the evaluation to help set the stage for the next experiment, demonstration, discussion, or problem-solving activity, and students are directly involved in establishing the work schedule.

Toward the end of the class session, you would again ask students to summarize the information they have learned and the learning experiences they have had that day using the aim of the lesson as their operating framework.

Have they gathered enough information to answer the specific question or solve the problem?

What homework assignment can now be given that stems directly from, and is related directly to, this learning experience?

What additional problems or questions were raised that will require attention at the next class session or lab or workshop?

You and the class will be using the chalkboard outline you developed to help summarize your work, apply it to the specific aim of the lesson, and define answers or solutions. The outline provides students with an organized, coherent summary.

Following each class session you should evaluate the entire lesson for its effectiveness and continuity. In particular, look at the aim and the motivation you used; ask yourself the same questions you used in your preliminary work on these two facets of the interaction. If they did the job you intended them to do, make a note of this. Perhaps you will use them in combination again.

If the motivation didn't elicit the aim you expected, determine how it might be changed, or what other motivation could be used in its place. If the motivation was challenging, and engaging, but caused students to move out on some tangential line of investigation, try to determine why this happened. If a motivation really fell flat, and failed to serve its function, you must understand the reasons for this failure.

☐ What had you not considered about the wording, or questions, or activities you used, that resulted in the kind of response you got?

☐ What changes did you have to make "on the spot" to salvage a motivation?

☐ How effective were the changes you made?

☐ What modifications might be made to increase the specificity of the motivation, and direct attention to an aim?

Remember that aim and motivation, as two of your most important considerations in planning and developing teaching–learning interactions, need evaluation before and after each class session.

☐ A motivation that works well with one class, does not work with another. *WHY?*

☐ An aim that is relatively easy to elicit from one group is not easy to elicit from another. *WHY?*

☐ Some transitions seem effortless. Others seem strained and contrived. *WHY?*

☐ Some summaries seem to fit in naturally. Others seem artificial. *WHY?*

The function of your pre-class and post-class evaluation is to help you more realistically and profitably answer these questions.

PROBLEMS, QUESTIONS, AND ACTIVITIES

5.1 Evaluate each of the following as a motivation for a forty-minute class session.

Proposed Aim:
To Study Robert Frost's "Mending Wall."

Motivation

1. Ask question: How many students in this class have gone to Town Hall to hear modern poets reading their poetry?
2. Ask question: What are the dangers of isolationism?
3. Ask question: Should one always observe traditions?
4. Ask question: Why do we fear strangers?
5. Show film clips or pictures of:
   The Great Wall of China
   The Berlin wall
   A New England stone fence

5.2 "The teacher must elicit the aim from the students." This educational truism has been challenged. Some educators feel that only the teacher can know the aim of a lesson, and that trying to elicit the aim is an exercise in guessing. From your experience comment on this question.

5.3 Evaluate the aims listed below, each one for a lesson of about forty minutes. Rewrite those you find to be unsatisfactory.

1. To learn the use of the semicolon.
2. To define all the causes of racial tension in the world today.
3. To study the uses of the slide rule.
4. To review French music of the Baroque Era.
5. To construct a graph illustrating the fluctuation of rainfall from 1870 to 1970.

5.4 One of your classes is an eleventh year class of students. The class is termed "average," indicating that it is not modified, or advanced level.

Evaluate each of the following as a possible means of capturing their interest.

1. A discussion of the question of Caesar's justification for crossing the Rubicon with his troops when he returned to Rome after his conquests in Gaul.
2. The playing of the record of Winston Churchill's "Blood, sweat, and tears" speech.
3. The review of a current movie in today's newspaper.
4. A picture of a current pop singer.
5. Your relating a detailed anecdote about yourself at the age of seventeen.

Show how a motivation of your own could be used to sustain the interest of this class throughout a class lesson in your subject area.

NOTES

NOTES

6
Questioning

WHAT IS A QUESTION?

As children we start to question almost as soon as we learn to talk; we are curious about everything, so we ask what? why? where? when? Thus we learn, and throughout our lives, questions—whether they are being asked or being answered—remain a primary teaching–learning force. Therefore, one of the most important skills for you, the teacher, to learn is questioning.

A question is a series of words

which are understood by the listener

and propel him into an intellectual endeavor

in order to make a response

which is understood by the questioner.

Questioning is really a dynamic process. In the classroom, questions facilitate the movement of information from student to teacher, teacher to student, and student to student.

All participants are actively involved, and can benefit from this inter-change.

WHY ASK QUESTIONS?

Each question asked in class by you or by a student has a specific function.

1. *Recalling data or facts.* These questions focus on specific facts or figures that may be required during a lesson.

☐ What formula is used to determine the roots of a quadratic formula?

☐ In what year was the first amendment added to the Constitution?

Data questions

2. *Establishing the student's experiential background in an area.* This type of question calls for a somewhat broader answer than simple recall. It uses facts already at the student's disposal and serves as a bridge to further work.

Background questions

☐ Why must oxidation and reduction occur simultaneously?

☐ How does the problem just done illustrate the use of the Pythagorean theorem?

3. *Helping to pinpoint problem areas.* This question, usually stated in imperative form, draws the students' attention to a specific problem encountered in their work.

Problem-pinpointing questions

☐ Many of you used the indicative instead of the subjunctive in the third sentence of your test. Explain the reason for such a choice. (Why did you use this form?)

4. *Focusing attention on or summarizing crucial points in the development of the lesson.* Such questions can serve to summarize, and crystallize thinking in an area before using that material for further study or application.

Summarizing questions

How does the atomic structure of carbon explain why carbon forms so many different compounds?

How would you arrange, in decreasing order of importance, the reasons given by your classmates for the French Revolution?

5. *Stimulating interest.* This kind of question helps to actively involve the student and make the material relevant to him.

Interest-getting questions

What advice would you have given Macbeth had he repeated to you his encounter with the apparitions?

If you were a member of the State Legislature, which of the plans we just discussed would you sponsor?

6. *Increasing student involvement.* This question requires the student to apply some of the former learnings to a current, and realistic problem at hand.

Involvement questions

Select one recipe from those listed on page 37 of your text. How would you adapt or modify it for use at an informal luncheon for eight?

7. *Satisfying curiosity.* Sometimes a word or a statement puzzles a student or you, and so a question is asked to satisfy curiosity. These questions often serve to focus attention or pinpoint problem areas.

Curiosity questions

Why did you add the acid to the water, and not the other way round?

Why did you remove some of the bottom leaves from the plant after you transplanted it to a different pot?

Usually the questions you design and ask will serve more than one function in the class, so that they provide a most important, and vital, means of communication for all the participants in the lesson.

HOW DO YOU FORMULATE QUESTIONS?

Effective, challenging questions, like all other facets of your lesson, require careful preparation and planning. Not all questions can be preplanned. Most grow out of what you are doing at a particular time. You want students to supply some data, for example, and so you ask a question to enlist their participation in a given manner. Although you might not be able to preplan all your questions, all the questions you ask should reflect your awareness of the basics of question construction.

Question shoulds and should-nots

1. *Questions should be concise.* "In what year did a distinguished engineer, who had been highly praised for his service as a food administrator in World War I, Herbert Hoover, receive the honor of becoming the highest elected official in our country?" is an exercise in endurance—both yours and the students—but is not a good question. Lengthy, involved questions confuse some, and discourage most students; they are hard to follow as to their intent or direction, and inhibit, rather than foster, participation. This question could have been phrased, "In what year did Herbert Hoover become President of the United States?"

2. *Some questions should be used that require thought and an extended answer.* These questions are really pivotal in nature and are intended to summarize or call attention to key aspects of the lesson's development. A question such as, "What are some of the effects of Sputnik's launching on American education?" requires quite a bit of recollection, organization, and synthesis of information by the student before he can answer with any degree of accuracy, completion, or confidence. Students will need time to formulate a reply to a question like this. Be sure to provide it, and do not be disturbed if students do not respond immediately.

3. *A question should not suggest its own answer.* Few teachers would ask a question as obvious as, "In what year did the war of 1812 begin?" unless they were having some fun. However, you must be sure not to fall into a similar trap as you formulate questions on the spot. You will find that as you speak, you are thinking ahead to the answer, or to what you are going to do next. In some cases these advance thoughts about the answer creep into the question.

4. *Questions should not suggest a "right" answer.* A subtle way of suggesting the "right" answer is illustrated by the question "Why do you think that Verdi was a greater composer than Wagner?" Only a dauntless student would object and say, "I don't. I think Wagner's music dramas are greater than Verdi's operas because . . . ." Such questions involving individual aesthetic preferences can be valuable to stimulate discussion, but are not suitable otherwise.

5. *Questions should not be worded so as to call for a* yes *or* no *answer.* "Does water enter a plant through the root hairs?" The *yes* answer to this question gets the class nowhere. A student has a fifty–fifty chance of being right, and this guessing contributes nothing to the learning process. A better question might be, "How does water reach a cell in a leaf or a plant?" The answer to this question will call upon the student to describe the structures and functions that a plant uses to secure water.

6. *Students should not be required to participate in a guessing game to find out what your answer is.* In this kind of game a teacher has the one "right" answer in mind, that is the one in his plan, and he will accept no substitutes. When he asks, "What does *allegro* mean?", he will accept only lively as the answer. Joyful, vivacious, and gay are all completely rejected. You must think of alternatives to the answer you might have in mind—alternatives that are adequate, or better than, the one you originally considered, and that are within the vocabulary range of your students.

7. *The vocabulary you use should be clear to the students.* The word *tragedy,* for example, does not mean the same in a literary context as it does in colloquial usage. "Why is King Lear a tragedy?" would not be answered properly in a literary discussion if the emphasis were to be placed on a poor old man wandering around in a storm. Terms in science, mathematics, and the arts, as well as in every other subject area, must be clearly defined, and their meaning in each context understood.

8. *The contrast between your experience background and that of your students must be considered.* Sometimes a question may be perfectly clear to you because you have a broad content background of knowledge in the subject area. However, the question may be quite ambiguous to your students. A question such as, "How would you classify Chekhov's short stories?" might be a perfectly obvious question to one of your colleagues who has just finished reading Maugham's contrast between his own concept of a short story and that of Chekhov. However, without this or a similar literary experience, the student would have great difficulty answering the question, nor would the question have much meaning to him.

9. *Every question should carry the lesson forward.* Questions should not be asked in a vacuum. They are a means for stimulating thinking and focusing attention. They should serve to develop a sense of totality in the lesson. Asking for the same information several times with no additions by different students is merely a time-waster. It does not foster student development, or enhance the teaching–learning interaction.

10. *Design questions that differ in their order of difficulty.* Students in almost every class vary in ability, even in those classes where an attempt has been made at homogeneous grouping. You should make sure that you have questions of varying difficulty and depth so that you can call upon and more actively involve students of all levels of ability.

WHAT IS A POOR QUESTION?

Many lessons could be vastly more stimulating and worthwhile learning experiences if you used a variety of effective questions and questioning techniques. This problem is not a new one—it has been around since Socrates. After you design a question, ask it to yourself out loud. See how it sounds. You can often detect poor questions, faulty terminology, or other flaws, if you see and hear the question.

The most commonly found poor questions have even been given titles. Some of these stand out as really ineffective, and should be avoided.

1. *The Double Question.* The student is asked to answer two or more questions that are usually interrelated, and is asked to simultaneously consider them.

Question mistakes

> What are the reasons why Cassius did not wish Anthony to speak, and why did Brutus fail to take his advice?
>
> Where is the stomach and how does it work?

2. *The Ambiguous Question.* The student is presented with a question whose meaning is not clear to him. He is puzzled as to what information he is expected to supply.

> How does the cost of food rise?
>
> Why do you like that water color?

3. *The Indefinite Question.* The student is presented with a question lacking definition, limitation as to scope, and purpose.

> What did Count Rumford do?
>
> What's the Stock Market all about?

4. *The Guessing Question.* The student is asked to supply an answer that is only a matter of guesswork.

> Why do you think Schubert failed to complete his Unfinished Symphony?
>
> Do you think more people own red or blue cars today?

5. *The Echo Question.* This question involves the repetition of one or two key words of the question.

> John said, "Hamlet was Mad." Mad? Bill?

The answer to Harriet's second question is four. Four, Ethel?

Question mistakes

6. *The Tugging Question*. The student is asked to furnish additional but not really meaningful information.

> Now that we have four words to describe this mammal, who can give me one more?
>
> Who can give me one more word to describe this painting?

7. *The Pumping Question*. This is a question in which the student is furnished with some letters or words of the answer and he is to supply the rest.

> The gas we breath is Ox ____?
>
> The painter of this work is Leonardo da _____?

8. *The* Yes *or* No *Question*. This question is answered *yes* or *no*, and calls for no further response. An additional question would have to be asked for more information.

> Is an antidote used to nullify the effects of a poison?
>
> Would you say that this shorthand outline is correct?

9. *The Whiplash Question*. This question starts as a declarative sentence and ends up with a question.

> The function of the mitochondria is what?
>
> Edison invented the electric light in his laboratory at where?

These questions will slow up, reduce the effectiveness, and minimize the impact of any activity you are using. The guidelines offered for use and the identification of those types of questions to be avoided are only your starting point. Even with a good, well-worded question in mind the next phase of questioning to consider is the *asking* of that question.

HOW CAN QUESTIONS BE PRESENTED EFFECTIVELY?

How to ask a question

1. *Ask the question first, and then select the person to answer it.* Asking, "John, what principle of mechanics explains this process?" during a demonstration, can mean that almost every student except John would cease to be interested in that question.

Once the person to respond has been selected, interest in the question may drop off and other students not directly involved tend to "relax." Questions should be addressed to the entire class.

2. *If you ask a question requiring some thought, then provide the time for students to formulate and phrase an adequate response.* A well thought-out question merits a well thought-out answer.

3. *If several partial answers are given, a student might be asked to summarize these responses.* Such a procedure encourages careful listening, and gives practice in the organization of a complete answer. Reserve some of these summary activities for the less articulate students to encourage their participation.

4. *Try to involve as many of your students in a lesson as possible.* When you ask a question, some students will volunteer to answer; others will not. Some students almost always volunteer, even if they have only the slightest inkling of the answer. Some students never volunteer, even though they know the answer or have a valuable contribution to make. Students in this latter category may be acting from shyness, apathy, hostility toward the subject or the teacher, lack of knowledge, or other personal considerations. Getting the group involved is always one of your prime concerns. Three aspects of this problem to consider are: The challenge of your questions, your attitude, and the student's attitude.

5. *Bring nonvolunteers into the lesson by learning about their hobbies, interests, school activities, and athletic interests.* Use these as the basis for their involvement. In short, get to know your students—their strengths, their weaknesses, and their interests. In the case of a chronic non-volunteer, consult with other subject teachers, and guidance personnel for suggestions and information on behavior patterns and/or physical handicaps, like impaired hearing or sight, which may be at the heart of the problem. When a habitual non-volunteer answers well, he can be briefly commended.

6. *Do not discourage volunteering.* Snapping out a question with the tone and tempo of a television district attorney who is trying to confuse a hostile witness certainly discourages volunteers. Sarcastic responses or snide comments on students' answers also serve to discourage participation.

7. *A student who gives a good answer should be complimented.* A nod, a smile, or a brief word of praise is always appreciated. The praise should never deteriorate into a ritualistic "very good," or "that's fine" after every contribution. All of us like deserved praise, but we quickly relegate the undeserved compliment to the category of conventional social noise. A student quickly learns to evaluate the worth and sincerity of a teacher's comment on an answer.

8. *Maintain a balance between calling on volunteers and on nonvolunteers.* Encourage all students to actively participate. Occasionally, you may find a student who volunteers to answer every question asked. Such a student should be talked to after class in an attempt to find out the reasons for his need for attention, so that you can decide how best to help both him and all the other students in the class. This is another instance where you should seek the advice of the guidance counselor.

9. *There should be no predictable system for calling on students.* Students quickly learn to recognize any pattern in your questioning. They then tend to cease being active listeners and become merely "hearers" for a safe interval of time after they have been called on.

How to ask a question

10. *Avoid repeating answers or questions.* Because a student did not listen, you may be tempted to repeat a question. Because a student spoke almost inaudibly, you may be tempted to repeat his answer for the rest of the class. Do not succumb to these temptations. Your repetition of answers and questions encourages students not to listen attentively, and not to speak loudly, for they believe you will repeat for them. Instead of your repeating answers and questions, ask another student to rephrase the answer, or tell why he agrees with a particular answer given by a particular student. In this way, you get more complete participation in the lesson, encourage student evaluation of answers and questions, and underscore the importance of careful listening and clear, audible responses.

11. *Students should always be expected to evaluate the responses made in class.* Whether a student is asked to correct a factual error, support or refute a viewpoint expressed by another student on a controversial issue, no student should be encouraged to accept unchallenged what he hears from any source. This does not mean that each answer is to be contradicted merely for the sake of argument. It does mean that critical listening and thinking are to be encouraged and made integral parts of each lesson.

12. *Constantly listen to your own questions with the same critical listening ability you wish to instill in your students.* If a question which you have clearly stated, and has been heard by the class, fails to elicit a response, or elicits inadequate or erroneous responses, you should reevaluate the question. Was it poorly worded? Was it ambiguous? Was the question calling for a more sophisticated background than the students presently have? A question which elicits these kinds of responses should be completely discarded, and a new one, covering the same material quickly substituted. You must develop the ability to think on your feet during the interactions. However, do not fall into the habit of verbally revising a question two or three times as you ask it, throwing not one, but two or three questions at the students. This gives the impression that you are asking many different questions all at once, and usually serves to confuse rather than clarify. Give a good deal of attention to the content, the purpose, the construction, and the delivery of the questions you ask so that each one adds dimension to the learning experience.

HOW CAN STUDENT RESPONSES BE USED EFFECTIVELY?

No matter how good your questions are, you must always be keenly aware of the students' responses in order to take advantage of them and build on them. The way your students answer your questions will guide you in recognizing those areas where they are progressing successfully and those areas where they need more work. Student responses are as much a learning experience for you as for them.

You will encounter many response situations; in fact, each time you ask a question and receive an answer you will be dealing with a singular case. However, despite their basically individual nature, some of the more difficult response-situations are indicated and suggestions are offered for handling them.

1.   *One student alone may seem unable to grasp a significant point.* Frequently a brief, personal, conference with the student on other than class time will help to clear up the difficulty. If the student needs several tutoring sessions, then you might meet with him during your preparation period or the period you are relieved of an administrative assignment, or during an extended homeroom period when he is not at an assembly.

How to use an answer

2.   *Sometimes you will have to deflect an irrelevant question.* Although it may be a good one, such a question requires an answer that takes the class too far afield. If the question is of general interest and serves a real function in your program you might make a brief response or incorporate it into the next or a subsequent lesson. If the interest is limited to the student who asked it, refer him to a source, or discuss the question with him after class or during a supervised study session.

3.   *The technique of handling an incorrect response will vary with the answer itself, and with the question that elicited it.* If a student answers "1566," when asked the date of the Spanish Armada's unsuccessful attempt to invade England, the most efficient thing for you to do is to call on another student without comment. However, there are many times when it is profitable for that student, and the rest of the class to find out why a response was incorrect. In math, for example, a student who says that $X^2(X^3 - 1) = X^6 - X^2$, should be asked to explain and verify each step of this work until he sees the error. You must decide, each time this problem arises, whether to devote the time to this kind of work because it will be of assistance to everyone, or whether working with a student in this fashion will slow up the group. In any case, a student should not feel as if he were being badgered or belittled instead of being helped.

4.   *There are answers which are neither correct nor incorrect for they involve matters of opinion.* Granting the initial premise that a student has an understanding of the information on which his opinion is based, he may with perfect justice be a minority of one in his maintenance of his position. He can be challenged to cite his proof but once that has been done and all the facts are there for everyone to weigh, further attempts to change his mind would be time consuming and pointless and not in the tradition of the democratic classroom.

How to use an answer

5. *Expressions such as, "You're wrong," are not conducive to the development of a flexible, receptive classroom atmosphere.* However, you must let a student know when he has given an incorrect response. In the case of the math example given earlier, a student giving an incorrect answer can be helped to understand the correct answer if you call upon another student to state the rules applying to exponents in this system. Then you might have the original student work through the problem again. If you have created an atmosphere in which everyone is interested in searching out answers, rather than identifying those who gave incorrect answers, you will find students more than willing to help each other learn.

6. *Sometimes the students will ask questions to which you do not have the answers.* In that event, it is best to admit it. You can say that you will check on the item and see if you can determine an answer; you can give the student who asked the question a reference, let him uncover the particular answer himself and then share it with the entire class. Do not try to bluff your way out of such a situation. Students are quick to recognize a bluff or a phoney, and really resent a "snow-job" kind of response.

7. *Some questions are directed to you and would seem to indicate that you are the only information source available.* Try to engage the efforts of all the students in the solution of a problem. Avoid asking questions which say "Tell me . . . ," and instead use the phrase, "Tell us. . . ." This helps to establish a broad framework in which all students can participate in the learning process.

It is important to keep in mind that questioning is a dynamic, ongoing process in which there is great potential for real teaching–learning interactions. It is one of the most important of the skills you will develop. Questioning is both a keen diagnostic tool, and a bridge from the known to the unknown.

PROBLEMS, QUESTIONS, AND ACTIVITIES

6.1 Evaluate the phrasing of each question below. Where you find it faulty, reword the question so that it will be more effective. Justify discarding the question entirely if you choose to do so.

1. Do you think Andrew Jackson was a greater President than William McKinley?

2. Why is oxygen necessary for life?

3. In the sentence, "John is tall.", what is the syntax of *tall*?

4. Many people favor the abolition of the Electoral College. Why do you agree with them?

5. Why does an isosceles triangle have two equal sides?

6. If A is greater than B, why is B greater than C?

7. Define the word *hero* in a literary context.

8. Why did the Embargo Act embitter ship owners in one section of the country and what were its effects throughout the United States?

9. How do you spell *achieve?*

10. Howard and Jason, have you done your homework? Put it on the board, please.

6.2 What would be your very next remark if you received each of the responses given below (1–6) in answer to the following question:

Compare and contrast Alexander Hamilton's attitude toward the common people with that of Thomas Jefferson.

1. "I didn't hear the question."

2. "Hamilton was against them. Jefferson was for them."

3. "I was absent yesterday."

4. "Jefferson was a very versatile man. He was interested in many fields including music and architecture. He believed in education for all. He was a liberal."

5. "I don't know."

6. Silence.

6.3 Evaluate the following questions used in a classroom situation. Rewrite those that you think need revision. Indicate why you would discard some completely. Select those you might use as they stand; tell why you find them to be satisfactory.

1. Why did so few of you do your homework?

2. Is that clear?

3. Where did our lesson end yesterday?

4. Why did you find example #3 so hard?

5. How many of you saw the news last night?

6. Do you all hear me?

7. Who put yesterday's homework on the board?

8. Will you please stop talking, Jane?

9. How do you spell *stationary?*

10. What time does this period end?

6.4 You find that many of your lessons fail to achieve the aim that you had planned although you asked the pivotal questions you designed. Too much class time is lost in interesting but insignificant digressions and irrelevancies. What steps would you take to remedy this defect and improve the lessons?

6.5 Select one specific topic in your own subject area. Make up a series of seven questions, each illustrating one of the functions listed in this chapter.

NOTES

NOTES

7

Demonstrations

WHAT IS A DEMONSTRATION?

This is the *Age of Visualization*. People at all age levels are accustomed to visual communication. The visual approach, and the visual media —pictures, posters, films, television—are all a very real part of our daily existence. In schools too the emphasis on visualization is becoming increasingly prominent. In the elementary grades there is wide use of "show and tell" sessions where students bring in a petrified rock specimen, a leaf from an unusual tree, a sea shell, a book, a picture. They show it to their classmates and tell something about it: where they found it, how they came to be at that location, what is interesting or important about it. This activity lets students share in some experiences of their classmates and thus enriches the experiential background of the entire class.

At all levels of learning there is a need for this kind of "show and tell":

Everyday demonstrations

Department stores have people demonstrate food blenders while telling customers about them.

Television commercials show you a product while its characteristics are discussed.

"How-to" books and magazines include, along with the instructions, pictures or sketches of the steps in making an object.

In schools, where the greatest emphasis should be on individualized learning experiences and the total involvement of the student, there is more and more a practical need today to show the student how something works, how a principle is applied, and how a technique is to be used so that he can then undertake more individualized investigation or study. These show activities are termed *demonstrations*.

The students are shown some technique, skill, or object, and then learn how it works, operates, or is applied. Demonstrations can precede, complement, or follow lab experiences so that students can derive more direct benefit from such activity. Demonstrations like lab experiences help to translate the theoretical concept, vague idea, or verbal description into concrete reality. Just as lab experiences are not limited to science classes, and discussions are not used only in English classes, so demonstrations are not limited to any one subject area. In each area there is a need for this kind of show dimension in a lesson in order to broaden the base upon which learning interactions are built.

WHY USE DEMONSTRATIONS?

As with every other facet of a lesson, there are many different but specific reasons for using demonstrations in an interaction.

The functions of demonstrations

1. *Motivating interest.* Cutting into a decorated seven-layer cake or serving portions of an aspic can serve to stimulate interest in how they are made.

2. *Focusing attention on a specific question or problem.* Illustrating the differences in conductivity of water solutions of salts, acids, bases, and alcohols can direct the student's attention to the question of why substances differ in their electrical conductivity.

3. *Explaining a principle.* Using a series of lines from poetry or prose to illustrate stream of consciousness can be the best way to give students a practical experience with this type of style.

4. *Developing critical listening and looking.* Using a taped or recorded segment of a dated political speech and/or showing pictures of candidates of various eras may start students listening for important phrases and looking for crowd-pleasing techniques.

5. *Illustrating a technique.* Demonstrating the preparation of a silk screen for making prints is the best way to let students get an idea of what the steps in the process are like.

6. *Summarizing.* Using a transparency to diagram how the territorial boundaries of the United States changed from 1780 to 1890 can help to summarize some of the major problems of that period in our history.

7. *Applying a principle.* Working through an entire problem in mathematics using all data provided can illustrate how a formula or mathematical principle is applied and used to determine a solution.

8. *Demonstrating a skill.* Showing how to operate a typewriter or a key punch machine may be the best method of teaching students how to use them.

9. *Reviewing.* Working out a complete procedure for the election of a class president—setting up qualifications, nominations, campaigning, voting, and counting ballots—is the best experience in reviewing an election system.

Each demonstration you introduce can serve more than one function in a lesson. However, there is much more than just function to consider; these activities, to be of maximum use, must be carefully planned and pretested to be sure that they work, and illustrate what you intend them to.

WHAT ARE THE ADVANTAGES AND LIMITATIONS OF DEMONSTRATIONS?

Each technique you use has its own inherent assets and liabilities. In order to use a technique effectively you must be aware of both, so that you can use the tool to its maximum potential. Do no expect your demonstration to do something it is not equipped to do.

Some of the advantages of demonstrations are:

The advantages of demonstrations

1. *They are economical of time.* With your greater familiarity with equipment and procedures, it will usually take you much less time to do a task than it would any of your students. You know how to set up equipment; you know what you want to do; you know what comes next.

2. *They are economical of materials.* You might use ten grams of a chemical for a demonstration. If fifteen groups or thirty individual students perform the same task you will need $15 \times 10 = 150$ grams or $30 \times 10 = 300$ grams of that chemical. This may be important if your supply is low, and you cannot count on immediate delivery of replacements.

3. *They let you introduce equipment and materials available in too small an amount to be used in a laboratory experience.* You might have only one oscilloscope in the school; you might have only one potter's wheel. A demonstration lets everyone in the class see the instrument, and how it works.

4. *They are safer.* Some demonstrations may be hazardous or risky for the less knowledgeable or less experienced. Adding wooden splints to molten potassium chlorate or using an antique slicing machine may be too hazardous for students; yet you would like them to see the process or the object, so a demonstration is the only safe procedure.

5. *They let you telescope time.* Some events take place over a long period of time—too long to be conveniently handled in a brief demonstration in a class. The metamorphosis of a tadpole into a frog can be "speeded up" if you illustrate the process with seven or nine different frogs and tadpoles, each at a different stage of development.

6. *They let you "stop the clock."* Some events take place too quickly to be seen by the unaided eye. Some processes are so lengthy and in-

volved that you really have to consider them in sections. In both these cases you want to stop the event or process and take a look at it. Filming the operation of a drill press and then viewing it at reduced speed helps you see how the machine really operates. The digestion of foods takes place in different areas of the body under the influence of different enzymes. This entire process is too complex to consider in toto. Demonstrations can be used to illustrate different phases of the digestive process and give you ample time to discuss them.

The advantages of demonstrations

7. *They let you focus and direct attention.* Demonstrations often give you the opportunity to direct the student's attention to a particular technique, skill, or process. You can emphasize important characteristics or implications. You can demonstrate an equilibrium system and show the effect of certain variables on it. You can illustrate the particular shorthand outline for a word; you can show how a graph is to be constructed.

Demonstrations have limitations including:

1. *They permit only limited student involvement.* This is the most obvious limitation of the activity. Some students can be directly involved to record or graph data, to assist in presenting some phase of the demonstration, or in diagramming or completing a chalkboard outline. However, the degree of direct involvement is usually limited. The students watching the demonstration are involved to the extent that they are making notes, recording data, and listening, but this is not the direct experience they get if they perform the experiment or investigation themselves in a laboratory or workshop situation.

The limitations of demonstrations

2. *They may not be readily visible.* If the equipment you use is standard or micro-size, then students in the middle and rear of the room may not be able to see what you are doing. In chemistry, for example, when illustrating the formation of a precipitate, only one or two students up front will directly participate. The other students have to take your word that something is happening in a test tube or flask. This limitation can be overcome by using larger equipment or doing reactions in Petri dishes on the stage of an overhead projector. You sometimes can safely bring all the students up to the front of the room where you are working and let them gather round to see what is happening. At times this will be the best you can do.

3. *They may unduly accelerate the pace of work.* A demonstration that you are doing can sometimes set too rapid a pace for comprehension of purpose or procedure. You may with your additional skill and knowledge be moving so rapidly that the students don't have an opportunity to follow what you are doing or why you are doing it. They do not have the chance to ask why something happened until the demonstration is over. Some matters of the procedure or technique used may be puzzling, and completely obscure the intent of the activity. When you plan and then pretest a demonstration, be sure that you allow time for brief stops—to answer questions, explain procedures or safety factors. You must always consider the pace you are establishing for the students to follow.

The limitations of demonstrations

4. *They may not be the most effective way to introduce a topic.* A demonstration, usually economical of time and materials, may not be the best method to use if you consider the long-range view and the side-effect benefits of other techniques. It is relatively easy for you to have pre-set-up a series of demonstrations illustrating Spallanzani's work showing that living things do not originate in dead matter. Different demonstrations highlight the different controls Spallanzani used and the entire system can be handled in a brief time span. However, if students perform this experiment given only rudimentary directions, they will have to identify and then provide the different controls and experimental conditions needed in a complete investigation. Admittedly, this kind of trial and error workshop or laboratory approach takes time. But the investment is well worth it. Students will get first-hand experience in experimentation, providing "controls," recording data. They will also get an appreciation of the fact that experiments take time—that there is no instant success in the solution of real problems.

5. *They may confuse students.* You may have complete understanding of what the demonstration indicates or illustrates. However, you may not have introduced or presented the work in such a way that the students also understand. In the planning and presentation stages, keep in mind the need for clarification of purposes, and procedures. You should share with the students the reasons for using a specific piece of equipment. To give practice in the area of making estimates and calculated guesses, you can ask them to suggest what the outcomes of a demonstration will be. The students must understand what you are doing and why you are doing it if the activity is going to have any meaning to them.

6. *They may encourage excessive lecturing.* One of the most unnerving things in a lesson is the silence that follows a question or the silence that follows your comments on a demonstration you are doing—the silence seems to last for hours when really only a few seconds have gone by. If the question you asked was a "good" one, requiring an extended answer, then you have to give students time to consider facts and formulate the answer. If you are engaged in a demonstration, and perhaps have just commented on some aspect of it, then stop talking and give your students a chance to:

Make notes

Sketch the equipment

Record data

Formulate a question

Ask a question

Don't be fearful of the moment of silence at this point. Instead, learn to appreciate its function, and use it as a significant part of the lesson.

7. *They may encourage hasty generalizations.* Just as one apple does not indicate whether the rest of the bushel is good, so one demonstration does not always prove the rule either. You must constantly emphasize this when you are presenting a demonstration or the students are doing individual lab work. One experiment or investigation can be used to illustrate a principle or help formulate a rule, but many repetitions and variations of that experiment are needed before any rules, or laws are established or confirmed.

The limitations of demonstrations

Demonstrations like other types of learning activities have a role to play in your instructional program. The idea is to use them to advantage, to make the most of what they offer and minimize their limitations. If you have examined all the alternative activities and have decided that the demonstration technique is the best one to use, your next tasks are to plan and pretest the specific activity.

HOW DO YOU PREPARE A DEMONSTRATION?

The first job here is to decide specifically what you are going to demonstrate. Where do you look for suggestions?

Ideas for demonstrations

- ☐ The textbook your class is using may include—along with exercises, additional readings, and projects—demonstrations or workshop experiences which will enrich the subject matter.

- ☐ There may be a teacher's guide designed by your local or state Department of Education specifically for your subject area.

- ☐ There may be guidebooks available from the U.S. Superintendent of Documents that you can order and purchase.

- ☐ There may be demonstration or activity handbooks specific to your area. Titles can be secured from publishers' catalogues or the local or school library card catalogue.

- ☐ During your student teaching experience you may see lessons utilizing workable and effective demonstrations that you can make note of for later use.

- ☐ Your supervisor or colleagues may be using demonstrations they have developed and refined which you can explore for your own use.

- ☐ Journals and newsletters published by national or state organizations in your subject area often contain articles about techniques, materials, demonstrations and workshop activities developed by teachers in different parts of the country.

Your sources for demonstration ideas are virtually inexhaustible. Once you have identified or designed a particular demonstration to fill a specific function in a lesson, you are ready to assemble the materials and try it out. The following checklist indicates the questions you should consider during this phase of the demonstration preparation.

PREPARATION CHECKLIST FOR DEMONSTRATION

Yes No

1. ☐ ☐ Have you prepared a list of all the materials and equipment you will need?

2. ☐ ☐ Have you ordered one extra set-up for pretesting and calculating the total amount of materials you will need for all your classes?

3. Will the materials be assembled and prepared by you or by some technician, paraprofessional, or teacher aide?

4. Where are all materials gathered?

   ☐ ☐ On a truck?

   ☐ ☐ In some transportable container?

   ☐ ☐ At your work area?

5. ☐ ☐ Have you assembled all the parts of the equipment and tried it out for leaks, points of stress, and operability?

6. ☐ ☐ Will you need water and electricity in the area in which you now work and then in the classroom?

7. ☐ ☐ Does the equipment work?

8. ☐ ☐ Have you considered all the safety factors?

   ☐ ☐ Will it be necessary to clear students out of front rows when doing the demonstration?

   ☐ ☐ Will you need a safety screen or safety goggles when working?

9. How much time will the demonstration take?

   With no stops?

   With stops for your recording data, making drawings, and sketching equipment?

10. ☐ ☐ Can the demonstration be safely stopped at any point for discussion or some related activity?

11. ☐ ☐ Will you demonstrate a technique or process once and then use a prepared supply of the material made to conduct further work?

12. What snags might you encounter?

13. ☐ ☐ Can the materials be seen from different sections of the room?

14. ☐ ☐ Is it possible to modify the demonstration equipment to use larger sizes, or in some way make it more visible?

15. ☐ ☐ Do you make what you are doing clear?

16. How much time will be needed?

   For introduction?

   For student discussion and analysis?

   For clean up?

Yes No

| | | **What provisions must be made for dismantling, and clearning the work area?** | 17. |

| | | **When, during the activity, is the best time to distribute printed materials or specimens to examine?** | 18. |

☐ ☐   **Will the data gathered or the technique illustrated be used again in the lesson or in some subsequent activity?** 19.

How can students safely and meaningfully assist during the work? 20.

☐ ☐   Drawing diagrams?

☐ ☐   Doing some of the work?

☐ ☐   Recording data?

☐ ☐   **Will any of the information developed during the demonstration be used as part of a homework or study assignment?** 21.

Your preliminary testing of a demonstration must go far beyond just the manipulation of some equipment or handling some objects. It involves your evaluation of the materials, the procedures, the timing, and the impact of a given demonstration. It also involves a great investment of time. Much of this pretesting work can be done during your preparation periods, for usually you will not have the equipment or source materials at home. Your preparation of requests for materials, and designing of homework assignments, data tables, diagrammatic flow charts or materials for duplication and distribution can probably best be done at home.

Many demonstrations that you read about sound excellent, but after trying them out yourself you may find that they are not as easy or as pertinent to your topic as you first thought. Some demonstrations may not be right for the present work but may have potential use later on. You should, therefore, keep a card catalogue or reference system on this work—on both the "good" ones and the "not so good" ones. This will help you repeat your successes and not your failures. Index cards (5 by 8-inch) are suitable for this purpose; they are usually large enough so that you can tape on or write in the directions, and a materials list as well as your comments about the demonstration.

After this preliminary screening, and pretesting, you are ready for the real test—the use of the demonstration in class.

HOW DO YOU PRESENT DEMONSTRATIONS?

Before you start on your program of demonstration work, try to observe other teachers at this type of activity. Secure the necessary clearances from the teachers and supervisors involved, and then sit in on several classes.

Try to identify the most effective and the most limiting features of the demonstration observed, which techniques of presentation and timing were workable and which were not. From your vantage point as a spectator you have the opportunity to see a demonstration that you may perhaps use one day, and that you certainly can learn from. You can learn the good points of presentation and the pitfalls to avoid. Perhaps your supervisor can recommend a teacher who is particularly gifted in demonstration work.

The following groups of questions were designed for you to first use as you critically evaluate the demonstration content, timing, presentation, and impact. Later you can use the same criteria for setting up and later assessing the effectiveness of your own demonstrations.

PRESENTATION CHECKLIST FOR DEMONSTRATIONS

Yes No

1. **How was the demonstration introduced?**

☐ ☐ Was its purpose clear?

☐ ☐ Was it appropriate to the topic?

☐ ☐ Did students receive any guidelines for watching or recording information?

Was any preliminary information given about the demonstration, or was it used "cold" to start students thinking?

2. ☐ ☐ **Was the purpose of the demonstration clear?**

Was it used as a motivation, to illustrate a principle, or to introduce a technique?

Was the role of the demonstration explained by the teacher or elicited from the students?

☐ ☐ Was the demonstration appropriate at that point in the lesson?

3. ☐ ☐ **Were all the materials ready?**

What materials were preassembled?

Which might have been?

How were materials organized in preparation for use?

☐ ☐ Were there any unnecessary materials present?

4. **How were materials displayed?**

☐ ☐ Was the table or work area cleared and ready?

☐ ☐ Was any special table covering used for visual contrast?

☐ ☐ Was the equipment organized and set up quickly?

☐ ☐ If a series of demonstrations was used, was each one sufficiently separated from the others to clearly stand out?

☐ ☐ Was time lost in handling materials and searching for missing pieces?

5. ☐ ☐ **Was the demonstration visible?**

☐ ☐ Was the equipment large enough to be seen?

☐ ☐ Was the lighting adequate?

Yes No

☐ ☐ Was a suitable background provided?

☐ ☐ Did students gather around the work table?

☐ ☐ Were any samples passed around for study?

☐ ☐ Were materials passed around for study, stored in suitable containers?

☐ ☐ Were labels large and visible?

☐ ☐ **Were safety precautions observed?**   6.

☐ ☐ Was a fire extinguisher ready at hand in the room?

☐ ☐ Were safety goggles or a safety shield used?

☐ ☐ Was it necessary to move students away from the work area? Why?

How were students directly involved in the demonstration?   7.

☐ ☐ Did they draw diagrams and record data?

☐ ☐ Did they assist in the demonstration?

☐ ☐ Did they perform some part of the demonstration?

How were printed materials for distribution handled?   8.

☐ ☐ Were materials previously counted out in batches?

When were materials distributed?

☐ ☐ Was this the best time?

What system was used for distribution?

☐ ☐ Were any materials to be collected? How?

☐ ☐ Was the function of these materials clear?

How much time was involved?   9.

How much time was needed for an introduction?

How long did the demonstration itself take?

What time was needed to record data?

What time was provided for discussion and evaluation?

How much time was needed for asking questions?

How much time was needed for cleaning up?

How much talking was involved?   10.

☐ ☐ Did the teacher do all the talking?

☐ ☐ Did any students ask questions?

☐ ☐ Was there time provided for students to just watch the demonstration, consider it and digest what they had seen?

☐ ☐ Was the talking and working pace so rapid that students seemed overwhelmed?

☐ ☐ Was the pace so rapid that some important facets of a demonstration were overlooked?

☐ ☐ Was the vocabulary too sophisticated?

Yes No

☐ ☐ Were terms used defined?

11. **How was the chalkboard utilized?**

☐ ☐ Was an outline completed?

☐ ☐ Was a data table organized and used?

☐ ☐ Were any diagrams drawn?

☐ ☐ Was the outline used again during the lesson?

12. ☐ ☐ **Were any long-range demonstrations set up?**

What provision was made for checking on progress and reporting to class?

Where were the materials to be left?

13. **What provision was made for clean-up?**

☐ ☐ Was the clean-up done while students were completing some portion of the work, or their notes?

☐ ☐ Was the area cleaned up and ready for use by the next class?

14. ☐ ☐ **Did the demonstration work?**

☐ ☐ Did the equipment work?

☐ ☐ Were there any snags?

☐ ☐ Did it serve its function?

15. **What assignment or further work grew out of the demonstration?**

How was it identified?

How was the assignment given?

There is a great deal to be learned by watching a demonstration with these guidelines in mind. In addition to observing other teachers, ask your supervisor to come into one of your classes to observe a demonstration. Later you can discuss its more successful and less successful features.

Another profitable possibility for getting experience with demonstrations or any other type of learning activity is to watch those of others with your supervisor and several fellow teachers. If you watch a lesson together, either a live lesson or a video-taped lesson, and then discuss it in detail, you can examine each facet of the activity. In the case of the video-taped lesson, you can play a segment back and watch it again. This method affords a greater degree of objectivity in your evaluation. You will not be psychologically tied to any part of the lesson, and can with greater ease critically and objectively evaluate it.

WHAT IS THE "FUTURE" OF A DEMONSTRATION?

After you present a demonstration, you should evaluate the extent to which it has been successful, and has done what you intended it to do.

This evaluation should take place as soon after the lesson as possible while your recollections about it are still fresh. As soon as you can — if possible before your next class — modify the procedures, the questions, the time sequence, or the materials you used in order to eliminate those "snags" which developed but which you had not anticipated. The next time you do the demonstration it will be in the light of:

☐ Your first experience in the preclass testing

☐ Your use of it in class

Makes notes on what procedures or sequences you changed or the different materials you substituted. Add these notes to the index card you have already prepared on the demonstration. Each time you do a demonstration you will perhaps use it in a different context, for a different purpose, and with different materials. Your previous experiences with a demonstration will come in handy as you try to adapt it for different uses.

A demonstration, like all other aspects of a teaching–learning interaction, should be evaluated before, during, and after each class session if it is to:

☐ Be carefully examined and prepared for use

☐ Serve a specific purpose, and be a relevant, pertinent, learning experience for you and the students

☐ Have an extended lifetime of use in this or some other context

PROBLEMS, QUESTIONS, AND ACTIVITIES

7.1 During a demonstration you will frequently find that you must use words or expressions unfamiliar to your class. What methods can you use to be sure that these words when they are first used do not interrupt the continuity of the lesson and do not impede communication with the students?

7.2 Make up a checklist you would use to prepare materials and equipment for a specific demonstration in your area. Be sure to include safety considerations.

7.3 Briefly describe a demonstration in your subject area. Write out the instructions or information you would furnish the students before the demonstration.

What activity would immediately follow the demonstration?

7.4 Design a demonstration that you would use for each of the following purposes:

1. Motivation
2. Summary
3. Review
4. Enrichment

7.5 How would you handle a demonstration that failed to work in class?

NOTES

NOTES

8
Audio-Visual Aids

WHAT ARE AUDIO-VISUAL AIDS?

Highly effective and meaningful learning experiences are usually those in which students are active, enthusiastic participants. High premium must be placed on learning by doing—the vital need for direct, first-hand experiences. All learning is multi-sensory in nature, and each of your senses—hearing, sight, touch, smell, and taste—plays a role in formulating your reactions to any stimulus. Each adds yet another dimension and makes a unique contribution to the learning process. Of prime concern is the need for planning and providing for as many first-hand learning experiences as possible in your instructional program. There are times, however, when such direct experiences are not feasible. Then you must turn to one or more of a variety of materials, equipment, and techniques designed to act as worthwhile but vicarious experiences for your students. Most of these substitutes involve sight and hearing more than the other senses; thus the term, *audio-visual aids*, has come to characterize these materials.

Audio-visual aids are devices which permit a more effective use of a multi-sensory approach to learning than just words can provide. Many different types of materials are included under this heading:

Audio-visual aids

- ☐ Projectors
- ☐ Charts
- ☐ Models
- ☐ Chalkboards
- ☐ Recording machines
- ☐ Maps
- ☐ Radio and television

The use of these audio-visual aids involves many different skills and techniques. Each aid has a spectrum of functions restricted only by the physical equipment and your creative imagination. Each provides the concrete, illustrative material so necessary in any real teaching–learning interaction. Another aspect of your planning, then, is centered about the use of these aids in your programs. As you look about your school and participate in professional activities, you will find that there is a wide variety of equipment and materials to choose from. There is a wide spectrum of quality as well as quantity.

You will find that there are marked differences in the extent to which audio-visual aids are used by teachers in real situations: some use few aids; some use a variety of aids; some use too many aids and negate the value of any one of them. Your first job is to determine what the potential uses of these materials are in your programs.

WHY USE AUDIO-VISUAL AIDS IN YOUR PROGRAM?

In essence, you use an audio-visual aid because you cannot use the "real thing" or you find it impractical to do so. Reasons for making this decision include:

1. *Overcoming inaccessibility.* Some places cannot be visited or viewed directly or at all. We all could not be aboard *Apollo 11* or the lunar module *Eagle* on its epic journey and landing on the moon in July 1969. However, the pictures and film taken by Neil Armstrong and Edwin Aldrin help us see some of what they saw. Tapes of their remarks help us relive, as often as we wish, some of their wonder and excitement in this great human and technological achievement.

Functions of audio-visual aids

2. *Reducing or enlarging size — the microscopic and the macroscopic.* Some objects and organisms are too small to be viewed directly. Even greatly magnified, bacteria are too elusive and small to be readily studied for structure and function. Microphotographs — photographs taken through an electron microscope — permit preliminary identification of structures prior to individualized, independent lab studies. These audio-visual aids enable us, as an entire group or individually, to examine a greatly magnified virus without direct access to a microscope or an electron microscope. Macroscopic systems, such as the solar system, the skyline of a city, or a large dairy farm are difficult to survey and study simply because of their magnitude. Models and pictures of buildings, theaters, and geologic phenomena permit gross analysis and comparison of components and lead to greater understanding of the entire structure.

3. *Insuring safety of students and teachers.* Some processes or pieces of equipment cannot be examined or used with even a moderate degree of safety to the investigator. Films of television pictures of the interior of a working nuclear reactor fill the need for information about the operation of such equipment and yet do not expose the learners to the hazards associated with the equipment.

4. *Capturing the infrequent occurrence.* The successful voyage of the *Kon-Tiki* or the sinking of the *Ra* have already added to the folklore of the world, and are examples of events that occur so infrequently in time that we cannot easily incorporate them into our teaching pro-

Functions of audio-visual aids

grams, no matter how flexible our schedule may be. Tapes, films, and pictures of such occurrences make them readily available for introduction at any moment you select. Students should be encouraged, whenever it is feasible, to personally witness natural events, exhibits, or history-in-the-making events. They should be encouraged to do as many things as they can—paint a picture, bake a cake, fly a model plane—and go to as many places as possible—museums, zoos, concerts, operas, the folk music festivals. It is in this way that they will build up a rich background of experiences. Tapes, films, and other audio-visual aids then permit us to consider such events or phenomena later, at a more significant moment in a class session, and so add further dimension to lessons, motivate interest in new areas, and provoke thought about events. The photographs of Mars taken by *Mariner VI* and *VII* in 1969 were interesting to see as they were beamed to earth. Still photographs of these pictures can be a most meaningful part of a science class study of the solar system.

5.   *Extending capabilities.* As direct observers, we are limited to the visible portion of the electromagnetic spectrum. We cannot see ultraviolet, radio, or infrared radiation. However, an analytical instrument such as an infrared spectrophotometer permits the study of structure in organic compounds not possible in any other manner.

Time lapse studies such as stop-action photographs permit you to analyze events occurring too rapidly or too slowly for convenient study. No matter how interesting a teacher's voice and style may be, a change is often welcome. The voice of Marlon Brando on tape or record speaking some of the lines of Marc Antony from Shakespeare's *Julius Caesar,* or of Dylan Thomas reading his own "Do Not Go Gentle into That Good Night" can be spine-tingling to a student. The teacher may be an excellent reader, and he should read aloud; the students may be developing into good readers, and they should be encouraged to read aloud too, but why keep talents like Richard Burton, James Mason, or Lawrence Olivier out of the classroom? Tapes and records can bring these people into the learning scene as valuable resource personnel.

Films, too, extend our capabilities. A class studying *A Tale of Two Cities* gets an instant picture of the hunger that Dickens describes in his novel when they see the film version, showing the nobles tossing meaty bones to their mastiffs, and the emaciated people trying to snatch the bones from the dogs. The reading becomes more meaningful, and greater understanding is possible when you use audio-visual aids in combination with reading and study.

Tapes of news conferences, scientific events, or theatrical or musical performances enable you to look back on these events as often as you wish. Tapes of students debating and discussing topics provide you with permanent records for repeated consultation. Recording your own and your students' readings provides you with a means of listening to yourselves, and of evaluating the effectiveness of speech and content as well as helping you to detect speech defects and flaws in logical presentation. For example, a group of seniors might want to discuss how their school regulations could be changed for the incoming freshmen. Your experience in the past may have shown that the majority of such discussions dealt with food and physical comforts, and you might play back a tape of a prior discussion to illustrate that important intangibles like cooperation, responsibility, and initiative had been ignored by previous groups. Further discussion of this topic can thus take on greater meaning and significance.

*Functions of
audio-visual aids*

Transparencies—transparent reproductions of materials for use on the overhead projector—of themes, essays, or poems written by students permit an entire class to study one work at a time, focusing attention on structure, style, or grammar in a manner not easily afforded otherwise. These transparencies are easily made in about twenty seconds using specially prepared films and an office copy machine.

These techniques and materials often generate much excitement and enthusiasm and can serve to move the learning experience on to broader horizons and greater student involvement.

6. *Coping with perishability.* Some materials are highly perishable and must be studied in their original locale. The Book of Kells in Trinity College, Ireland, can be seen only under protective glass. But for a study of caligraphy, or art style, still photographs of it can let us all look at this famous work and share in its appreciation and use in a classroom lesson. Films, photographs, and models of unobtainable materials provide for their introduction into the learning scene. Without the use of audio-visual aids, the students might not be introduced to these objects at all.

Some live specimens cannot be brought to the ocean surface for study without damage or destruction to the organism. Photographs let us study these creatures without going down to investigate them or bringing them to the surface and thus destroying them.

7. *Capsuling time.* Some processes or events take place over too long a period to be studied in the time you have available. A flower developing or the hatching of a chick or the erection of a bridge seen through time-lapse photographs gives the important highlights and a complete overview. These are aids that help us compress time.

8. *Combating cost.* Some materials are prohibitively costly for their inclusion in your programs. A Renoir or a Vermeer, for example, is beyond your department or school budget. However, a fine reproduction or a color stereo photograph serves to acquaint the student with the work of a particular artist and to stimulate him to view the originals and study the painter in greater detail.

WHICH AUDIO-VISUAL AIDS ARE BEST FOR YOUR PROGRAM?

There is no one right audio-visual aid to use in any given situation. Some are better than others for a specific task. The one you select will depend on those available to you, those you can prepare yourself, the time allotted, and the type of interaction involved—large group, small group, or individual study. As you survey the materials and equipment immediately available to you in your school, you will begin to recognize areas in which aids would be of help in your program, and what types would be the most effective.

Talk to your colleagues—see what aids they are using for a specific task and what they have developed to meet the need of their programs. Send away for catalogues of equipment, prepared aids, and materials available from commercial sources. All these will give you ideas for selecting or creating what best suits your purposes. For example, there is available commercially a set of cardboard cubes, each representing one of the chemical elements. The sides of the cubes list some physical and chemical data on each element, such as atomic weight and number. The set represents about sixty of the known elements. You can easily construct such oaktag cubes. Organize the information you want to use into six groups—one for each face—and print this information on the faces of the cube before you paste or glue the cube together. Be sure to put the same type of information on the same face of each cube so that the sequence of information on the cube faces will all be the same. Oaktag cubes of this type can be

FIGURE 8.1
Model for an oaktag cube

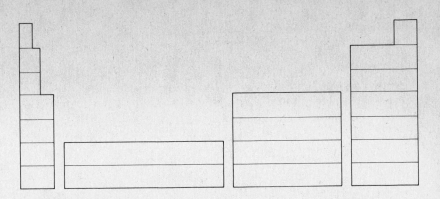

FIGURE 8.2
Shelves for periodic table cubes

used in many subject areas—epochs of history, conjugations of foreign language verbs, movements in art. In addition, you can construct shelves to hold this set of models, and thus create your own periodic table of elements in three dimensions. Such an aid can be used for studying the periodicity of properties of elements in groups or periods, and would be a useful adjunct to any science class. You can have the wood cut to size in a lumber yard and then easily assemble the shelves in sections for ease in storage. Your students can often do the carpentry work; a woodworking class might be able to do the entire project for you.

As you read, talk about, and investigate the various channels for securing and preparing audio-visual aids, you will learn to keep your eyes and ears open for new ways of doing things and new ways of using older aids. You must keep critically evaluating the learning scene for areas in which audio-visual aids will provide the needed motivation, experience, or stimulus to thinking.

WHAT ARE SOME TYPES OF AUDIO-VISUAL AIDS?

There are a vast number of different audio-visual materials and equipment available to you today. Each can be used to advantage in your program and add dimension to it. You should be familiar with most of the principal types of aids in order to more effectively use them. Some of the major categories of audio-visual aids include:

☐ Models and specimens

☐ Bulletin boards and display cases

☐ Charts and maps

☐ Chalkboards

☐ Photographs and pictures

☐ Mass media—television, radio, newspapers

☐ Textbook illustrations

☐ Recordings and tapes

☐ Film, filmstrip, slide, loop projectors

Categories of audio-visual aids

☐ Microprojectors

☐ Opaque projectors

☐ Overhead projectors

☐ Electrically prepared stencils and duplicating machines

You should at your earliest opportunity determine those aids available in your school, learn how to operate them, and then use them in your classes and see their effects.

Models and Specimens

This composite category contains two types of aids of overlapping definition—models and specimens. **Models** as aids representing smaller or larger than real objects can be categorized as:

Types of specimens and models

Those showing gross or surface features such as a relief map of a volcanic area

Those that are dissectible to show the relation of components such as a modern, three dimensional model of an animal cell

Those that are working simulations of real pieces of equipment or organisms such as lift pumps, thermostats, motors, or mechanical hearts

Each type of model serves a different purpose ranging from preliminary, cursory analysis to application or illustration of a principle. The size of the model will play an important role in its use. If it is too small to be seen easily, a diagram, transparency, or picture might be better than the model. You must consider the size of the group when selecting the most effective aid to use. Some models, such as rock specimens, can be mounted on stands to extend their visibility range.

A simple mounting stand can be made from a large coffee can, inverted and covered with construction paper, or from a large empty wire spool. These spools, 4 or 6 inches in diameter, can be obtained from the science department or from the maintenance staff in your

FIGURE 8.3
Using discarded items as mounts for models

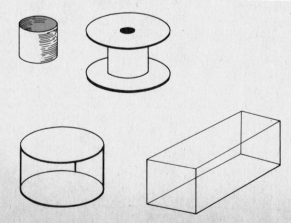

school. The school cafeteria uses large size cans of food too. You can ask that the empty cans, with the tops removed, be retained for you. After washing them thoroughly and drying them, paint or cover them with an opaque, adhesive material. They make excellent storage containers for small objects too. Another easily obtainable mounting base is the rotating type of plastic kitchen shelf organizer. This revolves easily and often has two layers to extend both use and elevation. A variety of wooden boxes, or plastic shoe boxes can also be used for supporting a model while examining and displaying it.

The most complex and costly models often come with an instruction manual for assembling parts and using the model. Keep these manuals on file for consultation and to provide the name and address of the manufacturer should you need a replacement part or some accessory equipment.

Before you purchase any model consider its use in a variety of situations.

Does it lend itself to more than a one-time per year exposure?

Does it seem durable? Cardboard, oaktag, and paper models can quickly deteriorate after a few uses if not carefully handled.

Is it accurate in that which it purports to represent?

Are the moving parts easy to move, or is there a good chance of snapping pieces off with the application of just a little pressure?

Does the model present up-to-date concepts or is it already out of date?

Can it be modified for further, more extensive, use?

Are the parts labeled? Can labels be covered or masked so that the model does not give away most of the answers?

What to know about a model

Examine models already available in your school carefully before recommending the purchase of others. Determine the weak points or drawbacks of each. Find the best, most effective model. Look over the equipment offered by a variety of companies. You can secure copies of their catalogues by writing on your school letterhead and requesting them. You can also have them add your name to their mailing list for new leaflets and announcements.

You can design and build your own models. Some of your students are very skilled in assembling kits. This is a cost saver and offers students a means of participating in class work which is not otherwise possible for them. A kit can be used for a laboratory exercise as well. For example, a set of DNA models for use in genetics studies can be constructed as a lab experience from kits, or a motor can be assembled from a kit in a physics class, or a model of a theater set in an English class. Each can be a rewarding and worthwhile learning experience, particularly if these models help to explain or visualize specific concepts and serve a practical purpose.

Specimens, as another class of materials, can be divided into two major categories—*living* and *nonliving*.

Living plants and animals pose unique opportunities and problems for use in a classroom setting. They require supervision, controlled climate, temperature and lighting, adequate food and water. You should be aware of these facets of their care before undertaking the responsibility of including them in your activities.

Terraria are important additions to any classroom. They can represent different ecological environments or simply be decorative. Several different terraria—desert, woodland, and bog—are highly recommended. Each can be set up in a large glass aquarium tank, or a plastic sweater box. About one-third of the container should be filled with pebbles or gravel to provide for adequate drainage. A layer of coarse sand is added next, the surface being contoured to add interest. Then the soil should be added—rich and loamy for woodlands, and sandy for deserts. Finally the plants are placed in an interesting arrangement. A local nursery or greenhouse can advise you about the best plants and soils to use.

FIGURE 8.4
Basic terrarium container

FIGURE 8.5
Terrarium arrangement

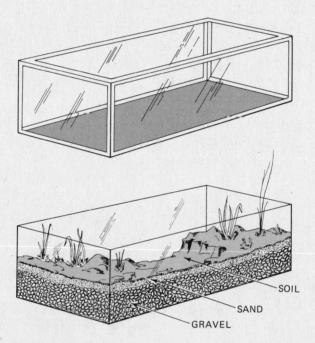

SOIL

SAND

GRAVEL

Vertebrate animals commonly introduced into school programs include mice, rats, guinea pigs, hamsters, and gerbils, as well as goldfish and tropical fish. Live animals require housing and careful, constant attention. They should be housed in a separate room and locks should be provided for their cages. They should be kept away from inquisitive fingers until you are ready to introduce them and can supervise the activity. The animals can be easily frightened and can inflict painful and sometimes serious bites simply because they were startled and then panicked. Animals must be fed and watered, and cages or containers cleaned on a regular basis. Adequate light, fresh air, and heating must be provided.

Aquaria, both fresh and salt water, are valuable assets to almost any program. You can secure detailed bulletins from a number of companies concerning setting up aquaria and maintaining them. Salt water aquaria are usually difficult to establish and maintain. A local tropical fish supplier can be of great assistance in helping you set up and care for the aquaria in your school.

Consider the care of terraria and aquaria before you introduce them. They will require daily attention, attention during weekends, vacation periods, and during the summer period. Some of your students may have aquaria at home and can be of assistance in maintaining the ones you establish in class. They may even take care of small animals at home during vacation periods as part of their own collections — with their parents' approval and consent, of course. However, the major responsibility for these projects is yours and cannot be delegated to any student. Consult with your supervisor or principal before you undertake any such activity. He will acquaint you with some of the regulations concerning live animals which are specific to your school district and offer his experience in developing a program using these materials.

Even small organisms like bacterial cultures, protozoa, worms, insects, and frogs require special provision for their maintenance and use. Your use of any of these specimens will be determined by the facilities available, your program, and your own interest. It is very easy to rush into incubating fertilized chicken eggs to study the embryonic development of the chick. However, what if the eggs are left to hatch? The chicks may hatch during a weekend and suffocate before you reach them. If they successfully come through the hatching, you have to provide a safe incubator that is not a fire or electrical hazard. Then you will have to make provision for the growing chicks. You will have to obtain parental consent (in writing) from those students who wish to take them home as pets. Keep in mind that these are small living creatures that you are introducing to your classes, and your attitude toward these animals will condition your students' attitude toward them. Your concern for them, and a reverence for living creatures, can have a marked effect on how your students react to and treat all animals.

The *nonliving specimens* used in class include rock samples, art works, adding machines, and fabric samples, to name but a few. Keep the following in mind when selecting any such specimens for class use:

The size of the specimen must be consistent with the size of the group.

What to consider about specimens

A series of specimens should be numbered instead of named. This extends their usefulness to practical exams and does not predetermine reactions to them.

Specimens should not, if possible, have any jagged edges or be too heavy to move about easily.

Specimens must be durable to withstand frequent handling. Fragile specimens should be supported on plastic or mounted in boxes, so that they can be passed around for inspection and not be damaged.

A variety of specimens should be provided to insure that students do not get the idea that all specimens of one family or species look exactly alike. This gives practice in looking for basic similarities and not accepting superficial ones.

Educational toys are considered specimens too. Many of the newer toys, models, and games produced today can be valuable additions to your program. Polarization of light experiments can be done with some toys; center of gravity and equilibrium experiments with others; spelling can be drilled; geography can be reviewed. Visit the toy and game department of major stores in your city from time to time and check on what is new in the toy line.

Bulletin Boards and Display Areas

How to use display areas

Bulletin boards and display areas are other important and often poorly utilized aspects of an instructional program. They can be used to motivate interest in an area, extend the textbook with pictures and data, summarize and review, compare materials or processes, and recognize student achievement. Effective bulletin boards require planning as does every other aspect of your program. The materials to be displayed should be assembled and only the best selected. Critically evaluate what you have available. Pictures of the highest clarity should be used. Printing should be as large as possible. Each item should be clearly labeled. A variety of different size pictures and items adds visual interest. Mount pictures, drawings, and photographs on colored construction paper or oaktag. These mounts are more durable than the unmounted materials and can more easily be removed and kept for use in a different display at a later date.

Your bulletin boards and displays should have a specific theme; they should not be a hodge-podge. Arrange items in a logical, but eye-catching manner. You may find that numbering the items or panels helps in guiding the viewer's attention. Experiment with various arrangements of materials. Use thumb tacks to pin up the different items while you are doing this. Then you can staple the display materials on the board when you decide on the most effective groupings.

Do not leave the display up for too long, but do not remove it prematurely. Give your students ample time and opportunity to study the display and consult it a number of times. You might devote a portion of a workshop or laboratory experience to examining and using the display in a specific lesson. If you leave the display up too long, students will ignore it, and then it has lost its impact.

The space available for the display must be considered too. Some schools have major display areas in each corridor, or on their main floor. They may be for general use, or may be assigned to departments or activities on a rotating basis. One person may be in charge of booking them; you will have to determine the specific set-up in your own school. The person in charge of this activity can often make valuable suggestions concerning any display you are planning. The art department in your school can be a source of ideas and suggestions when you want to try this kind of audio-visual aid.

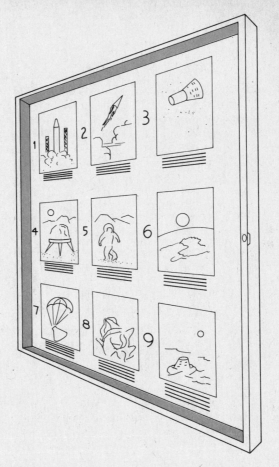

FIGURE 8.6
Picture panel arrangement

You may even have access to your school's major display area, for example, a large display board in the range of forty to fifty feet by six or eight feet, or several glass enclosed display cases equipped with locks. In one case the exhibit for an area this extensive illustrated the flight of *Apollo II*. Some of the steps in preparing this display were as follows:

The display materials were divided into two categories:
Pictures and articles taken from magazines or special pictorial editions. These were used on the large display board. Photographs taken of the live television transmission of the flight, which were mounted and put into the glass case.

Each day during the voyage, two copies of the major papers were purchased and pertinent articles and pictures gathered (two copies were usually necessary because of printing on both sides of a page). Shortly after the return to earth, color and black and white photographs were released and appeared in magazines. Again two copies of each magazine were purchased.

Assembling a major display

About ninety photographs taken of the live television transmission from space and from the moon were assembled and organized on oaktag panels. Each photograph was numbered and a caption was written beneath it. These panels of photographs covering the launch, the trip to the moon, the lunar walk, the trip back to earth, the splashdown, and the quarantine were put up in the display cases—taped to the inside of the glass doors. The photographs were thus protected and yet easily viewed. Spare magazine pictures not used on the large display board were used as a background in the cases.

The exhibit was titled, "The Epic Journey of *Apollo II*." This title was printed on an 8-by 1½ foot banner and mounted on top of the display board. The pictures were organized into segments which corresponded to those in the display case—Launch; To the Moon; On the Moon, Men from Earth; Home to Earth; Splashdown; Quarantine—and the different groupings arranged on the display board. Major titles were made by cutting out six-inch letters of white poster board and mounting them on heavy construction paper so that they stood out from the wall. This mounting added a three-dimensional effect to the otherwise flat display.

FIGURE 8.7
Display letters

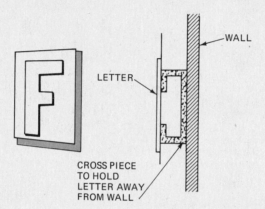

The complete display was quite comprehensive and integrated the scientific, historic, geographical, social, and poetic aspects of this event. Most displays can be handled in a similar manner, but on a smaller scale. Samples of different styles of lettering are available in newspapers, books, and magazines and are easily adapted to the type and size of your display. Each time you develop a set of letters, make them in cardboard or oaktag so they can be used again in future displays. Boards lined with cork readily accept staples or tacks, but tacks are less effective because they are usually too shiny, distract from the display, and can be too easily removed by passersby. Ready-made display letters are available from art stores in various colors. They are plastic and have prongs so that you can simply press them into a cork board and remove them again for later use.

Another technique to consider is a series of standing folding-screen panels on the stage of the auditorium or in a hallway. An effective walk-through pictorial display can be arranged using these fixtures.

In order to have handy a reservoir of pictures and articles, you should start a file. *Life* and *National Geographic* are excellent sources of both pictures and articles on a wide variety of subjects. *Life* also offers a series of reprints of specific collections of feature articles. Your daily newspapers supply current information about conferences, events, people, and places. Not too long ago, for example, ribonuclease, an enzyme, was synthesized. The amino acid sequence in this protein was detailed in major newspapers. Several students in one class drew a large wall chart (6 by 10 feet) of the enzyme using different outlines for the different amino acid residues, with all the chemical elements in different colors. The chart was posted on a wall in a school's science wing and visited by all the science classes in that school. It made a valuable contribution to the studies underway in general science, biology, and chemistry classes.

There are numerous examples of interesting and informative displays and bulletin boards you might like to try, for instance:

☐ An honor roll of achievement in a subject area

☐ Art work of a display or craft class or a major art class

☐ The work of a hobby club—photography, jewelry, or pottery

☐ A display of the elements of a computer system, and some of the careers possible in this field

☐ A pictorial description of how the school newspaper is prepared—from news items to finished product

☐ A display of some of the highlights of the senior play, or a school field trip

Ideas for bulletin boards

Your displays should answer questions, provide information, and raise new questions. They can extend your instructional programs into areas not officially a part of the formal curriculum, but of great interest and use to your students. This makes for a built-in updating mechanism for your programs by introducing current discoveries and theories long before they can be incorporated into a textbook.

Charts and Maps

This is a category of audio-visual aids common to virtually every subject area in a school, and it includes:

☐ Geographical and relief maps

☐ Typewriter keyboard representations

☐ Basic food groups charts

☐ Spectral colors and musical scales charts

☐ Tables of scientific data

☐ Graphical representations of math functions

☐ Diagrams and flow charts

☐ Stage set diagrams

☐ Athletic game plays

☐ Parts of a sentence

Types of charts and maps

Most of these aids are printed on heavyweight cardboard or treated cloth that can be rolled up when not in use; they are usually portable. In your school, select those you need for class use with the size of the class in mind. Do not pick a chart or map with lettering or diagrams too small to be readily seen. Instead of a single wall map, you might find a transparency for the overhead projector or a picture for the opaque projector to be a more effective audio-visual aid to use. Stenciled copies (8½ by 11-inch size) to help the students follow a scheme or outline are of major assistance in assuring that everyone in an interaction is looking at the same item at the same time.

Keep the chart or map you select rolled up or out of sight until you are ready to use it. This way you lose none of its potential impact. (As with all audio-visual aids, the element of timing is critical.)

There are times when you feel that no chart is quite what you want, and then you turn to preparing your own. Keep the following items in mind when planning any chart:

Reminders for making charts

☐ Lettering should be large and thick enough to be easily seen

☐ Vivid colors, fluorescent paints, and shiny textures enhance eye-appeal

☐ Information represented must be accurate

☐ The use of identifying labels should be planned

Charts need not always be designed to be hung on a wall bracket. They can be mounted on heavy cardboard or thin plywood and displayed on an easel or music stand. These fixtures are display assets for any classroom. They permit you to display charts, pictures, diagrams and the like without taking up valuable boardspace.

As you preview charts for purchase, or look through catalogues for new acquisitions, keep in mind the need for accuracy, visibility, and current appeal. Explore the possibility of modifying the charts you have on hand in order to extend their useful lifetime. If you and your supervisor or instructional leader decide that a chart is too old to repair or continue to maintain, you can select parts of it for stencil preparation or for the preparation of an overhead projection transparency. This may seem to be penny-pinching but it does permit the continued use of worthwhile materials in new and different forms.

Chalkboards

One of the most widely used—and widely abused—audio-visual aids is the old standby, the chalkboard. There are some things a chalkboard is not; for instance, it is not a place for uncoordinated scribbling or inaccuracies. It must play an integral part in the lesson, and you must plan its use carefully just as you plan each segment or activity in a lesson. Get to know the available boardspace in each room in which you teach. Organize the data and diagrams to be recorded on the boards so that you fully utilize the space. Plan and practice diagrams so that you can expertly draw them with minimal time lost in consulting sketches. You may find it more efficient to prepare transparencies of complex diagrams and prepare rexographed or mimeographed copies for distribution to students. Remember to distribute the materials *when* you are ready to use them—not before.

Generally the first item to be recorded on the board is the aim of the lesson. You can then use an outline system of noting major, and some minor, points. Remember the importance of orderly boardwork as a teaching mechanism; use parallel structure and a consistent method of numbering or lettering items. Well-organized outlines on a chalkboard provide the latecomer with a means of quickly assessing what is the aim of the lesson, and bringing him up to date on what has been done. It is an excellent device to use in summarizing. It helps to develop the skill of outlining and structuring notes.

Decide whether it is best for you to write or print. Go to the back of the room and look at your own boardwork.

Is your handwriting legible?

Is the writing large enough to be seen?

Have you observed parallel structure in outlining?

Does the outline make sense?

Does the outline follow a logical order, and help organize information about key factors?

How effective is your boardwork?

Colored chalk—vivid greens, reds, and yellows—often can highlight diagrams and underline important phrases, but do not overdo it; use color only for emphasis.

Student boardwork should also be carefully planned. Standards and procedures for recording such work can easily be worked out at the start of a semester. As the students enter the room, you distribute at random slips of paper or cards on which you have indicated the work each one is to do at the board—a problem to be solved, a question to be answered, or a diagram to be drawn and labeled. These "board slips" provide both you and the student with a ready reference to the exact question or problem that he has done at the board. If this work is to have value for the students doing the work, the students observing, and you, it must be used in the lesson. The work must be examined and evaluated by you and the class. Errors should be identified and corrected. Your students should actively participate in this work—both the written and the oral evaluations.

Photographs and Pictures

Photographs and pictures are valuable resource materials in any lesson. They help explore geographical and historical settings; they assist in analyzing structures; they permit us to examine organisms too small or too large to be easily handled; they can turn time backward.

Using photographs

As with all other audio-visual aids, you must consider the visibility problem. Enlargements large enough for use in most classes are costly. However, smaller sizes are easily magnified with the opaque projector, and the visibility is improved for all. Magazines are a good source of colorful, informative, up-to-date, or sometimes very old, pictures. You should keep folders of pictures with your other resource materials for a particular unit or topic. Museums, particularly those with educational services departments, often have collections of pictures and photographs which you can borrow on request.

Photographs you and your students take make valuable additions to lessons too. They encourage student involvement and emphasize their contribution. Photographs of different facets of student activities—football games, rallies, dances, musical performances, student art shows, science fairs, and club activities—make a most interesting and attention-getting display. You might even try to produce your own 8- or 16-mm film about different aspects of your school's programs. This could be shown at student assemblies, orientations for new or prospective students and new teachers, and parent association meetings. You can add to and periodically update this kind of audio-visual aid with new film clips. The audio-visual coordinator, photography instructor, or a teacher whose hobby is photography can offer valuable ideas and assistance in such a project.

Mass Media—Television, Radio, Newspapers

Using mass media

Television and *radio* are widely available resource materials but are often underutilized in a school's programs. They permit the student to watch and listen to history-in-the-making events. The viewers are eyewitnesses to concerts, plays, musicals, scientific events, and explorations. Your students no longer have to rely on a textbook, or a newspaper account, or your retelling of an event. Instead, they can see things for themselves and get the direct experience that is so valuable in the teaching–learning interaction. These media should play an important role in your total instructional program. You should include television and radio programs in your planning. Weekly program guides are available in the Sunday newspapers, or in weekly published guides. Specials are often given much advance publicity. Check these schedules for particular programs each week as a routine matter. Announce the program to your classes; prepare "fliers" about it and put these up on bulletin boards around your school building.

In recent years some of the major television channels have distributed outline sheets on special programs and designed discussion questions and reading lists pertaining to the topic to be explored. In some cases, they have provided a rexograph or ditto master announcing the program so that you can run off enough copies for posting and forwarding to other teachers in the school. Write to the education department of your major television networks for such materials. Not all of the programs may fit immediately into your lessons. However, students can view the specific programs and take notes for use later when the class investigates the same or a related topic. When advance notices are sent to schools about a program, there may be time for you to prepare a set of questions specific to the program, to be used by the students following the viewing.

Be sure to inquire about the availability of the television at students' homes. A student who does not have access to a set will not be able to participate in the assignment. You cannot make these assignments mandatory.

There are a number of educational television channels that offer a broad spectrum of classes and programs for your use. If your school has a television set with VHF and UHF channels, you can arrange for viewing some programs directly in class. If possible plan a discussion period immediately after the program to highlight the skills of critical listening and looking. Understanding some of the background helps make seeing the program a richer, deeper experience for the student, so be sure to provide some introduction. Develop some idea of the significance of the program in your current lessons. For major events, the television can be set up in an auditorium or library work area and used for larger group viewing. Ask your supervisor who arranges for these showings and works out the details for moving classes and booking viewing spaces in your school.

A recent development on the audio-visual aid scene is the video tape. For several years, sports fans have enjoyed the luxury of "instant replay" of football plays, golf shots, or baseball runs. This has been made possible by the development of video tape. Now this kind of aid is available to schools, and systems are marketed that permit you to:

Ideas for using video tape

☐ Video-tape a television program right off your television set and replay it at your convenience

☐ Video-tape programs even when you are not present through the use of a preset timing mechanism

☐ Prepare movies of lessons, demonstrations, field trips, or school events and then play them back through your television set

☐ Show cartridged video tapes of courses, programs, historic events, movies, plays, or dramatic readings

With this type of audio-visual aid you can film a moon-walk, a television special on ecology, or a performance of *Aida,* and use it in your classes, or for individualized instruction, any time that it best fits in with the course work you are doing.

Newspapers bring the student a plethora of information and extend the classroom into the real world. The paper provides more than just the news or advertisements: you can use the graphs presented in an issue to demonstrate some of the techniques used in representing data; you can use other items to develop skills in map reading, build vocabulary, study display techniques, investigate lettering systems, and show the difference between news reports and editorials.

Each of the mass media adds another facet to your array of tools and extends the horizons of your programs. You can look beneath the sea, visit a Broadway play, or listen to a poet. By using the mass media, your students can today learn more about many of these areas than you could ever teach them directly. Use these media in your programs, and plan for their inclusion as active ingredients in your lessons.

Textbook Illustrations

Using textbook illustrations

Another often neglected audio-visual aid is the textbook illustration. Pick up a current text and one of the first things you notice is the wealth of pictures, diagrams, sketches, and graphs. Newer refinements of color photography and printing techniques have permitted this facet of the printed text to really come of age. The illustrations, graphs, and flow charts are often far better than those you have available in chart form or on filmstrips or transparencies; yet they seem to go begging. Use them as you would any other audio-visual aid. The opaque projector can introduce textbook illustrations directly into your program, or transparencies of them can be made with the new copy machines. The maps and graphs in texts are a rich area for resource materials. You can make a detailed analysis of the graphs in your textbook and often go further in an in-depth study of them than the author intended or indicated. You may want students to interpolate or extrapolate values on these graphs in order to explore relationships of variables in a problem. You can use detailed maps for comparison or as a takeoff point for a discussion of some current problem or event. Plan the direct use of textbook illustrations and graphs in your lessons. For instance, use them in a supervised study lesson, where students can, with supervision, plot data provided in the text, and improve their skills in constructing and analyzing graphs from the data provided.

Professional journals and advertisements keep you informed about the publication of new texts in your field. Write to the major publishing houses who are particularly active in your specialty and have them add your name to their mailing lists. Your department chairman or supervisor often receives complimentary examination copies of new texts which are used in determining the adoption of future texts in various subject areas. But they can be a fine resource for you as well. No matter how good, challenging, or exciting illustrations are, they are of no value if not properly used. They can serve you in many ways: for preparation of stencils or transparencies; for bulletin boards; for student project ideas; as the basis for homework assignments; for workshop experiences.

Recordings and Tapes

A one-man show, a live performance, a great moment in history—each happens only once in its unique setting. Then it is gone forever, unless it is captured on record or tape. Earlier in this chapter, mention was made of the use of dramatic readings by talented actors to add further dimension to lessons in literature or drama. The same principle holds true for almost every subject area. Special concerts, reports, and discussions can become a permanent part of your audio-visual aid library, to be used when most appropriate.

Records need special care. Scratches are easily made on them and cannot be removed, and the sound made by scratches is distracting and annoying when the record is used. It is generally difficult to select specific segments of a record, and hunting for passages by trial and error detracts from the effectiveness of what you wish to present.

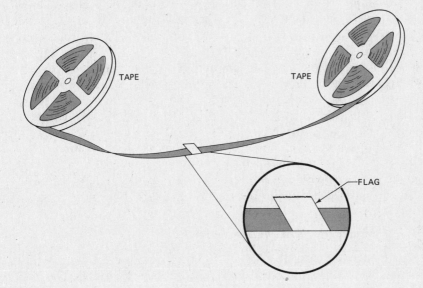

FIGURE 8.8
Flagging magnetic tapes

Tapes overcome this difficulty. Sections can be readily cut out and the ends spliced together with tape. You can select the segments to be used during a lesson, and mark the appropriate spot with a small "flag" made of the same tape. A tape recorder with six- to eight-inch reels can add a great deal of flexibility to your program. The small size reel players have shorter playing and recording times, and often give poor reproduction of musical tones. They are, however, fine for recording oral descriptions and reports. The smaller size recorders and some of the cassette recorders are easily portable and can be used to record any activity. Some operate on batteries; others have adapters so they can be used with batteries or house current.

A recorder gives you a unique opportunity to listen to yourself. When you plan a motivation, a series of questions, or an explanation, you think about what you are going to say, and then write out the questions or key phrases. However, what you think you say is not always what you actually say. You may be assuming a technical background your audience does not have; the question may be ambiguous; or the sequence of ideas presented not logical. The tape recorder gives you the opportunity to listen to your own questions and explanations and critically evaluate them before using them in a classroom setting. In addition you can tape segments of lessons or entire lessons as they actually develop. Later you can evaluate your students' responses and questions, summaries, or any other specific area of concern in a given lesson.

Using recordings and tapes

The tape permits you to relive the lesson now as an observer. It assists you in determining the extent to which the lesson accomplished its aim, how effective a technique was, or how logical was the development of a series of ideas. Some aspects of your teaching techniques, such as questioning, motivation, summarizing, or giving assignments can in this way be identified as those areas which need improvement. Your supervisor can be of great assistance to you here. Together you can listen to the taped lesson. It is best if the supervisor can be present at the live session as well to assess boardwork, and the visual components of the interaction. Ideally, a video tape would capture an entire lesson and permit detailed, comprehensive examination by you, your supervisor, and other specialists in specific skills. You and your supervisor can then plan a program of self-improvement to increase your effectiveness as a teacher. Your program should be assessed periodically using a similar taping technique. You will find that standing away from your lesson and examining it as an objective observer may not be easy for you but can give you greater insight into your own strengths and weaknesses, and increase your impact as a key participant in all teaching–learning interactions.

Film, Filmstrip, Slide, and Loop Projectors

Each of these projection devices serves to bring photographed events, people, and places into your lessons at any time you require or desire them. They provide a direct input of information and can enrich your program. The one guideline applicable to all of them is the need for you to become familiar with the operation and use of each of the different types of projectors. This is basic policy for all new equipment.

Learning to use the projector

After reading the instruction manual, request that the supervisor or someone skilled in the use of the equipment check you out in its operation. Before using these materials in class, preview the films, filmstrips, or slides to decide which parts you consider most applicable or pertinent. If you want to show only a segment of a film, thread the film through the projector to that section before class and then shut off the machine. You are now ready to go. You can work up a guide sheet or set of questions to accompany a particular film, and tailor it to your class activities.

Experiment with the location of projectors in your classrooms until you find the best position for maximum visibility and enlargement.

Remember to order your accessories and supplies: spare bulbs, adapter, and extension cords. Be sure to secure a screen for the area. If you find that screens are a problem, you can easily mount a large white window shade on wall brackets at the top of the chalkboard or some other location in the room. The plastic shades can be cleaned with detergent and a damp cloth and can in some cases be written on with colored crayon or chalk. A beige or white chalkboard or white oaktag board can also be used for this purpose.

One way to enlarge your collection of slides and films is to take your own pictures on field trips or summer vacations. Thirty-five-millimeter slides in color of animals on game reserves, plant specimens in their natural environment, or pieces of sculpture can add to your lessons. These aids have more meaning since they represent a personal experience or input of energy by the participants in the learning activity.

Making slides

Kits are available for mounting your slides or for making two by two-inch slides. You can type on transparent cellophane by sandwiching it between two sheets of carbon paper. This can then be mounted between two glass slides and used for titles or captions.

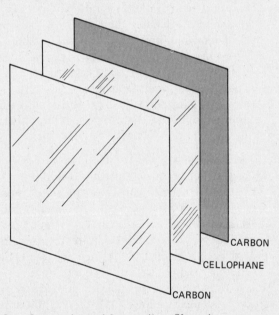

FIGURE 8.9
Making your own slides

CARBON

CELLOPHANE

CARBON

To prepare a glass surface for tracing with pencil or fiber-tip pen, use the following procedure:

Preparing glass for slides

☐ Put a clean glass slide on a few thicknesses of newspaper, sprinkle a bit of silicon carbide powder on the slide, add a drop or two of water, and cover with a second slide

☐ Rub one slide over the other, using a circular motion, adding powder and water as needed until both slides are uniformly ground. Rinse off both slides periodically, dry them, and hold them up to the light to determine the uniformity of grinding

☐ When they are completely and uniformly ground, wash off the slides and dry them. You can keep the silicon carbide powder for reuse

☐ You can now draw on these slides with a No. 2 pencil sharpened to a fine point. To protect the slide you have prepared, cover the ground surface on which you have drawn your diagram with another (unground) glass slide and bind the two together with masking tape or lantern slide tape

Slide projectors

Some filmstrip projectors have an attachment that converts the machine for use with slides. When using the equipment with filmstrips, you should take care in operating the windup mechanism. Be careful not to tear the sprocket holes on the side of the film or you will render it virtually unusable in that machine. It may be necessary, with some machines, to remove the windup mechanism in order to avoid this problem. You will have to wind up the film by hand. If you have some filmstrips damaged in this way, you can clip out individual frames and mount them in cardboard slide holders for use as slides.

Some slide projectors require that the slides be inserted individually. These models require your attention all during their operation. Slides must be maintained in proper position, upside down and backward, and should be kept in that arrangement when you remove them from the machine to facilitate their use later that day in another class. This kind of machine limits your movement about the room and ties you to the projector. Other projectors require that the slides be fitted into rectangular or circular trays. Once the set of slides is organized, it can be conveniently used repeatedly with a minimum of effort. If your slides are organized this way, be sure to preview the entire set before using them to insure that they are relevant to the lesson and arranged in the most logical order.

Some projectors permit you to advance slides and then go back to look at earlier ones for comparison and review. Other projectors have an automatic timer to advance the slides; some have remote control mechanisms. When you are in the market for a new projector, carefully consider all those available to select the one with the greatest versatility, and adaptability within your price range. Visit a large camera shop to see some of the newer models in operation before you decide on any purchase or recommend any to your supervisor. Consult *Consumers Guide* magazine for frequency-of-repair records and studies on performance. When you do order a specific machine, make sure you know how to operate it. Find out how it works, how to change the bulbs, how to fill slide trays or wind up the film, and so forth. Be sure to order several spare bulbs and keep your stock up to date.

Film-loop projectors

In the past few years, a newer type of projector has taken the market by storm—the film-loop projector. Film loops are short motion pictures dealing with a single concept, idea, or technique. The film comes in a plastic, sealed cartridge, is continuous, and needs no rewinding by hand. The film loop will recycle itself in the cartridge. To use this machine, you simply push the cartridge into the slot provided for it in the projector, following the up–down guide on the cartridge itself, turn on the current, and you are on your way. The projector can be stopped at any time, to study one frame or to remove the entire cartridge. The film loops because of their limited picture size are best for work with small groups and for use by individuals but can be used for somewhat larger groups as well. A corner of a room can be converted for small group use. You can use a portable viewing screen sold by the projector manufacturer or you can use a rear projection technique to avoid image reversal. Rear projection involves reflecting the image from a mirror onto a translucent screen. If such a setup is not available, use a conventional screen. Film loops were originally designed in 8mm but have recently changed to what is termed "Super-8mm" film. This film provides a better, clearer, sharper picture. Be alert to the difference when you order these loops and projectors, because the cartridges for the two types of film are not interchangeable.

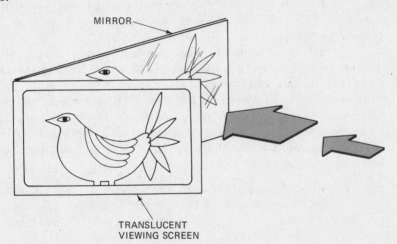

MIRROR

TRANSLUCENT
VIEWING SCREEN

FIGURE 8.10
Rear projection

Film loops

The film loops add a great measure of flexibility to your lessons. Students can use them during their free time for review or to see a new technique being demonstrated. They can look at the film over and over again—as many times as they wish—until they are familiar with the material. Film loops can be used as motivation devices, for specific demonstrations that are too complex or lengthy to be conveniently done in class, for supervised study sessions, for summary; the list can go on and on. A number of companies market film loops today. Obtain catalogues from them, and if possible preview the loops before you purchase them to see if they are geared to your needs. Many films, in many different subject areas and on various levels of difficulty are available, and make this type of aid one of the most worthwhile on the market today.

Microprojectors

When students work with microscopes, particularly in their early investigations, you often wonder if they are really observing the

Microprojectors

specimen or portion of a specimen about which you are speaking, or if they are looking at a dust particle, an oil droplet, or a smudge on the glass. The microprojector provides a means for an entire class to look at a prepared microscope slide, or a live microscopic specimen at the same time. This work is generally preliminary to their own individual lab work with the microscope. Perhaps because of limited availability of specimens or their extreme perishability, this may be the only way that a live specimen may be introduced into a lesson. The projector is equipped with high and low power objectives just as is a standard microscope. An oil immersion objective and a polarizing device can be purchased as accessories. Specimens are placed on the stage and the image can be directed to the table top or by means of a mirror to a wall screen.

The projector requires the same type of care given a standard microscope. Clean the lenses with lens paper and keep the mirror clean. Read the instruction manual carefully for focusing instructions particular to each model. You can use the microprojector to make tracings from slides for mimeographing, stenciling, transparency preparation, or preparing diagrams for bulletin boards or displays, but its major advantage is that the entire class can view an organism at the same time. This makes efficient use of time and materials and enables students to more competently locate and identify specimens using their own microscopes. It is also possible to take microphotographs using your camera and a standard microscope. Bulletins are available from Eastman Kodak describing the most frequently used techniques with simple cameras.

As with all other audio-visual aids, you will have to become familiar with the specific limitations of the projectors in your school. Use a projector several times before using it in class, to establish familiarity and to determine how dark your room must be made to ensure adequate viewing conditions on sunny days.

Opaque Projectors

Opaque projectors

The opaque projector permits the projection of pictures and prints from books, magazines, and newspapers so that the entire class can look at an item together. Only one copy of a print or a book may be available, and handing it about the room for examination is not an efficient procedure. By inserting it in the opaque projector the material can be seen by everyone at the same time. Books do not have to be torn up to get a picture or a chart. The entire book, open to the right page, can be placed in the projector for viewing. It is important to remember that only opaque materials and printed matter can be viewed in these machines. A great deal of heat is generated by their lighting systems so that they cannot be used for the study of live specimens; they would be cooked while you looked at them, and cultures or solutions would dry up. Keep this heating problem in mind in regard to printed matter as well, for paper will also get hot, and fragile old prints could be damaged if left in the projector with the light on for too long a period of time. Be careful of the glass cover plate which holds books in a flat position for it also gets very hot.

Although it is relatively easy to manage, the opaque projector is bulky and mounting it on a small rolling cart or dolly will facilitate its use. You can purchase a set of casters and bolt or fit them to a suitable table or to a board and make a dolly for moving the projector about.

This is an audio-visual aid designed for a specific purpose — viewing opaque, non living materials. For looking at a rock sample, a diagram, a picture, or a map, it is a fine aid; but keep its limitations in mind as you select materials for use in it.

Overhead Projectors

The most versatile audio-visual aid which may be at your disposal is the overhead projector. The overheads are portable or are easily movable. They require some darkening of the room for best viewing, but enable you to continue facing the students while presenting materials or demonstrating on the projector. This aid permits the introduction of materials and concepts not otherwise easily visualized or demonstrated; at the same time its facility of operation maintains the continuity of a lesson.

Care and use of the machine. As with the other optical instruments you use, remember to:

☐ Keep a spare bulb or two on hand

☐ Clean the stage, mirrors, and glass surfaces

☐ Locate the on–off and focusing knobs

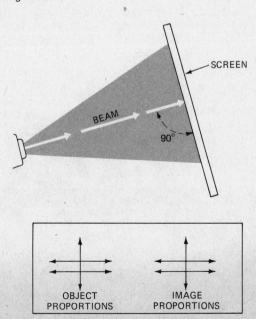

FIGURE 8.11
Projector alignment

You should inspect the interior portions of the projector from time to time and clean it thoroughly. The problem of keystoning is a real one with all projectors. Keystoning is the image distortion caused when the projected beam does not hit the screen directly at a ninety-degree angle.

FIGURE 8.12
Keystoning

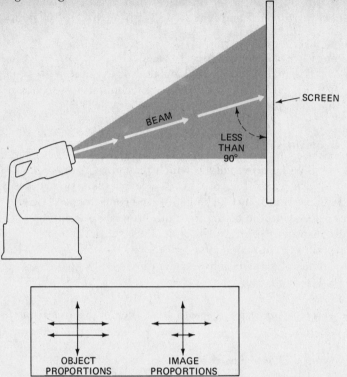

If it strikes at any other angle, the image is wider at one end than at the other. The screen can be tilted, or the level of the front of the

FIGURE 8.13
Correction for keystoning

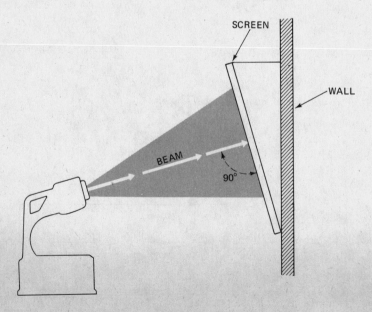

projector can be adjusted to overcome this problem. You will have to experiment with the specific location of the overhead projector just as with all the others you use. This projector should be located toward the front of the room or at the side area of the room. Be sure that the projector itself does not interfere with the students' view of the screen or chalkboard area on which you project the image.

Materials for transparencies. A number of firms manufacture materials for preparing transparencies by hand:

- ☐ Marking pencils and acetate inks in a spectrum of colors
- ☐ Drawing pens
- ☐ Pressure sensitive tapes for making lines and diagrams
- ☐ Transparent, colored sheets of acetate for adding color highlights to a transparency
- ☐ Pressure sensitive letters that you merely rub off a sheet onto the acetate sheet for making titles

Transparency materials

Making transparencies. One process for preparing permanent projectuals involves a diazo-coupling reaction. This process results in a product with the colored lines, diagrams, or words permanently recorded in the acetate. Or it can be used to produce a reversal of this system—a colored background with the diagrams colorless. Special equipment is needed for this process as are specially treated, light-sensitive films. The benefit of these projectuals is that they last a lifetime and can be used over and over again. You can write on them with a wax pencil and erase them just as you do untreated acetate sheets. This process requires that you first prepare a master and then from it make the finished product. This procedure is relatively long and requires a good deal of effort, but if you can devote the time and energy, the finished product is well worth it.

Start your experimentation in transparency preparation with a wax marking pencil and a transparent acetate sheet. The marks you make can be easily rubbed off the acetate sheet with a soft, dry cloth. The sheet can then be used again. The acetate inks can be washed off the acetate sheets with water. If you wait for several months before washing off the ink, you may find that some leave a yellow residue on the acetate. Once you have a transparency or projectual that you think fills a specific need in your program, have class-tested it several times, and then completely reviewed it for accuracy and workability, you can redraw the diagram in acetate ink or make it permanent in one of several ways.

You can use the copy machine in your school office or your department to prepare another type of transparency in just a few seconds. In this process you place the original picture, article, or diagram under a special film in a transparent, plastic carrier and let it move through the copy machine just as you would any master you want reproduced. Your finished transparency is ready in less than a minute.

You can prepare a ditto stencil of the diagram at the same time, or you can prepare a stencil master for preparing paper copies of the same material for distribution. Another development for the overhead is a type of ditto master that gives you a transparency that you first use as a master for making paper copies for your students and then use as the transparency for the overhead. This needs no copy machine—you just write on the master and you have the completed master and transparency.

The method you select for the preparation of transparencies or projectuals will depend on the facilities, the time available, and the needs of your own program. You may decide to purchase prepared transparencies from any one of a number of companies across the country. Whichever method you use, you should keep the following guidelines in mind when dealing with individual transparencies:

Mounting single transparencies

You may want to mount single acetate sheet transparencies in cardboard or oaktag frames which are commercially available

With single sheets, it is not always necessary to mount in a frame. If you use the heavier gauge acetate sheets, you can simply punch holes in them for storage in a looseleaf or a ring binder

If you decide to mount the sheet, place the frame, face down, on a flat surface; invert the transparency and center it over the frame. Tape the sheet to the frame in the order indicated in Figure 8.14 to smooth the sheet and keep it secure on the frame

FIGURE 8.14
Anchoring a projectual static

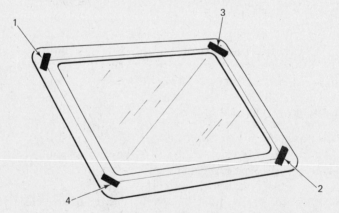

You are not limited to the single—static—sheet in the transparency. You may decide that you would like to add information, a bit at a time, to that included on the static sheet. This means that you will have to use a series of overlay sheets, mounted on the front of the frame and added to the picture one at a time.

For example, you want to design a projectual to summarize the solution to the following math problem: Plot the graph of the equation $y = x^2 - 2x - 8$ between the limits $x = -4$ to $x = +6$.

Mounting multi-layered transparencies

☐ The first step is to prepare a complete diagram of exactly what you want the finished transparency to contain. In this case, this would be arranged in three general areas:

A statement of the problem

An area for solving the equation

An area for graphing data

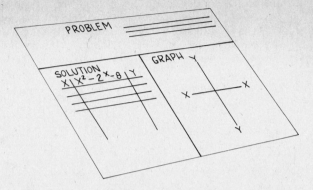

FIGURE 8.15
*Diagram for a
complete transparency*

☐ Place an acetate sheet over your completed diagram, and trace those parts of the diagram that will go on the static sheet. Remember that the static sheet is the sheet that contains those parts of the picture that will be on view at all times, unless you physically cover them with a piece of paper. You will find that taping the acetate down over the diagram on a flat, hard surface helps keep the materials from moving about as you trace the lines.

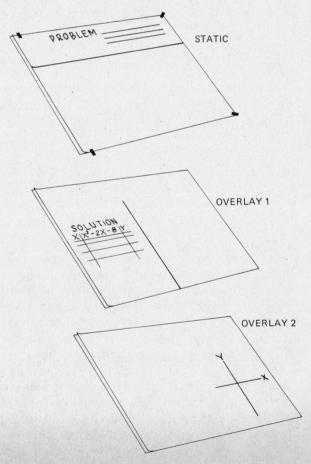

FIGURE 8.16
Sections of a projectual

☐ Remove this first acetate sheet and replace it with a second one. Trace onto this sheet those parts you want on the first overlay, which will be added to the static when you are ready to do so. Repeat the procedure with the third sheet of acetate and draw your second overlay. The three sheets, when registered or superimposed over one another, should show the completed diagram.

☐ Mount the static in a frame, as described above, and mount the other two sheets on the front of the frame. To mount the overlays, attach two mylar hinges on each sheet and staple to the frame. You can hinge the overlay sheets from the same side of the frame, or from different sides. The option is yours, but the second procedure gives you more flexibility in adding information to the screen. This way you can add or remove one sheet at a time, and in any order.

FIGURE 8.17
Completing the projectual

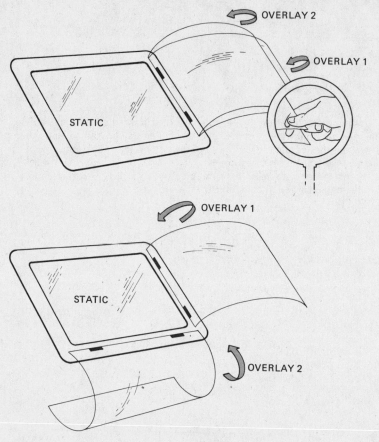

Acetate sheets with carbon backing on which you can write with a ballpoint pen are available. As you write on these sheets the carbon is removed from the back of the sheet. This provides you with a transparency with a black background and transparent lines and diagrams. Inclusion of one or more of these transparencies in a series adds variety to your presentation. You can tape strips of tinted transparent acetate tape to the back of these sheets to achieve the effect of several colors against a black background. This is particularly effective when you are examining graphs and trying to determine the effect of several different variables on a system. These carbon-backed acetate sheets are particularly perishable. Any mark you make on the sheet will remove the carbon, so it is best to sandwich your finished carbon-backed acetate sheet between two clear, heavy-gauge-acetate sheets and tape the laminated product at the sides.

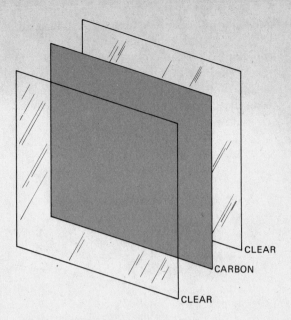

FIGURE 8.18
Protecting a carbon-backed acetate

CLEAR
CARBON
CLEAR

Before you purchase any of the prepared transparencies or projectuals, make a few simple ones and use them in your classes. See how your students respond to them and how you can use them best. Develop some facility in introducing them and handling them during a class. You will then be in a better position to judge what types you should have in your program, and will avoid buying "blind."

As we have shown, some projectuals can be quite easily made, but more complex ones require only a bit more effort. For example, a pair of acetate sheets arranged so that one rotates over the other can be prepared with a kit for making belts, secured from your local notions store. Punch a hole in the two sheets with a compass point or sharp tack, install a grommet as you would for a belt, and then hammer the grommet down as the kit instructions indicate. You can pre-

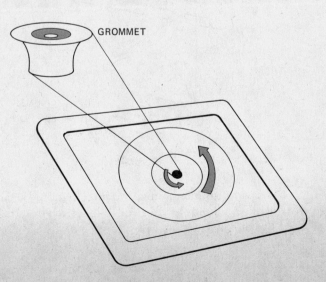

GROMMET

FIGURE 8.19
Circular motion in a projectual

cut the top sheet in the form of a circle, a square, or any polygon, and, with the grommet in place, it will rotate above the static sheet. With this kind of arrangement you can show why we see only one side of the moon here on earth or, with two rotating sheets, demonstrate how to tell time. Again, be sure to prepare a master sketch and decide what material will go on the static and what on the rotating overlay(s).

FIGURE 8.20
Sample circular projectual

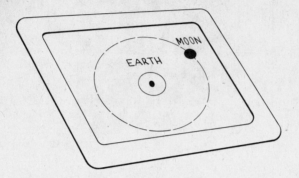

You can also purchase plastic tracks when you order the acetate sheets and frames. These tracks are stapled to the frame and permit you to slide a sheet over the face of the static. You can thus mask or cover portions of the static and reveal them again at any time.

FIGURE 8.21
Linear motion in a projectual

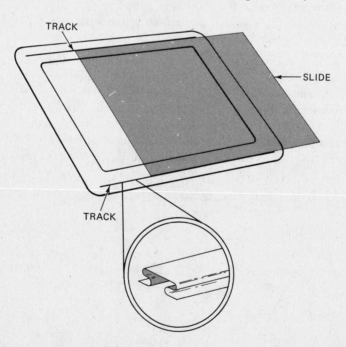

With simple equipment, time, and imagination you can produce many worthwhile additions to your collection, each designed to fit a specific need of your instructional program.

Using the overhead without transparencies. You can also operate the overhead projector with materials other than acetate sheets so that it can be adapted to scores of uses specifically tailored to your program.

Halves of petri dishes can be placed directly on the stage of the overhead and chemical reactions performed in them. You can demonstrate:

Other uses for the overhead

The miscibility of liquids (alcohol plus water)

The degree of concentration of a solution

The addition of a solid to water (a crystal of $KMnO_4$ plus water vs. a particle of sulfur to water)

The reaction of a metal with a salt solution (copper plus silver nitrate solution)

The addition of a crystal of solute to a supersaturated solution of that material (sodium thiosulfate in water)

You can use transparent rulers and slide rules to demonstrate measuring instruments and develop skills at making measurements

You can use plastic or wooden gears to demonstrate some principle of mechanics

You can prepare a transparency of a student's composition or essay and correct it with the class as direct observers and evaluators

You can prepare a transparency of bookkeeping or income tax forms and use it in conjunction with paper copies for the students

You can demonstrate the set designs for a play

You can diagram football maneuvers and basketball plays

An accessory unit has been manufactured for some types of lighter overhead models so that the unit can be used on its side. A small stage is provided on which science demonstrations in test tubes and simple heating reactions can be performed. Using the overhead in this manner, you have an image at least one foot high and visible all over the room. You can watch precipitations as they occur; you can perform color tests; you can heat solutions; you can watch chemical reactions in progress. A special projector has also been manufactured for this purpose which has a small stage, and high magnification. The stage can be used in the horizontal or the vertical positions, whichever best suits the work you are doing.

Of all the audio-visual aids available in schools today, the overhead projector stands out because of its versatility and flexibility in use. Write to the major companies in the field of transparency preparation for catalogues and descriptive brochures. Inquire about workshops and in-service sessions conducted by these companies to introduce you to the vast potential of this medium. For example, recently sets of biology projectuals have been reduced to 35mm slides and are marketed in a series of circular slide holders. These slides can be shown on the chalkboard. Students can then label diagrams, complete charts, and identify items right at the chalkboard. This technique uses the best of two worlds—the overhead and the slide projectors—in a blend that adds more flexibility to your lessons. Find out about existing programs in your school and school district, and consult with your supervisor and audio-visual coordinator about immediately available materials, and techniques.

Electrically-cut Stencils and Duplicating Machines

In recent years, many advances have been made in the field of mimeographing and stenciling materials. Mimeograph machines have been automated, and it is no longer necessary to turn them by hand or keep count of the copies they produce. The quality of the stencils has improved too, but complex diagrams still present quite a problem when many copies are needed. Whenever possible paper copies for distribution to students should be provided for the major transparencies you use. This way students can more easily follow the examination of a diagram or particular passage instead of trying to copy it from a chalkboard. There will be times when you need a diagram in large numbers, too large to be prepared from one spirit duplicating master. This problem has been solved: Instruments are now available from a number of companies that prepare a stencil from any page of printed material or copy. The stencil-maker electrically cuts the stencil in about twenty minutes, and furnishes you with a stencil capable of delivering several thousand copies. When using this technique, remember the following:

Making electrically-cut stencils

Secure the diagram or printed matter you want to copy. For example, you might want to prepare a stencil showing eight or nine different types of graphs clipped from newspapers—to be used in lessons on interpretation of graphs and techniques of graphing

Obtain paper of the size on which the finished product is to be printed (usually 8½ by 11-inch or 8½ by 14-inch) and paste one sheet on a cardboard or oaktag sheet. Draw margins on this paper to indicate the usable portion of the sheet for printing

FIGURE 8.22
Marking the limits

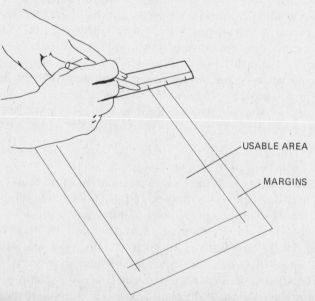

USABLE AREA

MARGINS

To prepare the master sheet for copying, put a blank sheet over the bordered one you have prepared, position the graphs on the paper and when you have found the best arrangement, paste the graphs on the paper with white glue or rubber cement. Do not use transparent tape, as it will leave marks on the stencil

Add any additional information, like numbers or titles, in black ink

Now that you are ready to use the machine and cut the stencil, check out its operation with the person in charge of it.

With this spectrum of different types of audio-visual aids at your disposal, you might get the impression that all of your teaching problems are solved. However, such is not the case; every aid has its own limitations and these, in large measure, will determine the extent to which you use each type.

WHAT ARE THE LIMITATIONS OF AUDIO-VISUAL AIDS?

The size of many aids limits their visibility and therefore their effectiveness. Many aids can be used easily with a small group or in individual study, but are not suitable for large group work. A one- by one-inch piece of quartz is not suitable for a class of thirty students; a five- by six-inch piece would be more effective.

Limitations of audio-visual aids

Most aids like photographs, maps, and charts are two dimensional — they lack depth perspective, a point which should be recognized when you order and use them. Relief maps and stereo photographs overcome this limitation but certainly add to the cost.

Some aids are not designed for the function for which they are sometimes used. A microprojector, for example, is a better audio-visual aid to use for the study of live protozoan cultures than is the opaque projector. The heat generated by the opaque projector and its limited magnification and resolving power make it the least effective means of studying these specimens.

Models, pictures, and diagrams can be misleading or inaccurate. You must determine in your preliminary planning and preparation whether an aid accurately illustrates the structure it purports to represent. Some aids are merely gimmicks, and should be recognized as such. They serve to attract notice, but do not accurately present real systems or equipment. They should be used in this vein, merely as attention-getters, and not be expected to develop understanding, or provide in-depth investigation.

Many aids lose most of their potential usefulness because the students have no orientation in their meaning or function. They may not grasp the relationship of the specific aid to the process or event it depicts or explains. The best models, films, and photographs can fall flat because the students do not know what they should be looking for. Admittedly there may be many times in a lesson when you want to present an idea, concept, or technique with minimal explanation, to stimulate the creative thinking of the group; but the important consideration is the student's individual contribution to the inter-action — the way *he* analyzes a specimen, tackles a problem, listens to a selection, or starts an investigation. With audio-visual aids it is generally more profitable and effective if you give the students a clear understanding of the significance of what they are about to see or hear—even if spontaneity must sometimes be sacrificed to explanation.

Before you introduce any audio-visual aid, you should be aware of the following considerations:

Guides to using audio-visual aids

☐ You will have to be the one who decides which aid you will use. The aid must fit your students, your program, your immediate topic, your time allotment, and you. Do not use an aid because another teacher told you it's terrific. Try it out yourself before class

☐ Get to know how to use the equipment and materials. Do not learn to use these items at the same time your students see them. The more facility you have in using any aid, the greater impact it can have on teaching—learning interactions, and the more it will reflect your own style and techniques of teaching

☐ Keep on the alert for new ideas and refinements of their use. As you gain experience in using these teaching aids, you will develop new aids yourself, find new ways of applying older aids, and should keep a fresh, inquiring outlook in your selection of materials for use.

WHERE DO YOU GET THE AUDIO-VISUAL AIDS?

The sources of audio-visual aids can be organized into four general areas:

Where to find audio-visual aids

In the school

Outside the school

Commercial sources

Yourself and others

In the School

Each teacher should begin by acquainting himself with those audio-visual aids in his own school. In some cases one teacher may be assigned as the audio-visual aids coordinator. It is his function to recommend purchases of equipment and associated materials for use by all segments of the school. The coordinator maintains a central inventory of all the audio-visual equipment and materials from which specific items can be drawn on request. He stores, repairs, and issues the equipment. When a teacher requests a specific film or projector, he has the item delivered to the classroom ready for use.

The audio-visual coordinator usually instructs a group of students in the operation of projectors and recorders. These students deliver the requested aids to the classroom and can operate them during the class session. Although on the surface this may seem quite a time and labor saver for you, there are many drawbacks to such a system. It does not permit you to preview films nor does it let you select those portions of a film or tape which are the most appropriate for a given class. Letting a student bring in the projector, set it up, and show a film means that you must take all or none of that aid. For maximum effectiveness you must be familiar with the operation of each of the various types of projectors in your school. You should be able to change a spent bulb and thread and rewind tapes and films. You must know how to select the best of what is available and use only that and nothing less.

In some schools subject departments have developed their own program of audio-visual aids. The department as a functioning unit maintains its own equipment and library of materials. These materials are more easily obtained than those one must compete for on a school-wide basis. In addition, the aids in your department collection are more specific to your needs and program requirements. The supervisor can be on the alert for talented teachers who can employ their imagination and initiative to build up the department's collection of audio-visual aids and encourage their use. Even though you may be new to the teaching field, you might be just the one to take on this type of responsibility. Each time you use a film, film loop, chart, tape, or any other aid, make notes on it. On a 5 by 8-inch index card indicate:

Information file for audio-visual aids

☐ Type of aid

☐ Title

☐ Running time for a film or tape; size for a chart or picture

☐ Location

☐ Number in stock

☐ Associated aids, printed materials, or kits

☐ Uses: Indicate topics, or units concerned

☐ Comments: Indicate segments most pertinent; condition of item; any inaccuracies; good questions to use; homework assignment or workshop suggestions

You can secure the comments of several of your colleagues and thus catalogue information about each audio-visual aid available to you.

It would be most desirable to have a reservoir of audio-visual materials and equipment located in each classroom and instantly available to you and your students. You could then easily use more than one aid at a time—a portion of a 16mm film, and a film loop—and not deprive anyone else of any of these items. This type of program involves considerable financial support, facilities for an audio-visual center in each room, and a talented, informed, resourceful staff. Very few schools can afford such an extensive audio-visual program. Therefore you will probably have to order the equipment and materials you want in advance from a department or school coordinator, and learn to share with your colleagues. Several other teachers will often require much the same material as you do, and at about the

Where to find audio-visual aids

same time. The ordering and sharing require advance planning and focus on the need for you to be familiar with all the aids available in your school. The materials survey described in Chapter 3 comes in handy when you have to select suitable alternatives for use in a lesson when you learn you cannot have the first selection you requested.

It is your responsibility to obtain from a coordinator, your supervisor, or an experienced colleague the instruction and maintenance manuals on the various pieces of equipment you will use. Check out their operation with the appropriate person. Preview the films, tapes, or transparencies during your preparation periods. Study the materials available. No one can do this job for you. Remember that this will take time. But the time you invest in this type of exploratory activity is well spent. It broadens your background and permits you a greater measure of flexibility in your teaching.

Outside the School

There may be central audio-visual coordinators in each school district who can help you in learning how to use specific aids or in developing materials for use with them. In the immediate future, you will find the need for more specialization in this area in order to meet the demands for the use of new, stimulating, and challenging aids, and audio-visual programs. The district coordinator may conduct workshops in the preparation and use of aids, either in specific subject areas, or in general terms.

There may also be a central district depository of films, tapes, and photographs that may be borrowed for a period of time. Central purchasing and maintenance decreases the financial burden of an audio-visual program in one school, but seriously handicaps the free and extensive use of the materials in a practical sense. You generally have to order items long in advance, and do not have much time to preview the materials for use.

Consult the major museums and libraries in your area for materials that you may borrow for use in your classes. Many of these institutions have educational service divisions that will send films on a free-loan basis (you need only pay the postage), or exhibits or dioramas for use in your school.

Commercial Sources

Many companies specialize in the production of audio-visual equipment and associated materials in many different subject areas. They also produce the materials with which you can prepare your own transparencies, films, or models. Some of the nationally known companies are listed in the appendix. Check your local yellow pages for companies in your area which specialize in such equipment. Consult your professional journals and publications for the names of major concerns in your field of specialization.

Some of the larger companies produce newsletters on audio-visual aids and preparation techniques; others conduct workshops for teachers. Some will send representatives to demonstrate new products and equipment at your department or faculty meetings. Write for catalogues and price lists, and have your name added to their mailing lists for bulletins, newsletters, and fliers on new products. This will help you keep alerted to new materials. In addition, consult the *Journal of Audio-Visual Materials* in a major public or college library for articles on new aids and techniques.

Where to find audio-visual aids

Yourself and Others

There is a field which you will enjoy exploring—making your own audio-visual aids. The aids you produce have more meaning to you and will have more value for your students. A sense of your involvement is quickly detected and appreciated by your students. Some of them will want to participate in this kind of activity and they too can produce many worthwhile aids. Some of your students may be more talented than you are in design, painting, woodworking, or metal craft. Do not neglect this talent. Perhaps teachers in other departments in your school will prove a valuable adjunct to your developing audio-visual program. All of these people—teachers and students—can prove a valuable resource of skills, talents, and imaginative ideas from which to draw.

The set of oaktag cubes described earlier in this chapter provides a good illustration of this cooperative spirit. Students can construct the cubes; others can do the lettering; still others can put the shelves together.

The ideas for bulletin boards, models, charts, and other types of audio-visual aids are limitless. Their construction can enlist the talents and creative spirit of your students, and increase the degree of their involvement in class activities. Segments of department conferences or workshop sessions can be devoted to exploring new techniques with other members of your department. One teacher particularly adept at making transparencies, for example, might conduct a workshop to introduce teachers to some techniques of preparation and presentation. Your ingenuity and creativity will make the sky the limit in your use of audio-visual aids.

HOW DO YOU USE AUDIO-VISUAL AIDS?

This is really a three-faceted question, which should read:

How to use audio-visual aids

☐ How do you use aids before class?

☐ How do you use aids in class?

☐ How do you handle aids after class?

Before Class

*How to use
audio-visual aids*

In your preparation periods in school and in your available time, establish a program for exploration of the equipment available to you. Obtain an inventory list of equipment and supplies from your supervisor, audio-visual coordinator, or specialist in your school in charge of the program. Set up a schedule with the person in charge so that you can get a particular aid, its instructions, and accessories when you want them and then provide a time for trying out the equipment, under supervision. This procedure must be repeated periodically to permit you to explore new materials as they become available. Experiment with threading tapes and films, using accessories and adapters, focusing, controlling volume, and adjusting the distance of projectors from screens.

Try out models, take them apart, and reassemble them several times before using them in class. See what the model can do, and what it cannot do. Decide which aids are ready for use with a given topic, and whether you think they will be a worthwhile contribution to the lesson. Remember, a bad audio-visual aid is worse than none at all, because the poor one will confuse issues and hinder understanding.

Early in your teaching career you will find that some audio-visual aids look terrific, but they do not do the job in the classroom. They seem clear to you, but not to the students. Perhaps you failed to recognize the high degree of sophistication assumed by the model or aid, and not yet present in your students.

Some aids are successful for one teacher and not for another. Some teachers feel comfortable using aids and others do not. Keep an open mind as you approach each type of aid and experiment with them all. See how your students react to them. Critically evaluate their impact on doing the task for which you used them.

*Evaluating an audio-
visual aid*

Did each do its job?

Were there any unexpected dividends?

Which aids should be modified for future use?

Is there any other aid that would do the job better?

This pretesting and preliminary work takes time. You cannot familiarize yourself with a piece of equipment or a model three or four minutes before a class. If you try to, your use of it in class will reflect this poor preparation.

In addition to the audio-visual aids themselves, you should carefully check over the rooms in which the materials will be used. Check on the following:

PRELIMINARY CHECKLIST FOR AUDIO-VISUAL USE

Look for the location of wall outlets, for electrical equipment: **1.**

Yes No

☐ ☐   Is the plug on the equipment two or three prong?

   What type of wall outlet is present?

☐ ☐   Are any adapters required for these outlets?

   Where can the adapters be secured?

   What type of current is required by the equipment and what type of current is available in the room?

Select the specific location for setting up the audio-visual aid: **2.**

   Will you use a table, desk, rolling cart, or cabinet?

☐ ☐   Do you need access to water?

☐ ☐   Does the location interfere with visibility?

Provide accessory items: **3.**

☐ ☐   Do you need spare slide cartridges or marking pencils for making notes on transparencies?

☐ ☐   Is there a fire extinguisher in the room?

☐ ☐   Are there spare bulbs for the equipment you are using? (Be sure you know how to change the bulb.)

☐ ☐   Is there a wiping cloth for surfaces and lens paper for mirrors and lenses?

☐ ☐   Do you have electrical adapters, extension cords, transparent tape, paper clips, and rubber bands?

☐ ☐   Do you have enough empty spools and blank tape for the recorders, empty reels for the projectors, or acetate sheets and marking pencils for overheads?

These are the items that you will most often require on an emergency basis. Keep them in a container in the room in which you teach, or make sure they are on the cart which transports the equipment to you. You must order these accessories when you order or secure the equipment.

Check the lighting: **4.**

Yes No

☐ ☐   Will the room have to be darkened for use of the aid?

☐ ☐   Are the shades in good order?

   Who fixes shades in need of repair?

☐ ☐   Can any lights be left on during the use of the aid?

Investigate seating: **5.**

☐ ☐   Can the seats be rearranged to permit maximum visibility or interaction?

   Which pattern of seating—if flexible seating is possible—is the best one to use?

How is the aid set up relative to the seating arrangement?

Where will a screen be placed?

As you gain experience in the use of these aids and the emergencies that arise or the specific problems you encounter in using them, develop your own checklist of emergency supplies to order, and decide on the best means for getting the equipment to your particular classroom locations.

In Class

How to use audio-visual aids

Once you have decided upon a particular audio-visual aid, and have done all the preliminary work concerning it, there comes the test of your planning—using the audio-visual aid in a real learning situation. Adjustment of shades, lighting, setting up the specific equipment ideally should be done in advance of the class meeting. However, this is not always possible. Other classes may use the room for other subject areas, and require a different arrangement of facilities. Be adaptable. As soon as you enter the room, do what must be done for your use of it. Students can help with the shades, lighting, and chalkboard and screen preparation. Use a rolling cart, if possible, for bringing equipment and materials into such rooms.

If you are not planning to use an aid at the beginning of the period, keep it off to one side, and do not draw attention to it until you are ready to use it and the students have been prepared for its introduction. Then speedy modification of the physical setting can be accomplished. It is important, particularly with younger students, to condition them to accept the dimming of lights as a signal for new work. Do not waste time setting up projectors or finding the start of a film. This gives students an uneasy feeling that you are not really prepared and that they are wasting time while you locate the correct starting point. When you are using slides, or photographs in sequence, and wish to use them again, in that order, number them on the back. As you introduce each put it face down in a pile so that the set will maintain its organization for your next use. If slide trays are available organize your set of slides in order of presentation. Be sure that each slide is inserted upside down and backward.

If you plan to develop a chalkboard outline, diagram, or sketch, first put the layout on paper as part of your lesson plan. Have a preliminary sketch of what you want to draw so that it will fit into the space available. Clear boards at the start of the period before students enter. Find out when the boards in your room are washed, and who does this task. The boards should be washed daily to provide a good working surface. Erasers should be cleaned periodically too.

Do not distribute rexographed or stenciled materials until you are ready to use them. Early distribution creates confusion and often "tips your hand" about a particular investigation or problem-solving

FIGURE 8.23
*Upside down and
backward*

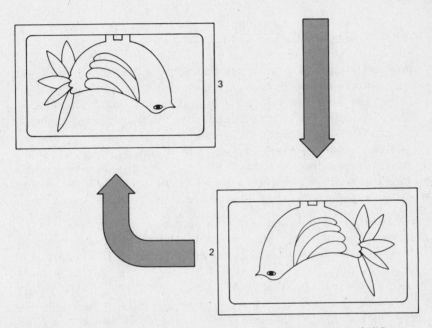

situation. Detailed planning, retesting of materials, and establishment
of routines for introducing and using the materials help insure
efficient and effective use of your time before and during the class
session.

After Class

*How to use
audio-visual aids*

After the preliminary work and the actual use in class, you have one
more operation—evaluation of results and disposition of equipment.
While the lesson is fresh in your mind make notes on your reactions
and those of your students to the different aids you used. Note the
good and the poor points, the time required for use, problems encountered, and the general effectiveness of the aid.

Discuss the specific audio-visual aid with your colleagues who have
used it in order to assess the overall picture of its use.

☐ Are they using the aid the way you did, or in a way radically different from
yours?

☐ Where do they introduce the material in a lesson?

☐ How do they introduce the use of that material?

*How to use
audio-visual aids*

This evaluation while the experience is fresh in your mind will prove of great value in all of your future teaching experience. You will not be using that specific lesson, in toto, again. The lesson, the class, and the times will be different. However, you will probably be using that audio-visual aid again, or one just like it. The experience you gain using a technique or a sequence of activities will influence all of your coming lessons. Your notes, made immediately after using an aid, will be valuable to you later when deciding whether to use a given aid again.

Be sure you report any equipment that needs repair immediately. Films, filmstrips, and tapes should be rewound and replaced in their respective cases. Slides and pictures should either be stacked for immediate reuse, or returned to their central depository. Maps and charts should be rolled up and replaced in the proper storage area. Torn or broken films, tapes, charts, and maps should be mended as soon as possible. Small repairs may be up to you, a lab specialist, a coordinator, or your supervisor. Major repairs on projectors, recorders, and other equipment are usually not done in the school itself. This equipment may be out of your working inventory for quite a period of time. The earlier you report the need for a repair, the earlier the equipment can be back in service.

Old, badly torn film and filmstrips that have been earmarked for disposal need not be simply discarded. Frequently there are sections of these materials that can be salvaged and reused. The film slip can be spliced to others for use later. Segments of film should be separated by blank film so that each segment can be used independently of the others on a reel. Each segment on a reel should be numbered and indexed on the film canister and an inventory list. Frames from filmstrips can be made into slides. Old posters and charts that are too torn to be used as such, can be reduced in size photographically for use in a transparency, or for the preparation of a stencil.

The more you explore the area of audio-visual aids, and the more experience you develop in their functions and use, the greater will be your capability for developing and modifying aids to meet the needs of your students.

WHEN DO YOU USE AUDIO-VISUAL AIDS?

*When to use
audio-visual aids*

Audio-visual aids should not be considered as separate entities, but as an integral part of the instructional program and lesson. They should be used when there is a need for them, and not just to fill time, amuse, entertain, or because someone else used them. *You* must be aware of the materials and equipment available to you, and *you* must decide upon the role you want the aids to play in a lesson. You might select an aid to help motivate a lesson. A model of a landform showing geological faults, different displaced strata, and intrusions might be used to initiate a study of diastropism or the reconstruction of an area retracing its geological history.

A tape of Robert Frost or Archibald MacLeish reading one of his own works might be used to stimulate thinking and discussion about a poetic style or the impact of a type of poetry on the current scene.

When to use audio-visual aids

Audio-visual aids can be used to introduce concepts into the evolving interaction. They can provide illustrations of the applications of theoretical concepts or principles; they can be used to compare materials or organisms; they can introduce historical figures or events; they can provide a varied and valuable input into the developing lesson; they can help create problem-solving situations; they can be used for review or in summary of ideas discussed in class.

In every case the use of the audio-visual aid is planned and it is used as an integral part of the lesson. It does not stand apart as a separate experience, unrelated to what came before and what comes after its introduction. Each aid is designed to be used to supply some aspect you think necessary in the program, which can be supplied in no other, more effective, way.

The following checklist is offered to guide you in gathering information about audio-visual equipment you might use in your instructional programs.

INFORMATION CHECKLIST FOR AUDIO-VISUAL AIDS

Charts and maps   1.

☐ Where are these materials located?

☐ How are they inventoried—alphabetically or numerically?

☐ Is there a master inventory list prepared for your use?

Models   2.

☐ Where are these materials stored?

☐ How can you secure them for preview and testing?

☐ Is there a master inventory list for your use?

Kits of materials   3.

☐ How many of each type of kit are available?

☐ Is the kit designed for a demonstration or for laboratory work by students?

☐ Is an instructional manual or teacher's guide provided for each?

☐ Is the kit for one-time use or is it for repeated assembly and disassembly?

Projectors: Film, filmstrip, film-loop, slide, opaque, overhead, micro   4.

☐ What is the manufacturer's name and model number of each?

☐ What is the reference number of the bulb to be used in each?

☐ What are the reference numbers of accessory items?

☐ Where is each stored?

☐ Is there a master inventory list prepared for you of all projectors and accessory items?

☐ Is there an instruction manual for each?

☐ How do you order each one for testing and use?

5. **Materials used with projectors: Films, slides, transparencies, film loops**

☐ Where is each type of material stored?

☐ How are these materials indexed—alphabetically or numerically?

☐ Is there a master inventory of materials arranged by associated type of projector?

☐ How do you order these for preview or use?

6. **Materials for preparation of transparencies**

What materials are in stock for making projectuals or transparencies?

☐ Pencils

☐ Acetate inks

☐ Drawing pens with different size points

☐ Press-on letters, numbers, and tapes

☐ Acetate sheets, and carbon-backed acetate sheets

☐ Rolls of acetate

☐ Frames

☐ Masking tape

☐ Tracks, grommets

☐ Templates for making drawings

☐ What types of films are available for preparing transparencies using copy machines?

☐ What types of films are available for preparing transparencies and duplicating or mimeograph masters?

7. **Copy machines**

☐ What is the name of the manufacturer and model number of each?

☐ Is the machine a photo-copier or a thermal copier?

☐ Are any plastic or silk screen carriers or paper holders required?

☐ Can you copy materials from books, or just from flat, single sheets of paper?

☐ What is the type and reference number of the film or paper to be used with the machine in order to make a:

Transparency

Paper copy

Spirit master for spirit duplicating machine

Mimeograph master for mimeograph machine

☐ Where is the machine located?

☐ Is there an instruction manual for each?

☐ Who is in charge of the machines?

Spirit duplicating machines: Rexograph or ditto machines   8.

☐ What is the manufacturer's name and model number of each?

☐ What type of paper is to be used in each?

☐ Where are the machines located?

☐ Where is the fluid for the machines stored?

☐ Where are the accessories stored, including extra wicks, fluid containers, and card attachment?

☐ What is the type and reference number of the master units to be used for preparing rexographed materials, including:

Standard master units (purple or black)

Masters for color duplication (red, green, blue, black)

Master units for preparing a transparency and a spirit master at the same time

☐ Is an instruction manual provided for each model?

Mimeograph machines   9.

☐ What is the manufacturer's name and model number of machine?

☐ Is there an instruction manual available?

☐ Where is the machine located?

☐ Is it a manual or an electric machine?

☐ What is the reference number of the stencils that can be ordered in your area?

☐ Where are the accessory items including:

Card printing attachment

Inks

Correction fluid

☐ What type of paper is used—sixteen- or twenty-pound? (With twenty-pound you can easily print on both sides of the paper.)

☐ How are stencils cleaned and stored for future use?

Electric stencil cutter   10.

☐ Where is the machine located?

☐ Who is in charge of its operation?

☐ What is the manufacturer's name and model number of machine?

☐ What is the reference number of stencils to be used?

GLOSSARY OF AUDIO-VISUAL AIDS

Acetate film. A transparent plastic material which is usually cut into 8½ by 11-inch sheets. It can also be purchased in a roll. Diagrams or words can be drawn on the material with acetate inks or marking pencils, and then used on the overhead projector for group viewing.

Audio-tape. Magnetic tape for recording sound. Spools or cassette cartridges are currently marketed.

Cartridge TV. A video tape encased in a plastic container or cartridge, which is inserted into a television player for viewing.

Copier (light or heat). A machine for producing either paper or transparent copies of diagrams or pictures. Heat and light are used with specially treated paper to reproduce diagrams, articles, or pictures.

Diazo-coupling reaction. A chemical reaction involving light that produces a light-fast and water-fast dye on an acetate sheet.

Diorama. A three-dimensional representation of a site or location.

Film-clip. A segment of an 8mm or a 16mm film that has been selected for viewing independently from the rest of the film.

Film-loop projector. A device for showing three to six minutes of 8mm or super-8mm film. The film is encased in a plastic cartridge for convenience and no handling or threading of film is required.

Filmstrip. A series of sequential frames of 35mm film.

Flow-chart. A chart indicating a sequence of operations, directions, or activities.

Frame. A cardboard holder for keeping transparencies both flat and protected.

Grommet. A small, metal insert for reinforcing holes made in leather or plastic.

Microphotograph. A photograph taken through the eyepiece of a microscope. An electron microphotograph would be a photograph of the material viewed with an electron microscope.

Microprojector. A device for group viewing of objects as seen through a microscope lens system. The image can be directed to a table top for small group viewing or to a wall screen.

Mimeograph. A machine for printing paper copies of material which has been typed or otherwise cut on a stencil.

Mylar hinge. A plastic, adhesive film used for attaching overlay acetate sheets to the frame of a projectual.

Oaktag. A heavyweight, smooth-surface, manila-colored type of paper used for mounting pictures or making charts.

Overlay. The acetate sheets added to the static sheet of a projectual.

Overhead projector. A device for casting images of transparent objects, prepared transparencies, or projectuals on a screen or wall.

Opaque projector. A device for casting a picture of a real but opaque object on a screen. This machine has a projecting tray for holding flat pictures, books, or small, nonliving objects such as rocks, shells, or small tools.

Periodic table. A chart, used in science studies, which depicts the arrangement of chemical elements according to their atomic numbers.

Petri dish. A flat, circular, glass or plastic dish provided with a glass cover that is used for bacterial studies and cultures.

Plastic track. A grooved, linear strip of plastic that can be attached to the frame of a projectual. It is used to guide acetate, paper, or opaque plastic sheets across the surface of a transparency or projectual.

Projectual (also see *Transparency*). A hand-drawn or lettered diagram on acetate sheets that is used on an overhead projector. In addition to the static sheet, a projectual can have several overlay sheets attached to the frame.

Relief map. A map on which elevations are indicated by raised, textured surfaces.

Silicon carbide. A chemical used to grind glass surfaces.

Spirit duplicating machines. Machines used for printing copies of material that has been typed, written, or drawn on a spirit duplicating master unit. This machine uses a liquid alcohol to transfer ink from the master unit to the paper copies.

Sprocket holes. The holes at the side of a film or filmstrip that govern the advance of the film through the projector.

Static. The bottom-most acetate sheet of a projectual that remains on view at all times when the projectual is used on the overhead projector.

Stencil. The master unit on which words or diagrams can be printed, drawn, typed, or electrically cut. This master unit is then placed on a mimeograph machine in order to produce a number of paper copies.

Stereo-photos. A pair of photographs of the same scene which, when viewed simultaneously, appear to give a three-dimensional image.

Stop-action photograph. A photograph taken by a camera with a shutter speed fast enough to "freeze" rapid action.

Supersaturated solution. A solution which has been induced to contain more dissolved material than it would ordinarily hold at a given temperature.

Template. A plastic or metal plate in which designs, numerals, figures, or letters are cut out. The plate is used for making drawings.

Transparency (also see *Projectual*). A reproduction of some printed or drawn material on specially treated acetate film that is used on the overhead projector. The reproduction is made by means of a copy machine.

PROBLEMS, QUESTIONS, AND ACTIVITIES

8.1 List at least five sources of audio-visual-aid materials in your subject area, other than those already available in your school.

8.2 Design and sketch the layout of a bulletin board on some topic in your subject area. How would you use it in a lesson?

8.3 Secure and preview a filmstrip in your subject from your department or school collection. Determine the topics emphasized.

    1. What specific use would you make of this filmstrip in a lesson?

    2. Indicate the nature of any written guide you would design for student use in viewing this filmstrip.

8.4 Design a projectual you can use in your subject area. Indicate how you would use it in a lesson.

8.5 Indicate which of the audio-visual aids discussed here would be of major use in your program.

    1. Which would not be applicable to your area?

    2. On what basis would you select the aids you want to use?

8.6 Briefly describe an original audio-visual aid which would enhance the presentation of a lesson in your subject area.

    1. Show specifically how you would prepare this aid.

    2. How would you use it during a lesson?

NOTES

NOTES

9
Summaries

WHAT IS A SUMMARY?

The last impression on a listener, a spectator, or a reader is of paramount importance. A political speech ends with the call, "Vote for . . . ." A television commercial signs off with two housewives, backed by a symphony orchestra, singing the product jingle. An editorial concludes with a vivid restatement of its chief theme, sometimes in BLOCK CAPITALS.

Similarly each lesson or discrete part of a lesson should end with an activity which leaves the student in possession of a clear, well-phrased statement of exactly what was learned during that time segment. Summaries will generally include a recapitulation of the aim of the lesson in terms of the extent to which it has been achieved.

WHAT ARE THE FUNCTIONS OF A SUMMARY?

Effective summaries help develop an awareness of the essential unity and purpose of what was done; they tie up the package in order to maximize the impact of each learning experience. The creative, dynamic summary can make cosmos out of chaos.

Functions of a summary

The purpose of any particular summary depends upon the learning activity that it is intended to complete. These purposes include:

Correlating Data

If students in a science class have been collecting data on the extent of solubility of potassium nitrate in water with change in temperature, a summary can be used to correlate the data gathered. Each team of students can work with different temperatures so that any one group does not needlessly repeat a procedure. Instead they use the laboratory time more profitably. At the end of the session, figures are recorded on a chart on the chalkboard. The entire class can then copy this information and share it in order to prepare a graphic representation of it, compare it to other such studies, and determine the generalizations this work illustrates. In a lesson based upon several uses of quotation marks, a summary may involve the restatement of the rules for their use and then provide for the creation of several original applications of these rules.

FIGURE 9.1
Chalkboard summary

Temperature (°C)	Number of grams of solid required to saturate 100 grams of water
0°	13.1
10	
20	31.4
40	
60	
80	
90	
100	245

This function of summaries is a supportive measure to give students practice in gathering isolated facts, correlating them, and using them to formulate broader generalizations.

Crystallizing an Idea or Concept

During a lesson, many facts or ideas may be introduced. Another function of the summary is to help students synthesize these ideas and formulate some statements or generalizations about them.

A class may be discussing different properties of some chemical elements discovered before 1865, in an attempt to work out a system of organization for these elements. The summary here would involve students relating some of these properties and actually designing a periodic table. They will have to leave blank spaces for elements yet unknown in 1865. This type of summary activity helps students to apply some of what they have learned, and to crystallize a statement about the periodic law.

An English class may be reading several poetry selections dealing with different views of war. A discussion centered about the students' reactions to these poems helps them to crystallize ideas about techniques of expression and communication of ideas and feelings. The summary activity here can help students to relate the themes of these poems to various opinions about events today.

Focusing on the Aim of the Lesson

The aim of a lesson must be carefully thought out, well stated, thoroughly understood, and accepted by the students. The final summary of that lesson should refocus the students' attention on that aim. They can then determine the extent to which it has been achieved; they can develop a sense of accomplishment and progress.

Functions of a summary

In a secretarial studies class, the aim of the lesson may have been to learn the use of a particular symbol. A summary would include a concise statement of the rules for using this symbol before and after consonants.

In a driver education class, where the aim was a consideration of traffic signs, the summary can center on the use of nonword symbols and sign shapes to communicate information to drivers and pedestrians.

In these cases, the summary brings the student "full circle" to the aim again, but this time it is with the advantage of the additional learnings of that class period.

Setting the Stage for Further Work

In addition to evaluating the work of the day, or the progress in a unit of work, many summaries help to set the stage for further investigations, research, or discussions. Medial summaries, those used during the course of a lesson, frequently are used for this purpose.

A lesson in an art class can be devoted to exploring the techniques used to convey a three-dimensional quality. A prepared sketch can be used as the medial summary. Students identify two techniques used and then continue to discuss and practice additional techniques illustrated in this summary sketch.

In a lesson on the causes of World War I, the economic factors might be emphasized. The final summary of that lesson can point the way to the need to also explore pertinent political and social factors as causative agents.

Developing Judgment

Occasionally the summary, by giving each student the chance to review concepts or principles just learned, presents him with the opportunity to pronounce an aesthetic judgment or show he has grasped some human value of which he might have been previously unaware.

The student in an art class who has just learned some of the characteristics of Baroque art will be summarizing findings when he explains why he would, or would not, consider a newly studied picture an example of that period.

Functions of a summary
Sometimes people have feelings or ideas about objects, events, or people without having any direct knowledge of them. In an English class the students can be asked to respond to certain words you call out. They find that some words are emotionally charged or offensive to some students, but not to others. Just learning to recognize and accept that different people react differently to the same word is a step toward developing real understanding among people.

A summary comparing opinions before and after a laboratory experiment or discussion can be a valuable and far-reaching learning device.

Taking Stock of Progress

Summary activity can allow a slower student in a class to catch up. At times, because a student may not be skilled at taking notes quickly or correlating information speedily, he can get the feeling of being swamped. A summary period gives him the opportunity to take stock of how much he has accomplished and get ready for the next segment of work. It gives the more gifted student a chance to add comments to his notes, or formulate some question that has been percolating during the lesson. At times, too, because the pace of a lesson has been rapid (maybe too rapid), a summary period is just the breathing space both you and the students need to look back in order to move ahead in the right direction.

WHEN DO YOU SUMMARIZE?

When to summarize
A summary is in order at any point in the lesson where a phase of a learning interaction comes to a logical end. The end of the class period is one point where a summary is essential; this is the *final summary*.

During the class period, there is frequently a need for a transition from one facet of a lesson to the next; this is the time for a *medial summary*. Some types of lessons lend themselves to more than one summary; others naturally require but one.

All summaries, medial or final, require careful planning to insure effective integration of the different aspects of that teaching–learning interaction.

HOW DO YOU SUMMARIZE?

How to summarize
It is not advisable to ask at the end of a lesson, "What did we learn today?" unless you know your class very well, for there may be a wise guy in the class who will answer, "Nothing." However, though that

question might not be the right one, a question is usually the way to start the summary activity. For example:

> What have we learned so far today about carbon?
>
> How does this example illustrate the law of conservation of energy?
>
> On the basis of what we have learned today, what functions does stage scenery play in a production?

Summary questions

These questions require that students look back over what they have just done, concisely state the key ideas developed in this time period, and apply what they have learned to a specific example or problem.

Many times, a summary may involve problem solving. A specific problem in math may be introduced which calls for the application of one or more theorems or principles investigated during the lesson. A contour map of an island can be used to illustrate and apply the principles used in communicating elevation, type of terrain, and man-made structures in an area.

A student must clearly understand a principle before he can apply it, and his summary statement of it will indicate to you how accurately and fully he has grasped it. His application of that principle to a real situation is the test of his full grasp of a particular concept. Knowledge of facts is important but the application and utilization of those facts is much more important.

Whatever technique you use to initiate the summary, it is imperative that the students, *not you,* do the summarizing. They must learn to *synthesize, crystallize,* and *apply.*

Active student involvement is the key to a summary's success just as it is a key to the success of any teaching–learning interaction. Many students need to develop skill in summarizing. Your plans, therefore, must include plenty of time for this activity. Admittedly, you can devote less time to a summary if you do the work, but then the real question to face is how much the students have learned. Unless you give them time to ask questions, develop generalizations, and, in short, get involved, you will not know if they are learning.

Part of your planning for this summary segment of a lesson should be devoted to the preparation of a working chalkboard outline—a valuable summary instrument. An outline prepared for a lesson on the Elizabethan theater might look like this:

I. The Elizabethan Theater

Summary outline

  A. *The Building*
    1. Location
    2. Shape and Size
    3. Contrast to Modern Buildings

  B. *The Audience*
    1. Composition
    2. Seating Arrangements
    3. Conduct

C. The Performance
  1. Stage(s)
  2. Actors
  3. Style of Acting
     a. special conventions
     b. comparison and contrast with that of today

Note that the outline has a regular sequence of Roman numerals, capital letters, and Arabic numbers, and makes use of parallel structure.

How to summarize

An outline can be readily copied by students while it is being developed on the board, and they can add comments as they progress. A carefully structured outline also provides a latecomer to class with a concise but accurate resume of what the class has done.

Another system you can try is to delay any notetaking by students. In this case the chalkboard outline you develop will have to be more detailed than the one given above. You can then provide a few moments following the medial or final summary for students to copy the outline and add any comments they wish. While they are doing this, you can be distributing or writing out the homework assignment for the following class meeting. One advantage of the restriction of note-taking time is that many students have the tendency to copy down every word that is said. They are so busy writing that they are not really listening to what was said or thinking about it. If they stop taking notes for awhile and listen — really listen — to what is going on, you find that they ask more questions, volunteer more answers, and generally participate more in the lesson. This system takes a bit of getting used to; it means that you must have a top-flight outline and that you provide time for copying it.

Another device is the preparation of rexographed or mimeographed sheets for students to use in working out summary problems, examples, or questions. These sheets, stating the problems or questions and giving directions for answering them, should be distributed when you are ready to use them, not before. If distributed too soon, they will distract from the work you are doing and give away the work you plan to do.

Crossword puzzles are another instrument you can use for a summary or a homework assignment. Start out with a list of the terms you want to include: pollution, sludge, detergents, phosphates, insecticides, potable, raw, sewage, seepage, oxygen, ozone, and so forth.

Spell them out on a sheet of graph paper until you have fitted in all those you can. Then number the boxes from left to right across each line. You need only put in the numbers of the first box for each word vertically or horizontally listed. Then shade in the areas not used. Put this prepared master over the inked page of a rexograph master and draw the lines you need and put in the pertinent numbers. The last thing to do is construct definitions for the terms you have included, correlated with the numbers across and down. This kind of

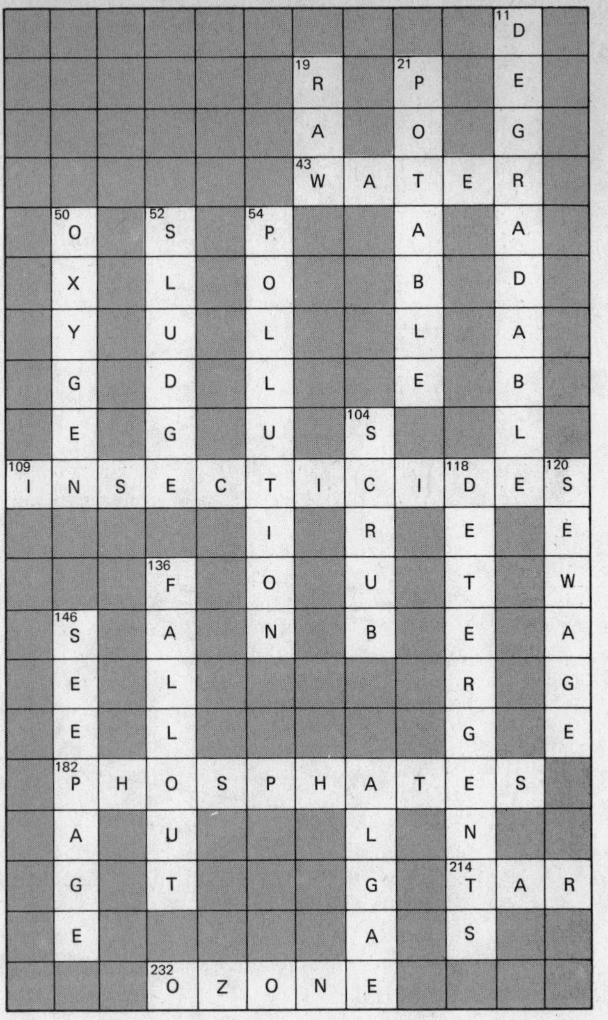

FIGURE 9.2
Crossword summary

```
                                              11
                                              D

                      19           21
                      R            P          E

                      A            O          G

                      43
                      W   A    T   E    R

50       52       54
O        S        P                A          A

X        L        O                B          D

Y        U        L                L          A

G        D        L                E          B

E        G        U   104
                      S                       L

109                                118       120
I   N    S   E    C   T   I   C    I   D   E   S

                      I       R        E          E

         136
         F            O       U        T          W

146
S        A            N       B        E          A

E        L                             R          G

E        L                             G          E

182
P   H    O   S    P   H   A   T    E   S

A        U                    L        N

                                       214
G        T                    G        T    A   R

E                             A        S

         232
         O   Z    O   N   E
```

activity can serve as a homework assignment, a summary, or as a bit of variety to the usual summary techniques you use. Students can also make up these puzzles as unit reviews.

A transparency can be a summary device. Students can complete diagrams, state principles, or identify pictures. If you used a graph during the lesson and want to illustrate a principle using much the same graph but in a different problem, plan a transparency for such use. Put the coordinates on the static. On the first overlay, have the data to be used in constructing the first graph. On a second overlay, have the data to be used in the second — the summary. Be sure that the two overlay sheets are carefully registered over the static sheet. Then assemble the transparency. Be sure to include an extra, blank transparent sheet on which you can work out the calculations, or make notes.

A film, filmstrip, film loop, a chart, a map, a model — all of these aids can be used during the summary segment of the lesson to aid students

FIGURE 9.3
*Making a summary
transparency,
first stage*

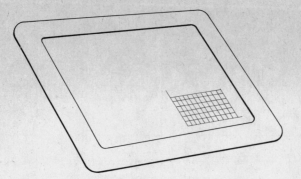

FIGURE 9.4
*Making a summary
transparency,
second stage*

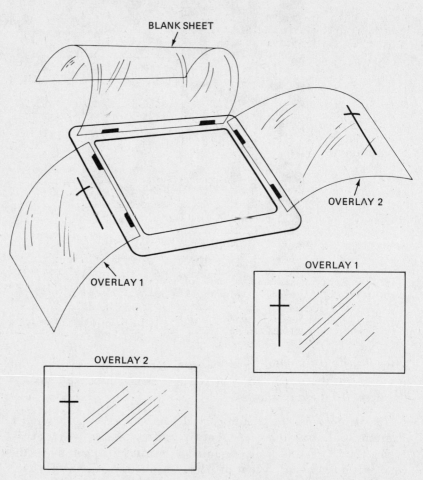

in assessing how far they have come in a study, and where they are going next.

Whatever instrument, device, question, or technique you employ to initiate or complement a summary be sure to:

Musts for a summary

Challenge students to do the work

Provide adequate time for the activity

Use the summary as a springboard for the next work

WHAT IS THE DIFFERENCE BETWEEN
A DRILL, A SUMMARY, AND A REVIEW?

Three terms—*drill, summary, review*—are sometimes used almost interchangeably. However they are not synonymous. Each involves a different concept and needs its own definition.

Drill

A drill is the purposeful reiteration of a necessary fact or basic skill. Sometimes the drill is not an identical repetition but an obvious application which is an extension or variation of the original item.

Practicing the index finger positions on a typewriter keyboard helps to gain speed and develop skill in touch-typing.

Writing chemical formulas by "crisscrossing" valences on ions gives practice in formula writing; the use of valence in constructing formulas is also underscored here.

```
DRILL
1,1,1,1,1,
2,2,2,2,2,
```

FIGURE 9.5
Drill by repetition

Summary

A summary is an activity which leaves the student with a clear-cut, well-phrased statement of just what was learned during the preceding segment of the lesson. Summary activities can be described in terms of the expression, "The whole is equal to the sum of its parts."

A definition of a price support system, a clear distinction between a stock and a bond, a statement of a physical law are all summaries.

The solution of a problem, the explanation of how an object works, the application of a principle just learned are also summaries.

```
SUMMARY

1 + 1 + 1 + 1 = 4
```

FIGURE 9.6
Summary is the sum of its parts

Review

A review is a comprehensive activity which looks at several sequential lessons to develop a new perspective that will enhance the mastery of what has been learned and encourage the student to see additional relationships.

A review has more far-reaching implications than does drill or summary. Any review is usually based on a summary which has provided the students with a firm foundation for building their intellectual ladder to broader generalizations and understanding in any area. The summary is usually a finite activity, but a review is limitless in scope.

As a review, you can ask a class to make up original examples in geometry based on the rules for finding the area of a triangle, circle, and square. You can tell the students that you will select several of the examples turned in and include them on the next exam you give. Each student will then have to summarize the rules and formulas he has learned, and use them in creating original problems.

As a review, you can visit an exhibit in the museum. Each student is furnished with a set of statements that he is to either support or refute on the basis of exhibits he sees, the information provided by the tour guide or lecturer, and the information he has gathered during the previous class work. This kind of field trip, involving summary, investigation, and synthesis illustrates the real meaning of review.

FIGURE 9.7
*Review is greater than
the sum of its parts*

REVIEW

$1 + 2 + 3 + 4 + X = 12$

A review goes far beyond a summary, and can be thought of in terms of the expression, "The whole is greater than the sum of its parts."

Each of these different activities—drill, summary, and review—has a place in your lessons, but only the summary will be part of *every* lesson. The summary serves to get the students thinking about what they are doing, expressing ideas in their own words, and developing confidence in their ability to undertake learning activities as individuals. The summary can get students more involved in the class work and less dependent on you.

PROBLEMS, QUESTIONS, AND ACTIVITIES

9.1 Collect three articles, news items, advertisements, or pictures that you could use to initiate a summary in a lesson in your subject area. Briefly indicate how you would use each one.

9.2 Write five questions, the response to each of which would begin the summary of a lesson. Assume that one of these responses is correct but inadequate as a good summary. Write the followup question(s) you would use.

9.3 As a result of your going over their notebooks with several of your students, you see that there is a pattern of good notes for individual parts of lessons. However you find few good summary statements that tie all the aspects of the learning activity together into some unity. How would you plan or modify your summary activities to remedy this weakness?

9.4 Prepare a diagrammatic representation of the material that you would include in a chalkboard outline for a specific lesson in your subject area. Include diagrams, and data tables if necessary. How would you use this outline in summarizing?

NOTES

NOTES

10
Assignments

WHAT IS AN ASSIGNMENT?

In simplest terms, an assignment is that learning activity you ask the student to do between the end of one lesson and the beginning of another. The activities that your students are performing—

Reading

Project work

Painting

Writing

Library research

Viewing

Listening

are examples of the types of assignments you can design. In addition to those that grow out of the daily lesson, there are a number of others for you to consider. Some may require a longer time span, for instance:

Two days to read a chapter in a novel, or a unit in a text

One week to write up a laboratory experiment done in class including some pertinent theory, statement of procedures, data gathered, graphs, and conclusions

One month to visit an art exhibit or display, read references in the library, and write a paper on the topic

One semester to write a term paper on a selected topic, or design, do, and write up a project in shop, science, or English literature

WHY GIVE ASSIGNMENTS?

Each assignment—if carefully planned with regard to the course of study, the students in the class, and the time available—should help the student expand his knowledge and skills base. It should provide each student an opportunity to respond individually and creatively. In doing his assignment, the student is fashioning a means of communicating directly with you, his teacher, and at times with other students in the class. The creativity with which he does the assignment depends upon:

Developing creativity

☐   How well he recognizes his own uniqueness and individuality

☐   The nature of the assignment you have designed

Individual expression should be a vital ingredient of each assignment in every subject area. Getting a student to participate actively in this part of the learning experience is helping him assume more responsibility for directing his own education. Creative expression involves the student's true reaction to an experience, expressed in a manner that is understood by others. Naturally, the poets come to mind because they are the masters of thought and language, and should most readily be able to convey their originality to others. But creative expression is as much an ingredient in science, math, art, and home economics, as it is in English. Your job will be to design and develop assignments that call forth the originality of your students. Assignments such as these can do just that:

Creative assignments

Imagine that you are a high school student in Georgia just before the outbreak of the Civil War. Describe a typical school day. Write your description in the form of a diary, or a newspaper account. Include your reactions.

On your way home today, look at a tree or shrub. Describe it in such a manner that someone who has never seen a tree would know what one is really like.

Look at the painting by ——— which is hanging in the library. After you have looked at it for several moments, describe what you saw. Describe your thoughts and feelings about the picture and what it depicts.

When you go to the cafeteria today, do not look at the menu or the food on the steam table. Look in another direction. Let the aroma of the food be your first introduction to the menu of the day. Can you discern any special aromas of dishes? After lunch describe your feelings about the unfamiliar foods that you smelled and then saw. What were your thoughts as you tasted some unfamiliar dish?

On your way home today, listen to all the sounds about you. Are they pleasant? Are they discordant? Which sound did you like the best? Did any sounds frighten you? Did any sounds make you sad? After thinking about these questions, and listening to the sounds, write your appraisal of several of the sounds you heard. Compare the sounds you selected with those you heard in the music we played in class today.

A teacher must think creatively, accept the unusual and the unique, and strive to understand the reaction that the student is expressing. The uniqueness of his response is the most vital part of the assignment. It is the key to unlocking a realization of his individual worth. By listening, reading carefully, and providing a variety of means for him to use in expressing his ideas, you are allowing room for his creativity and are developing the climate necessary for individual expression. Although creative expression—each student's unique response—should pervade every effective assignment you give, each assignment must also have some unique function depending on the aims and objectives of the learning activity of which it is an integral part. Some of these functions include:

Reenforcing and Applying Principles Already Introduced

An English class had explored the role of the multisensory approach in writing. Students had seen from an analysis of their previous writing that virtually all of their descriptive writing referred to what was seen, not what was heard or touched or smelled or tasted. To help them make progress in writing, each student was assigned to write a description of a specific location in the school, using hearing, touching, and sense of smell impressions, and minimizing what was seen. This assignment reenforced what was learned in class — that effective writers use word pictures to convey their total experience.

Reenforcing assignments

An American history class had discussed the precise nature of the Constitution and the interpretation of that document. The class also knew that members of the Supreme Court did not always unanimously agree with a particular interpretation of the law. To reenforce the principle of constitutional interpretation, a student committee was formed to draw up a set of rules governing conduct in the school cafeteria. The committee, which worked over a two-week period, was directed to construct the rules precisely so that they could be administered fairly and impartially. The set of rules they formulated, and the subsequent class analysis of this code, clearly showed that interpretation of these rules was needed.

A biology class had investigated the nutritional needs of plants and animals over the course of a month's time. Students were asked to plan a balanced aquarium or a balanced terrarium that could be organized in class during a subsequent laboratory session. They were to:

Detail how the foundation of the ecological system was to be built: gravel, rocks, sand, or shells

Detail the specific organism that should be included

Explain how the different materials were to be arranged

Outline the conditions required during the preparation and the maintenance of the system. This was putting information directly to work.

Relating New Skills to Previous Work

This kind of assignment can serve as a bridge from one learning activity to another, or between two topics linked in format, content, or skills required.

An assignment in math requiring the use of tables of roots and squares, and interpolation of such data, is good preparation for the use of more complex tables in math.

New-skills assignments

A class in Spanish might transpose the verb form from present to past tense in a reading selection.

A typing class can be assigned the job of setting up in column form, statistical data on dates and volume of sales for a given item. The original data is supplied in nontabular form, so that students must organize the data into meaningful columns and then calculate how to arrange it on a page or in a specific area on a page.

Motivation for Work to Be Done in Future Lessons

Motivation assignments

Students can be instructed to listen to conversations of other students their own age on the way to and from school, and note mentally certain pronunciations. It might be the flat "a" in "man" or the slurring of the "–ing" syllable in words such as "talking" and "walking." This kind of assignment is a prelude to a very exacting scrutiny of the student's own speech patterns and habits. Listening to others and then to our own speech characteristics is often quite an eye-opener.

An assignment to tour and examine a pictorial display on animal classification, as well as answering questions about segments of the display, will prepare the class for later lessons on the classification of living things. It informs them of the magnificent diversity of life forms on earth, and helps them see the need for a system of classifying data.

Providing for Individual Study

If an assignment is really going to teach a student how to learn for himself, then it must be structured to do that job. Not all students in a chemistry class are going to be research biochemists, just as not all students in an English class are going to be Pulitzer Prize-winning authors. But some may be one day. The assignment you design must provide for the entire spectrum of interest in your area, which is usually easier to say than to do. Textbooks rarely provide this kind of spread in their questions or problems. The author of any text does not know the particular students in your class, so he has not included all the questions or problems that you might like to use for that class. It will be up to you to prepare assignments that tap the individual differences.

Individual study assignments

If you are teaching writing, you can read a few sentences aloud from a story beginning that you made up and let each member of the class complete the story as he perceives it. The results will be most interesting, the task having permitted each student to respond within the framework of his own abilities. Such assignments will encourage students, hold their attention, and challenge those of all abilities in your class.

WHAT ARE SOME TYPES OF ASSIGNMENTS?

Reading is at the heart of virtually all assignments you develop for your classes. It may involve the text you are using, references in the library, or data gathered during a laboratory session or from a discussion. Aside from the reading component of all assignments, the remainder of the assignment can usually be classified as:

Categories of assignments

☐ Reading and answering questions

☐ Writing assignments

☐ Problem-solving

☐ Projects

Each type of assignment has specific advantages in that it attempts to develop yet another skill or talent of the student. On the other hand, each has certain limitations that must be recognized and, when possible, avoided.

Reading and Answering Questions

This is a commonly used type of assignment which generally appears as: "Read pages 29 to 34, and answer questions 1 to 4 on page 39." Such an assignment is commonly used because it is easy to give. However, you are using the text material and the questions designed by the author of that text. As easy as this type of work is to assign, there are several inherent and serious limitations to consider. It assumes that all the students have the same degree of reading ability, which is rarely true in any class. It may be that the factual material in the text is specifically what you want the students to work from, or perhaps a particular novel or essay is to be read. In such cases you must use the reading material as it appears, no matter how easy it may be for some students, or how difficult for others. As you gain experience, you will become alert for those texts or other reading materials more appropriate to the slower and to the advanced students in your class. These can then be introduced to provide each group of readers — the slower, the "average," and the advanced — with a meaningful, worthwhile reading assignment.

This kind of read-and-answer-questions assignment makes no provision for individual differences in ability, but could be improved if you modified the assignment to include:

☐ Attention to important vocabulary words

Modifying reading assignments

☐ A series of graded problems or questions. Each question you develop or use might be rated on a scale of 1 to 4

Problems or questions rated 1 and 2 could be done by all the students

Problems or questions rated 3 are of increased difficulty and could be done by a large number of students

Problems or questions rated 4 involve real "thought" processes that would challenge some of the more advanced students

Each assignment of the read-and-answer type could include problems from all four rating groups. Students would be instructed to try to do all the assigned questions. Each assignment you collect and check over or grade should be examined from the standpoint of correctness and the difficulty of the types of problems or questions done. If the student tries some of the more advanced questions but does not succeed with them, you might indicate some of the errors so that he will try difficult ones again. The slower students will not get discouraged this way, and the more advanced students will not get bored.

Try using some of the questions offered in the text and some you design yourself for a specific assignment. Also, many reference texts at your disposal have very practical exercises and questions. Take advantage of the work and experience of as many resource people as you can in order to offer relevant, pertinent, workable problems and questions to your students.

With these modifications, the reading- (a primary means for transmitting information) and-answering-questions (those selected or designed specifically for your group of students) assignments can provide a most effective means for stimulating and challenging your students.

Writing Assignments

Writing assignments can be sub-divided into:

Types of writing assignments

Those which are more creative in nature, including poems, essays, compositions, term papers, and character studies

Those which are primarily research reports or papers, including ones on laboratory work, field trips, research papers or literature studies in a given topic.

Creative writing assignments can be of short or long duration. The term paper is a frequently used assignment which can be a valuable teaching–learning experience but which must be distinguished from the research digest or survey. Both have many similar characteristics and both have value in an instructional program. Both are preceded by reading and notetaking; both have footnotes and a bibliography. However, the research survey is just that—a digest or survey of ideas of others. The student is presenting a great many ideas and opinions culled from many sources. Sometimes the ideas and opinions are in almost the exact words of the original author. Rarely in the research survey is the student reacting to what he has read, or questioning or evaluating it.

A term paper, on the other hand, can be a dynamic message from the student. The student has read several sources; he has investigated a problem; he has assimilated and synthesized what he has learned. In his term paper, the student is conversing with the reader in a style and language all his own. He is questioning and evaluating. He is quoting original sources where necessary. This kind of paper provides you with some insight into the student as he is reacting to a problem or exploring a topic. Both the term paper and the research survey require that you carefully:

Assigning term papers

Explain the scope and function of the paper

Set down guidelines for doing the work and presenting the finished product

Clearly define the time limits

A less comprehensive report than the term paper is the book report. If you are asking for a written report at the end of the reading of a book, be sure to tell the students what you want to know. The book report might be based entirely on a well-developed answer to statements such as:

> In literature as in life, an event which at the time it happened seemed to have very little significance may in the end play a large part in the lives of the characters. From the book you have read, give definite references to show that this is true.

> Conflict and challenge make for personal growth. Using the book you have just read as your reference, explain whether you think the author agrees or disagrees with this statement.

Statements such as these that are specific will evoke very interesting, original responses from your students and can be used with a variety of books. You may want students to:

> Make an analysis of a character in a book

> Compare the themes of two books

> Write a synopsis of one or several passages from the book

These reports, based on the reading of one or two books, can be exercises in creative writing and, in effect, research papers in miniature—they can be short- or long-range in scope. The main part of credit for the book report should go for the reading of the book. If the student has read a book honestly but has written a second-rate report, then the trouble is with the writing. Give your students a chance to report orally from time to time. This may increase their interest in reading and allow certain students to compensate in their oral reports for the shortcomings of their written reports. As often as possible follow up by means of individual conferences with those students who have writing difficulties and indicate how they can improve their writing.

Reports on specific laboratory experiences call for a high degree of organization, synthesis, and analysis. Most of these reports call for:

☐ Some background information

☐ A summary of data collected

☐ Conclusions developed

☐ Some explanation of sources of error in the work

☐ Some indication of further investigations

Papers on field trips can call for a factual, step-by-step approach in reporting what was seen and done. Other such papers may call for the students to describe their feelings about a concert, an exhibit, or a meeting. Such reports thus emphasize reactions to an experience.

Written reports, whether long or short in duration and scope, whether more creative or more data oriented in approach, all have a place in virtually every program of differentiated assignments. They emphasize various skills, help develop diverse talents, and provide a spectrum of challenges for your students.

Problem-Solving

This type of assignment can be a fascinating learning experience. Basically, there are two different types of problem-solving assignments:

Types of problems for solving

Those problems that can be solved

Those problems that a student can get more information about, but that he can really never solve

Did Marlowe write the works of Shakespeare? This is an example of the unsolvable problem; it is an exercise in investigation. It serves to help students to learn to gather data, organize information, and express an opinion logically.

How does one cell in your right big toe get energy from the hamburger you had for lunch today? This problem also calls for investigation, organization, synthesis, and analysis of information, but it is a question that can be accurately answered.

Problem-solving assignments can play a role in any subject area.

Using problem-solving assignments

How did the French *vous* come to be the accepted polite form?

Calculate how the figures on sales of ten stocks for the past two months can be organized into tabular and graphic form for posting in a ledger or on a sales graph.

Describe how you would use a piece of driftwood in creating a free-form sculpture.

How would you prepare a soufflé or bake a cake at a high-altitude summer resort?

Suppose you had a musical arrangement of "Home Sweet Home," written for a full band. How would you rescore it for your own small orchestra of: 4 violins, 2 cellos, 1 French horn, 1 clarinet, 1 piano, 1 viola, 1 double base, 1 trumpet, 1 flute, drums, and triangle.

These are the kinds of assignments that students like to tackle. Problems or puzzles are intriguing at all age levels.

The Project

This assignment involving something a student will do—projects, model making, painting, simple experiments, and investigations—is the type that relies least on the student's ability to read, but does permit him to communicate reactions, ideas, and feelings in a meaningful way.

Simple experiments or investigations can be conducted easily by the student in a moderate amount of time. It should be remembered that this type of activity is not restricted to the science area.

Project assignments

> A student translates five popular advertising slogans into a language he is studying.
>
> A student experiments and develops a recipe for a dessert or a vegetable dish and then discusses it in her home economics class.
>
> A student compares the active ingredients in ten commonly used bleaches to determine their similarities and differences.
>
> A student follows the prices of wheat futures for a period of time, predicts how he would invest in that market, and then follows the "investment" via the daily market reports in the newspapers.
>
> A student compares three magazine advertisements for style, arrangement, and balance, and then writes and designs one for himself.

These simple investigations are different from the standard assignments in that they call upon the student to move out of the textbook into the environment about him and use that environment in his homework. Some of these investigations can be done overnight; others might take several days.

In the case of the longer project several progress reports, written and oral, are required in order for you and the student, working together, to assess progress and direction. Again, this type of assignment is not restricted to science classes. The student in any subject area can do a project: he may design and make a dress, a model car, a collage, a stage set, or a balanced aquarium; he may collect seashells, travel posters, minerals, campaign buttons, postage stamps, or records.

This type of assignment taps yet another student talent—his ability to set up a work schedule, complete the unit of work, and develop tangible results. Students can work independently or in small groups on a project. An entire class can prepare an assembly program, which is really a project.

Each of these types of activities, once introduced, must be carefully planned and then used in the learning experience. Projects should not be handed in at the end of the last day of the term; you won't have time to evaluate either the project or the effort it represents. Moreover, you will then be the *only* person to see the work. The other students in the class will not benefit from the work, or share in learning about it. Project work should be submitted well before the end of a semester. It is helpful to collect small batches of such projects so that you have the time to evaluate them; the students can then present their work to the class in sessions you plan for and provide.

WHAT ARE THE GUIDELINES FOR CREATING EFFECTIVE ASSIGNMENTS?

In developing challenging, creative assignments you should keep in mind:

Components of an assignment

☐   Your students

☐   The available resources for you and for your students

☐   The best techniques to use for a specific unit of work

What to Know About Your Students

In order to create effective assignments you must get to know your class. Your first knowledge of them will come from your teaching–learning experiences with them, how you accept them, and how they react to you. Additional insight into specific talents and problems can come from an examination of their reading scores, their standardized math exams, and their interests in sports and other extracurricular activities like dramatics or music. Guidance counselors too can often help you with information on specific students which may help you to more adequately provide them with meaningful learning situations.

On this basis you can begin to develop your differentiated assignments. You will build into each modifications and variations that can interest and challenge virtually each student in the class.

What to Know About Available Resources

Resources for assignments

If your school has records to lend to your language students, use them. If your school library is well stocked, use it as a resource area. Ask that certain books be put on reserve so that all the students will have the same opportunity to use them.

If the assignment calls for journals or references not found in your school library, see if they are available in the local library. If you ask students to visit an exhibit at a distance from the school, determine if all the students can afford the transportation or admission fees. Most young people are very sensitive and may not admit any financial limitation, but remember financial considerations in making your assignments. Projects, for instance, should not be exercises in spending money but in the application of creative thought and talent.

In making assignments you should take into consideration that the student has a number of other major and minor subjects and may have homework in all of them. Some students must work after school and on Saturday and will not have as much time to devote to lengthy assignments. Some students may live in crowded apartments and not have the luxury of a quiet place to read or write.

What to Know About Assignment Preparing Techniques

You must have a clear understanding of what you want an assignment to do.

What an assignment should do

An assignment of typing practice every evening is reenforcing motor skills.

Listening to language records is training the ear to the sound of the new language.

Research problems, creative writing, and problem-solving are all designed to stimulate thinking.

Usually you will want one assignment to do a variety of things: motivate interest, reenforce learning or skills, summarize. As you plan each unit of work in your program, you should decide upon those assignments you think would be the most profitable experiences for your students. During the year you may run across questions, problems, articles, and advertisements that can serve as the basis for an assignment of short, medium, or long duration. Add these items to your resource file and use them when you design assignments. Some assignments will be the direct outgrowth of your work in class. Drill, remedial exercises, simple investigations, projects, or term papers might be generated as an outgrowth of a laboratory session or a discussion.

HOW ARE ASSIGNMENTS PRESENTED EFFECTIVELY?

No matter what the length of the assignment you can use the following presentation guidelines:

Presenting assignments

1. *Decide when you will give the assignment.* You can write the assignment on the board as soon as you enter the classroom. The advantages are that students expect to routinely copy this work as soon as they arrive. It also provides a quick way of getting down to work, and insures that you will not forget to give the assignment that day. Most assignments, however, should stem directly from the lesson and should not be given until the end of that lesson. Giving assignments at the start of a lesson may diminish interest in the day's work.

2. *Decide on how you will give the assignment.* Are you going to give it orally? This usually requires several repetitions and always involves some confusion. Are you going to write the assignment on the board? This requires time but it is clearly visible to all present and serves to decrease confusion about terms and references. Are you going to use rexographed assignment sheets? These sheets may have as many as twenty questions, examples, or suggestions, and span a two- or three-day assignment period. Once the sheet is duplicated, you can cut it up into segments and distribute one section at a time when needed. This saves class time and provides a means of furnishing absentee students with a record of the assignments they missed.

Shouting out the assignment at the end of the period after the bell has rung is worse than giving no assignment at all.

Presenting assignments

3. *Decide on timing.* There are several aspects of timing to consider — the time to give the assignment; the time to get progress reports if needed; the time for the students to do the work. Plan on providing time to explain the specific assignment. Early in the school year you should clearly outline with your students the manner in which you want daily homework and assignments done.

The daily assignment

☐ Do you want them in a notebook, or on looseleaf paper?

☐ Should they write out the questions first and then answer them?

☐ Should there be specific size margins for the teacher's comments?

☐ If you number the assignment you give, should students use this code number on their homework?

This preliminary time investment minimizes the time you must devote to explanations of format later on.

A major assignment — a term paper, project, or long-term assignment of any kind — should be announced in general terms on one of the first days of the term. Such advance notice and some preliminary discussion of guidelines develop an awareness of the scope and meaning of this long-range work. The first announcement should include the information that:

The major, long-term assignment

☐ The work will be required

☐ It should involve a topic from a specific area of work

☐ It should be of a minimum scope

☐ It will be due on a certain date

☐ You will discuss this work further before the end of the following week

During the next discussion of this work you will explore:

☐ The specific problems or questions that might be treated

☐ The format or structure to be followed

☐ Some of the references available in the department library, the school library, and the community

☐ The dates of progress reports

Be sure to schedule a number of progress report days. You can also use portions of supervised study sessions to have conferences with your students about this work. In your discussions be sure to stress to the student the importance of the "you" in the project or paper. The assignment thus becomes integrated with class work and students understand that it is an important learning experience.

One more important aspect of this work to consider is the public relations factor. The student's family, even if it is a young, modern family, may still think that there should be some written homework every night. The parents must know that if a student is sitting reading a book, pasting a display together, reading the newspaper, listening to a specific program, he is directly involved in a homework assignment. Since it is often difficult to meet with parents, you may encounter a communication problem which can be overcome by using the rexographed or duplicated assignment sheets to let the parents know what is being assigned. They can read about the project work that is going on, the reports that are due, the specific reading assignment that you made.

Parents are still your greatest ally in getting students to do homework. In some cases they can go over the homework with the student. They can check on completeness, listen to vocabulary, discuss reading passages, verify math problems, and be supportive and encouraging. During conferences with parents and at parent association meetings, the role of homework is a most worthwhile topic to explore.

HOW DO YOU USE COMPLETED ASSIGNMENTS?

Using the assignment

There is a gradation of choices open to you in your utilization of homework assignments. You can go all the way from doing nothing with them to an in-depth evaluation complete with comments and a grade.

Doing nothing with an assignment is a big mistake. If the homework is not worth using in some manner, why assign it at all? If you put such a low premium on an assignment, students will quickly abandon it as a meaningless, irrelevant waste of time.

If on the other hand you consider an assignment a valuable part of the teaching–learning interaction, then the problem facing you is how to handle it in light of the total number of students in your classes and the time required to examine assignments done at home. The logistics of the teacher's confrontation with homework is frightening to contemplate. If we assume that you have five classes, and that each class has thirty students, daily written homework (assuming one page per student) totals 150 pieces of paper each day, 750 pieces of paper each week, 3,000 pieces of paper per month. Even if you check each page in one minute, you must put in 750 minutes per week — that is over 12 hours each week. It is not rewarding to either you or the students to spend only one minute on each paper. You could scarcely evaluate a paragraph in that time, or hardly grade one or two problems. Is such perfunctory handling of assignments worth over 12 hours of your time per week? Most emphatically, no! Instead, you can spend that time in other work — developing demonstrations, lab sessions, discussions.

Using the assignment

What then do you do with the theoretical 150 papers each day? You can check highlights in class. While several students are at the board, and while the class is watching the board work, you can walk around the room and check on some of the work. The checking is not for a grade or an evaluation; it merely indicates that you have seen the work and that you recognize what the student has done. You can usually see a lot even as you glance over the paper. You can see something to commend or something to comment on. Even the words, "Good work," or an admonishment, "Be careful about the units." make the work more worthwhile. The value of the assignment is not in your checking it, but in the student's doing it. Your checking provides further motivation. This kind of checking also alerts you to those not doing the assignment. You can follow up on these students at the end of the period, during a study session, or in a workshop session.

Random sampling and spot checking are other techniques to use. You can collect five or ten assignments, at random, in a class. There should be no prescribed or obvious way in which you select the specific ones to collect. Students are very quick to discern patterns and will then be able to predict when it is "their turn." You can do a better job of evaluating these randomly selected papers because there are fewer of them to examine. You can set aside a section in your record book for indicating the times you have checked or evaluated homework for a student

($\checkmark$)   collected and acceptable
($\checkmark$−)   collected and unacceptable
($\checkmark$+)   collected and particularly well done

Make comments on these assignments where necessary and indicate strengths and weaknesses. Bring a few of the outstanding assignments to class and read or refer to sections which are particularly well done. You can make a transparency of a section of a composition, or of a problem solution, and using the overhead projector, examine it in detail with the entire class.

An in-depth evaluation is the other extreme in the range of possibilities in handling assignments. This calls for you to first briefly read over all the homework assignments, or look them over if they are models, projects, or the like. Get an idea of the scope of responses. From your general survey, you can formulate a model answer, a grading key, or some basis of comparison for judging the completed assignment. Then evaluate each assignment carefully, making comments where needed on content, style, logical presentation, or other significant aspects of the material.

The completed assignments should be discussed with the students to help them develop skills in answering questions, presenting ideas, organizing facts, or illustrating principles.

Projects or models should be evaluated after a discussion session in which the student presents his work, answers questions about it, and discusses some of the problems he encountered. This discussion develops the student's ability to "think on his feet" in discussing a topic with which he is familiar.

Using the assignment

If the assignment is a model, a chart, or a map, then you should display some of the most interesting ones. Be sure the student's name is clearly evident. When the work has been displayed for a sufficient period of time, then return it to the student who made it, on a day that he has the means for getting it home. Remember not to leave displays up too long—they lose their effectiveness. Be sure to schedule the submission of long-range assignments sufficiently before the end of the semester so that you will have ample time for this evaluation, discussion, and display.

Your development or selection of a variety of assignments is an important facet of your planning and requires all the careful attention you devote to developing demonstrations, lab work, or discussions. The assignment is that portion of an interaction in which the student works independently on some task and develops his own abilities and talents for learning.

PROBLEMS, QUESTIONS, AND ACTIVITIES

10.1 From your own experience as a student, a student-teacher, or a teacher, list the chief reasons why homework is not done.

Briefly analyze the significance of each reason listed. Tell how you would try to reduce the number of students not doing their assignments in each category you have noted.

10.2 Assume that you have been teaching for two months. You have fallen behind in several subject class and homeroom reports due in the assistant principal's office. In analyzing your work, you find that the preparation of your lessons and the reading and marking of nightly homework assignments take all of your time. What changes might you have to make in order to have sufficient time for all your work?

10.3 As a beginning teacher you note that your students write fluently but that there is little depth of thought evident in their written answers. You have decided that for a period of three weeks you will give assignments that involve outside reading, and then you will follow up with discussions and other workshop experiences. At the end of one week, Richard's parents ask if they may come to see you. They are irate because their son gets no "homework," which to them means no written assignments.

   1. How will you prepare for this interview so that Richard's parents will be assured that their son is engaged in worthwhile learning activities?

   2. What will you *say* to Richard's parents?

10.4 Describe three different assignments that you would give as part of a specific unit of work in your subject area. Each one should involve a different learning activity.

NOTES

NOTES

11
Enrichments

WHAT IS AN ENRICHMENT?

A well-prepared teacher, teaching a well-prepared lesson skillfully and vividly, is always enriching that lesson. However, from time to time the enrichment activities are deliberately chosen and directly planned. Examples of enrichment activities include:

Sources of enrichment

1. *The teacher's unique experience background.* A teacher who has traveled throughout the Southwest and taken a number of 35mm slides of that section of the country can introduce them in a unit in social studies on the growth of the Southwest, or in a unit in English on the American scene, or in a geology study in earth science.

A teacher who has worked in industry or a business firm can introduce pertinent anecdotes about procedures followed in such firms.

2. *The unique talents and experiences of students.* A student who plays the guitar can be called upon to illustrate some characteristics of different sounds in physics. A student who has lived in another country can describe the preparation of some dishes or special meals.

3. *The resources of a particular school or community.* The nearby park with its noteworthy rock outcroppings can be visited. The nearby public health station can be visited and different technicians and/or other personnel can speak to students about health problems in their community.

4. *The season of the year.* Introducing the Edna St. Vincent Millay poem, "Renascence," in the spring can elicit different responses than when used in the cold winter months. Collecting specimens of different plants and shrubs is easier in the early fall and late spring. These specimens can be preserved or pressed, and studied later during the winter.

5. *The occurrence of a natural phenomenon or an historical event.* The landing of the *Apollo 11* astronauts on the moon, or the suspenseful return of *Apollo 13* can be used as teaching–learning enrichments in many different subject areas. The enacting of a piece of legislation, or the delivery of the decision of the Supreme Court can make valuable contributions to some lessons.

The success of any lesson will not necessarily depend upon the inclusion of any enrichments, but an alert teacher will utilize any significant place or event to make the interactions lively and exciting, and to involve students. Enrichments do just this and enriching people, places, and objects surround you, no matter what subject you teach. Your major task is to identify those enrichments at your disposal, and utilize those which are most pertinent, stimulating, and challenging.

WHAT ARE SOME TYPES OF ENRICHMENTS?

Printed Materials

An enrichment which is almost always available is the printed word as it appears in books, magazines, newspapers, pamphlets, student publications, and other reading matter.

The gifted student, the "average" student, and the student who is a slow reader, may all find their contact with books enriched if you can suggest readings on suitable levels.

Printed materials as enrichment

Get to know the periodicals and books in your school library which are particularly of interest to your subject area. Make use of the texts, references, periodicals, microfilmed materials, and different collections in the library in your school and in the community nearest the school. The school librarian will usually, if asked, conduct a library lesson for your class. Indicate some of the special topics that you will be introducing in the program so that she can indicate some of the specific journal references she has on hand. A school library affords true enrichment not only when it provides resource materials for a given assignment, but also when a student discovers in browsing and in leisure reading the joy of books.

Exhibits

Exhibits, whether they are permanent or transient, in local museums, galleries, banks, and department stores are another source of enrichment. Museums are constantly planning and establishing new collections and displays. They often produce "trail guides"—pamphlets to use on a trip through the exhibit or collection which draw attention to important facets of the display. Some museums prepare displays, dioramas, and exhibits that they will send to your school on request. The exhibit is generally borrowed for a specific length of time.

Exhibits as enrichment

A number of banks display collections of ancient coins and various forms of currency. You can make arrangements with the particular bank for groups of your students to come to look at the collection. This kind of field trip lends a touch of variety by giving students a learning experience with a valuable collection that they would not have had otherwise.

Exhibits as enrichment

The window display of a local department store, or specialty shop, prepared as it frequently is by a professional, may well be used by the art teacher to develop in his students the skill of observing, mixing materials, achieving certain dramatic effects, and blending colors.

A collection of sea shells or paintings used by department stores to complement furniture displays can be valuable teaching devices. When you see these things on display, you should refer your students to them. You might be able to borrow all or part of such a collection for a period of time and display it in your school. Many firms are most willing to cooperate with schools in this way. Class display cases with locks in the library or main hall are most suitable for such displays. In these spots they will have maximum exposure and protection. Try to select a background that will enhance the effectiveness of your display. For example, a collection of sea shells and corals would be very eye-catching if displayed in a glass cabinet against a black fabric background. The specimens on glass shelves—some standing on the shelf, some in tall glass containers, some spread out in a fan-like arrangement—can be enjoyed by all. The display setting is of great importance in increasing the effectiveness of the display.

Canvass the teachers and students in your school for those with special hobbies or collections that they might be willing to display in suitable cases. If the collection is an exceptionally valuable one, it might be brought in for one lesson rather than displaying it over a longer period of time.

Bulletin Boards

Using bulletin boards for enrichment

Most classrooms and some main halls in schools have display boards. You can use them to maximum enrichment advantage too. In one school, there may be long display boards on each floor that are reserved for use by different departments. In other schools, the use of the display boards may be rotated from subject area to subject area. Keep alert for pictures and articles for use in these displays. Each time you see an advertisement, or get a flier from a company with a particularly interesting drawing, graph, or pictures, add it to your resource file.

The display boards are a wonderful means for exhibiting work done by the students—photographs taken as part of a study of the environment; sketches done on a field trip; drawings done in class; photographs of students involved in different aspects of school life. These enrichments add a measure of personalization to any teaching–learning interaction. Displays prepared by students, and about students at their work, can be a very effective extra way of involving them in learning.

Television and Radio

Television and radio programs are also sources of enrichment if you take advantage of those offerings which are significant and relevant to your work. So much history is now made before our eyes that we cannot minimize or ignore these devices as teaching instruments.

Using television and radio for enrichment

It is unwise to assign the viewing of a particular television program, or the listening to a specific radio program as a mandatory part of a homework assignment for an entire class. You can never be certain that a television set or a radio is under the exclusive control of that student. If there is a particularly important program on during school time, and if the school has a television set, you can arrange for your classes to see this program.

Projects

Students interested in a subject area frequently want to go much more deeply into that area than the time for class consideration permits. This is where special projects can be most valuable.

A student in the sciences may be encouraged to enter a local or national science fair competition. You can assist the student in defining the limits of an investigation, suggesting readings, and consulting with him periodically about his progress. To be of value, the work must be done by the student. Your role is to advise, recommend, and be alert to potential hazards, not do the work.

A teacher in any subject area may provide enrichment for an interested student by suggesting a series of readings beyond the text and then giving that student the opportunity to present his findings to the class. This kind of project emphasizes the student as a resource person in a special area.

People Resources

A great many teachers have professional interest, or travel experiences that can be helpful in enriching a lesson. However, an autobiographical digression, fascinating as it might be to the narrator and momentarily to the students (a captive audience), is justified only if it truly adds to the learning experience.

People as enrichment

Students can frequently enrich a lesson, not only by tangible evidence of topics studied and places visited, but also by their references to their out-of-school jobs or experiences in student government. A teacher should make himself aware of the variety of student experiences and interests in a class and then bring these into the lesson. A student, for example, who has worked during the summer with young people in another part of the country, served as a hospital volunteer, or spent some time in a school system in another country can bring enrichment to the lessons you plan. You might be able to combine several classes in one period so that more students can participate in this kind of enriching learning experience.

Inviting an outside speaker in to enrich a lesson for a group is another interesting addition. The advantages are that the speaker:

Using an outside speaker

May be an expert in a field

Can offer realistic vocational guidance to students

Can add a refreshing change of pace.

There can also be disadvantages in such a plan and they should be taken into consideration as well.

The visitor may not be a good speaker; he may be highly talented in his field but not experienced in talking before groups.

He might not have been apprised of the age level, and scholastic background of the group he will meet.

He may not be attuned to school schedules and could even arrive after the class has been dismissed.

You can take the following steps in preparing for an enrichment involving an invited speaker.

Preparing for an outside speaker

☐ Determine the school regulations regarding the appearance of speakers.

☐ Speak to your supervisor and colleagues for recommendations as to speakers.

☐ Write to the particular person inviting him and telling him:

The age level of the audience

The type of class involved—Advanced Biology; Economics; Modified English III

The date and time period for the visit

The specific topic you would like treated

The purpose of the visit—to fill in subject matter; to offer vocational guidance

The need for you to know about any audio-visual equipment he will require.

☐ Schedule preliminary discussions with your class; assign preliminary reading or investigations in order to get the most out of the visit.

☐ Secure a room large enough to accommodate the class or combined classes.

☐ Provide the materials needed by the speaker: chalkboard and chalk, overhead projector, microphone, slide projectors, extension cords, electrical outlets. If the room has to be darkened during the presentation, check the shades and lighting facilities.

☐ Prepare and post fliers announcing the guest speaker.

☐ Prepare an introduction for the speaker.

☐ The follow-up activities you can plan for include:

Discussion following the visit

Further suggested readings

Project work and laboratory experiences

A thank you note to the speaker for lending his time and talents.

Assembly Programs

An assembly program planned and presented by students is another form of enrichment. This kind of activity should be considered in terms of planning and rehearsal, presentation, and follow-up activities.

An example of a successful assembly program which was planned and executed by students took the form of a Consumer Quiz.

☐ Groups of students researched items in areas including: best buys in certain foods, labeling, packaging, advertising claims, ingredients in specific items, purchasing contracts, consumer protection.

Putting together an assembly

☐ Each item to be included was phrased as a question. Three possible choices were offered as answers. This combination of one question and three possible answers was printed on an acetate sheet and used as a transparency on the overhead projector. The three choices were covered by two pieces of oaktag: the bottom one cut to reveal the correct answer, and the upper one to completely mask all the choices.

FIGURE 11.1
Planning the transparency

☐ The transparencies were sequentially numbered, and then a script was written about the questions which had been developed. The questions had been grouped together so that two or three of them would focus on a particular issue. The script provided for some introductory information about a particular topic, then indicated the question, and possible answers.

FIGURE 11.2
Completing the transparency

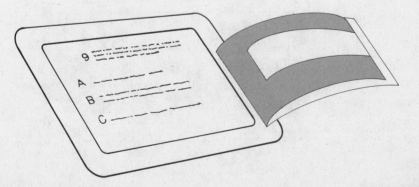

☐ Once the total number of questions and the script were completed, an answer sheet was prepared. Copies of this answer sheet were distributed to students as they came into the auditorium for the program. At the end of the program, the completed sheets were collected by designated students. Six students were directly involved as performance participants. Four were speakers and two handled the overhead projector. The number of rehearsals was minimal: one for familiarizing each student with his portion of the script; and two for working out stage positions, checking on audibility and visibility in all parts of the auditorium, correlating the spoken words with the introduction of the transparencies, and timing the entire program.

FIGURE 11.3
Sample answer sheet

		SCHOOLYEAR ———		
A	B	C	A	B	C
1 ☐ ☐ ☐			☐ ☐ ☐ 21		
2 ☐ ☐ ☐			☐ ☐ ☐ 22		
3 ☐ ☐ ☐			☐ ☐ ☐ 23		
4 ☐ ☐ ☐			☐ ☐ ☐ 24		
5 ☐ ☐ ☐			☐ ☐ ☐ 25		

20 ☐ ☐ ☐	☐ ☐ ☐ 40

TOTAL
CORRECT ———————

☐ Students positioned themselves as planned and screen and projection materials were arranged as shown in the diagram.

FIGURE 11.4
Stage layout

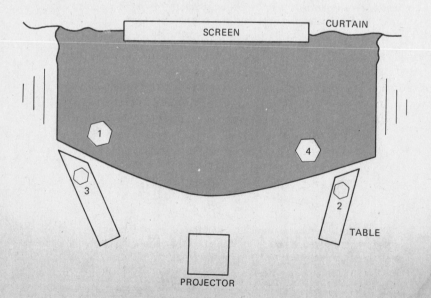

☐ As a student read the introduction and then the question, the question was flashed on the screen. Then the three choices were revealed as they were read by the speaker. Students in the audience were given ten seconds in which to record their answers on the answer sheets provided.

☐ The projector was turned off and the speaker briefly gave the explanation of the particular question and then the correct answer was flashed on the screen.

☐ The students in the audience, and the faculty members as well, became totally involved. They graded their own papers.

☐ Results of the questionnaire were treated as follows:

The total score on each paper was correlated with the year of the student: freshman, sophomore, etc.

Specific items were selected for determining the number scoring correctly on that specific item.

☐ Students in the program, and in the audience, were quick to recognize many of the different aspects involved in the program including economics, home economics, science, advertising, merchandising, art, and consumer psychology.

☐ Discussions followed the program in many different classes that day, and on subsequent days as more information was noted on the emerging consumer movement.

A Class Newsletter or Magazine

This is another instrument of enrichment for your classes. It provides an outlet for the journalistic and artistic talents of your students, and gives each student tangible evidence of his association with other students in this activity. Examples of this type of school publication include:

School publications

The magazine published by a language class, with articles, poems, and puzzles all in that language

The newsletter on current science events put together by a biology class

The history club newsletter on topics they had discussed or researched

These journalistic efforts are not made only during class sessions. The materials are prepared individually, evaluated by the student editors, and by you, and then prepared for publishing after school, or during the students' nonclass time in school.

Field Trips

Field trips fall into the category of enrichment. You can look at a picture of a sedimentary rock like limestone or you can examine a three by five-inch specimen of it; but how much more exciting to move out of the classroom to a limestone deposit and stand on an area that was probably once covered by the sea.

Field trips as enrichments

You can read about legislatures, parliamentary procedure, and debates; but how much more dynamic the experience if you go to see senators and representatives at work in a city council, a state legislature, or the Senate chambers in Washington, D.C.

As a teaching–learning interaction, a field trip might have a specific function in your program; however, its potential for enrichment cannot be ignored. The many areas to consider when planning a field trip, together with guidelines for organizing a field trip, are explored in Chaper 17.

Enrichments can add variety, challenge, and stimulation to your program. Enrichments, like the icing on a layer cake, are not absolutely vital, but they are certainly most welcome.

PROBLEMS, QUESTIONS, AND ACTIVITIES

11.1   Briefly describe three experiences in your own professional, academic, or travel background that you might draw upon to enrich a lesson in your field.

11.2   List, with a brief description of each, five sources which you could use to enrich the lessons in your area. Indicate which of these sources are permanent and which are transient in nature.

11.3   Select five items from today's newspaper which might serve as enrichments in your subject area.

11.4   Determine how an assembly program is scheduled in your school. Who sponsors it? Who prepares the backdrops? Who handles lighting? How are rehearsals scheduled?

11.5   Design an activity for a specific unit in your subject area that would be challenging, and interesting to:

1. A student with poor reading ability

2. A student with great interest in your specific field.

NOTES

NOTES

12

Evaluating the Interaction

WHAT ARE THE AVENUES OF EVALUATION?

As you prepare each unit of instruction, you should make some provision for checking, during the course of that unit, the effectiveness of your teaching and the extent of the students' learning. This is called evaluation.

There are many different activities that furnish you with information on a student's progress and development. Some, informal in nature, include:

Informal evaluations

The questions he asks during or after class

The responses he makes to questions

The way he explains an idea or process to others

The way he works in a laboratory or workshop situation

The manner in which he listens

The degree of his involvement in class discussions

The kind of challenges he either seeks out or accepts

Although these activities do not fit into any numerical grading system, they may be more significant than the results of some formal, written exams.

Other avenues of evaluation, more formal in nature, include:

Formal evaluations

Oral reports

Written exams

Practical examinations

Status reports on projects

Prepared materials like paintings, a batch of cookies, or a finished bookshelf

In all these more formal types of evaluation, the students should be aware of the criteria for judging their work long before the results of the evaluation are announced.

All these different and varied aspects of your evaluation program have one thing in common—they assist you in formulating an estimate of the achievement and development of a student. Each type of evaluation, formal or informal, furnishes a somewhat different perspective on the student and serves to add dimension to your total concept of him as an individual. Your awareness and utilization of all these sources of information assist you in crystallizing the picture of how well he is learning in your class.

WHEN DO YOU GIVE A FORMAL EXAM?

One of the most efficient methods for checking on the students' progress is giving some kind of written evaluation regularly. An examination may take a few moments at the start of a period; it may take half a period; it may take an entire class meeting. Examinations should be used as teaching devices, not instruments for threatening or punishing.

It is unwise for you to defer the entire written evaluation of a unit of work until its last days; perhaps a particular instructional procedure early in the unit of work was less than successful in reaching the students. This can be detected, and particular difficulties more easily overcome, if continuous evaluation is an on-going part of your planning.

An examination's length and format will depend on its specific function. When a unit of instruction is early in its planning stage, you should allot time for testing just as you do for all other phases of your work. For example, in a unit in biology, the following is a sample time schedule established for three segments of a unit:

Unit: The Study of Life   *Unit time schedule*

    I. The Concept of Life—2 days
        A. Definition of Life
        B. Activities of Life

    II. The Units of Life—8 days
        A. Cell Theory
            1. Historical background
            2. Current concepts
        B. Cell Study
            1. Techniques of study
                a. instrumentation
                b. measurement
            2. Structural components

Examination—1 day
Examination Follow-up—1 day

    III. The Chemistry of Life—11 days
        A. Elements
        B. Chemical Compounds
            1. Inorganic

            2. Organic
        C. Chemical Activity in Living Matter
            1. Enzymes
            2. Reactions

    Examination—1 day
    Examination Follow-up—1 day

Such a unit plan, in addition to giving you an overview of the time commitment for certain topics, also provides a built-in block of time reserved for examinations.

WHAT ARE THE FUNCTIONS OF WRITTEN EXAMS?

The most common functions of examinations include their use:

As a Quick Summary

The failure of many students to correctly answer a particular question will immediately alert you to the need for reteaching that aspect of the unit. This of course presumes that the examination question was well worded. This type of exam also serves to remind students of the need for keeping up to date in their work, and of the need to be "on top of their subject" all the time. Such quizzes also make the final or other important examination less awesome.

As an Encouragement to Do Homework and Independent Study

Sometimes a student does not see the relevancy or importance of the homework he is assigned. At times he may even stop doing homework, or independent, individualized study. You should then take stock of the assignments you are providing and determine if they are doing what you designed them to do. It is often good to include a question or two from homework topics which you consider important on a quiz.

There may also be times when you and the students explore the idea of a "contract" of work. In this scheme, the students undertake the learning of a unit of work outside the class activities. You detail the specific reading assignments or questions to be investigated, and you provide a guidesheet of directions for the student to follow in this independent learning experience. At the end of the period of time you have decided upon as sufficient for this work, you can give an examination to test the progress of the student. This exam helps you assess his progress in:

Evaluating individual study

An area where you have had no direct input into the learning process other than outlining it for him

His ability to "dig out" the important facts or key ideas and his ability to correlate and synthesize them

His ability to begin learning on his own

The examination that you construct for this evaluation should test broad generalizations and ideas, not the student's ability to memorize isolated, insignificant minutiae.

As a General Survey

Examinations given at the end of a unit of work generally fall into this category. This full-period exam, made up of short-answer questions, essay questions, or a mixture of these types of questions, permits comparison of achievement in a class. Each student has the same time and the same physical setting for his written evaluation. The students all have the same or very similar tasks to perform, skills to use, and problems to solve.

As an Opportunity to Demonstrate Creative Ability

This kind of evaluation includes such techniques as:

The development of a haiku

The writing of a paragraph or essay

The preparation of a full-length report

The assemblage and presentation of a project

Demonstrating creative ability

This kind of evaluation requires a clearly defined set of instructions, and carefully established criteria for judging. These are established by you, and must be understood and accepted by the participating students.

As a Means for Assigning a Grade

This function is all too often the sole purpose for which exams are administered. They are graded, the results are weighted and averaged, and a final grade is computed for the student.

An exam serves one or more of the functions described previously. A final grade should represent more than just a statistical average. It should reflect the student's total achievement:

How he has scored on practical, oral, and written exams

How he has learned to work independently

How he has developed skills and abilities

How he has progressed in reading ability, and reasoning ability

The final grade should reflect:

A final grade should reflect the total growth of a student, and so cannot be merely a statistically derived figure. It should be determined—not calculated—on the basis of the total growth of the student in that subject area. The grades he receives in other subject areas should not affect the grade you indicate for him, aside from alerting you to those areas in which he appears to be more successful, and those in which he seems to be less successful.

All evaluations, formal and informal, are more complex processes than merely grade giving. They involve the past, the present, and the future.

What evaluations do

They review and evaluate that which was learned in the past.

They provide a means for the student to prepare, organize, and present that which he has remembered and learned, and can apply at the present moment.

They reveal the student's strengths and weaknesses which will be the foundation for reteaching, enrichment, and further study.

WHAT ARE THE TYPES OF FORMAL EXAM?

There are essentially three different types of formal examinations available to you:

Formal exams

☐   The oral examination

☐   The written examination

☐   The practical examination

You must carefully decide the specific kind of exam that will best serve your purpose at a particular point in a program.

Oral Examinations

All classroom interactions can be considered oral examinations in the sense that you are continually using all the information the student furnishes you with in order to estimate his progress.

In a more formal sense, an oral examination involves a student delivering a speech in a given time period. He is aware of the criteria you have established for judging it. You may also wish to test his ability to deliver an impromptu speech about a topic you provide ten minutes before he is to speak. You might have all the students record their speeches on tape and then evaluate them after hearing them through several times.

Other types of oral examinations are the book report delivered in class, and the interpretation of a prose or poetry selection. In language studies, this kind of examination tests the pronunciation, inflection, rhythmic sense, and fluency of the student.

In social studies classes, science classes, and art appreciation classes, you might want to determine how well a student can "think on his feet." You pose problems or questions, and see how well the student can work through them, explaining as he goes, until he reaches a logical conclusion.

In essence you are evaluating not only what the student says but also the way in which he says it. You are evaluating the mental images he is communicating as well as the factual content he is introducing. This kind of examination gives you a perspective on the student's abilities which you can use in helping him to learn how to learn.

Written Examinations

Three of the most often used types of written exams are:

☐ The objective question examination

☐ The essay examination

☐ The examination which is a mixture of these two kinds of exams.

Strengths and weaknesses of written exams

Each type has its strengths and its weaknesses.

A test using only *objective questions* or the so-called short-answer question is a very popular device for measuring a student's knowledge of the facts in an area, formulas and data gathered from maps, charts, or graphs.

An *essay question,* which means that the answer will generally be in connected discourse in the student's own words, is used when the teacher wishes to give the student a chance to interpret a selection which allows for individual interpretation; to organize and present facts, concepts or opinions; to indulge in some creative activity.

The mixture or *hybrid examination* uses questions from both categories and provides variety and change of pace in the exam format. It provides a variety of means of responses and furnishes information on a variety of different thinking processes and expressional abilities.

The function of each specific examination will be the prime determinant of the type of exam questions you give.

Practical Examinations

These examinations evaluate how effectively and skillfully a student can perform a task, analyze a situation, identify objects, or evaluate alternatives. They furnish you with another perspective on the student's abilities. This kind of examination is used in classes in art, drama, shop, home economics, business machines, and science, to name but a few.

In a science class, for example, a teacher can set up thirty, single-concept demonstrations about the room. The demonstrations are numbered and a student examination sheet is prepared coded with the same item numbers.

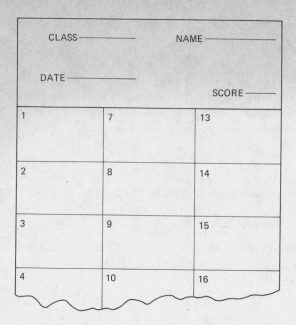

CLASS————   NAME————

DATE————

SCORE————

1	7	13
2	8	14
3	9	15
4	10	16

Just before the start of the examination the students are briefed on the positions they are to take at the start of the exam, the route they are to follow, the amount of time at each setup, and how they are to record their answers. A typical flow chart is shown in Figure 12.2. In this particular exam, there were eighteen items for consideration.

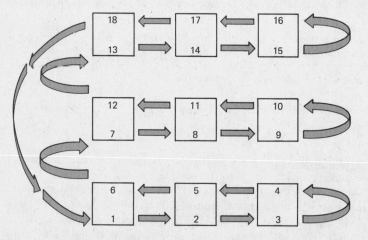

This kind of examination requires careful planning in that each demonstration included should test a different skill or concept, involve a simple procedure that can be done in the time provided each student, and be specific in what it illustrates or what the student is to determine about it. The time investment is well spent in that you can evaluate how the student works with materials, his manual dexterity, his ability to follow instructions, and his skill at examining and using equipment and materials.

The demonstrations, the pattern of movement during the exam, the grading system used, the answer sheet, the replenishment of materials during the exam, and the additional supervision required all need your careful attention. The number, and degree of complexity of the exam items must be considered in the light of the time available, the facilities to be used, and the number of students taking the exam.

The practical examination, with clearly defined activities and questions, can be used with some modification for several different classes. The instructions for each setup can be printed on an oaktag sheet and taped to the table next to the piece of equipment to be used, or the specimen to be identified. Plan several different questions for each test item.

You can coordinate this kind of examination with another teacher in your subject area. Together you can prepare the test items and questions to be used. You can, if the classes are relatively small and the facility large enough, combine classes for this examination if they happen to meet during the same time period. Both teachers would be supervising the exam while their students were at work on the test items. One can be the timekeeper and signal when it is time for students to move to a new location. The other teacher can be moving about the room, checking on the equipment and supplies, and supervising.

The scope of any quiz or examination you give should be clearly defined and understood by you and the students who are to take the exam. The students should know exactly what they are supposed to do, the nature of any special procedures they are to follow, how much time they have to do the work, and what use will be made of the exam results. Each of these items is important in helping to make an examination—oral, written, or practical—a teaching–learning device for both you and your students.

WHAT ARE THE TYPES OF OBJECTIVE QUESTIONS?

Objective questions, which are featured in the short-answer type of written examination, have many forms, including:

Objective questions

☐ The true–false question

☐ The matching question

☐ The completion question

☐ The modified true–false question

☐ The multiple-choice question

For a short quiz, or as part of a larger examination, the multiple-choice question appears to be the most useful. From the standpoint of their construction and administration, the other varieties of objective questions have definite limitations.

Limitations of objective questions

The true–false question gives the "guesser" very favorable odds. Unless at least 100 items are used the results are not very significant. The limited choice and the nature of the choice do not give you any clue as to why the student gave an incorrect response. Then too, students soon learn that words like "always" and "never" usually mean the answer is false.

True–false questions are very difficult to phrase, for if they are too involved they tend to become ambiguous. If they are too simply stated, the answer is usually quite obvious.

The matching question is limited by the fact that after a few answers have been correctly paired with their corresponding questions, the guessing becomes progressively easier. The scope too is limited for the distractors—the wrong answers—become increasingly obviously wrong as the right answers are eliminated.

Again there is little or no opportunity for you to see why a student selected an incorrect match. There is no clue as to where to begin a review of the topics considered.

The completion question must be worded very carefully so that there is only one possible answer. Again, this requirement sometimes tends to make the answer rather obvious, however, not so obvious as that noted for the true–false question. For example, in answer to the question, "The horse who brought the good news from Ghent to Aix was . . .", one very bright student wrote, correctly, "exhausted." This was not the answer the writer of the question intended. How easily the wording could have been modified to avoid this kind of answer. The question could read, "The name of the horse . . .". Even this refinement is open to some erroneous interpretation. The completion test also can cause some confusion in that sometimes we must decide whether or not we will accept a certain variation of an essentially correct answer. If the answer given is correct, but misspelled or the wrong form of the word is given (adjective instead of noun) does this answer receive the same credit as the one which is correct in all respects?

The modified true–false question is a slight improvement on the standard true–false question, in that it asks the student to evaluate whether an underlined, or italicized term or phrase in a statement, is correct in that context. If the designated term is correct in that context, the student would indicate true as the answer. However, if the term does not make the statement correct, then the student is called upon to furnish a term or phrase which will make it correct. Here then, there is some additional input of information called for, rather than simply indicating that a term is false.

Advantages of the multiple-choice question

The multiple-choice question has many advantages. The distractors may be so carefully chosen that you frequently can have some clue as to why an incorrect selection was made—a clue which will enable you to later clarify an ambiguous concept, or refine a definition. Then too the distractors may be of such a nature that the student is tested on his power to discriminate between nearly, but not entirely, correct answers. Even when the wrong answer is chosen, some degree of knowledge can be noted by the choice he makes; if the distractor he chooses is totally irrelevant, it indicates that he has no grasp of this area of knowledge.

In order to minimize the possibility of guessing correctly, you generally construct this kind of question to include one correct answer, and three or four incorrect distractors. The question usually takes the form of a declarative sentence of which the last item is omitted. The correct answer for this item is selected from a numbered or lettered group of choices. Remember to design all the choices, correct and distractors, so that each one when selected would make a grammatically correct sentence, even though it would not necessarily be a correct statement of content.

The construction of multiple-choice questions requires care and ingenuity. After a quiz has been marked, you would do well to study the results with the thought of discarding questions which have been proven worthless, rewording other questions that still have potential, and retaining those questions which truly measure proficiency. A quick way to estimate the way in which a question serves its purpose is to note how many students who did well on the exam got it right. Also note the number of students who did poorly that got it wrong. A question answered correctly by most of those who did well, and incorrectly by most of those who did poorly, is a good question to retain because it separates the good performers from the poorer ones on the test.

Construction of the multiple-choice question

A question which about the same number of high ranking students got right and got wrong, while most of the low ranking students got wrong, is a fairly good question. Questions that are correctly answered by half of both groups, or those questions few high ranking students got right should be completely reworded or, if necessary, discarded.

Evaluation of the multiple-choice question

Your continuous evaluation of exam items and questions in the light of the students' responses to them is a major requirement of an evaluation program that has any potential as a teaching device. These exam items alert students to those areas in which they are less skilled. The results of examinations alert you to those areas in which students will need additional help or instruction, those areas where individual students appear either particularly good, or particularly less successful. Unless you review the results of particular test items yourself, you will never get a feeling for the use of an exam as a teaching–learning instrument for both you and the students.

HOW ARE ESSAY QUESTIONS HANDLED?

Essay questions should also be carefully constructed so that the student knows:

☐ Exactly what he is to do

Preparation of an essay question

☐ The form in which he is to present his answer (outline, list, or continuous discourse)

☐ The time at his disposal

☐ The criteria for evaluation

☐ The distribution of credit, and use of part-credits in grading

Be sure that you do not ask an essay question which is really a fact-finding question.

"List the properties of sulfur." is not an essay question, because it merely calls for simple recall of factual information. It involves no evaluation or application of data or principles. An essay question could effectively elicit the same factual information and, in addition, require the student to add the dimensions of organization and judgment. For example: "In a paragraph of 150 to 200 words, explain how the complete absence of sulfur would significantly affect your daily activities."

Presentation of an essay question

Once you have prepared an essay question, you must decide on the manner of presenting it, and then on the marking criteria and guidelines you plan to use. If you want to use only one essay question as the entire examination, then you might decide to write it on the board for students to copy or simply read, and then answer. This will take some time to do unless the question is extremely brief. A more efficient means to use is rexographing copies of the question and the specific directions you want observed in answering it. These can be distributed to students when appropriate and they can start immediately. You can even duplicate the copies of the question on ruled paper, and then prepare a small exam packet in which you staple the top sheet containing question and directions to several sheets of ruled paper for use. This simplifies the distribution of the exam materials, and makes the question a permanent part of the answer papers so the student will have a complete copy of question and graded answer when you return corrected papers to him.

After you have prepared the essay question you want to use, you should develop a "model answer." You should list those items that you think should be included in a complete answer, and then indicate the distribution of credits you will assign to each segment of the question. Your model answer will probably be more complete than any student answer you receive—but this may not always be the case.

Evaluating an answer to an essay question

In the sulfur question indicated previously, you might feel that the five areas you think should be considered in the answer are: food, clothing, transportation, housing, and drugs. If the question is valued at 15 credits, then each area would be assigned three credits. This distribution of credits can then be modified to two credits for a less complete answer, one credit for reference to the area, or no credits if the student failed to mention this or a comparable area. Students should be informed about the total number of credits for the entire question, and given the information that you used in your construction of an answer—one fact–one credit.

Scoring an essay question

Before you begin the grading of the papers, you should select several papers at random and read them through. Determine the impact of the question on these students, and identify other suitable answers that they have included which you might have omitted in your preparation of a grading key or model answer. You should then modify your grading guide to include these items so that you will be grading in real terms and not in a vacuum. If several essay questions are given on one examination, one question should be completely marked on all papers before you proceed to the next question. This helps to insure greater uniformity and objectivity in the grading.

Before you administer your first essay exam—or objective examination for that matter—you would do well to consult your supervisor and together critically evaluate the questions you plan to use, the answering guidelines you have developed, and the grading system you have devised for that exam. Your grading system should not be mysterious or kept secret from the students. They should be familiar with the criteria you use in judging their work, and the rating systems or scales you use. Students are most familiar with the 0 to 10 or 0 to 100 grading systems. If you design an examination whose credit allotments do not total either 10 or 100, then you should convert this to a 100-base scale. For example, if the exam totals 60 credits, then 60 on the exam would be equivalent to 100.

If 60 = 100, then you can work out the rest of the scale from the formula $\frac{60}{100} = \frac{59}{x}$

Scoring an essay question

59 = 98
58 = 97
57 = 95
56 = 93
55 = 92
54 = 90

Both the raw score, and the score on the 100 scale should appear on the paper, and their meaning should be made clear to the students.

Be sure to keep in mind that while you are an expert in this field you will be reading papers written by students who are not majors in your field and may never be so, or who are taking this course "under protest" because they must do so. Your grading should be done in the light of the standards you have set, and the intellectual level of the students in the class. Some teachers seem to be proud of giving low marks because they feel students have not met the high standards they have established. Your standards must be set not only from your own knowledge base but also from that of the students in your class. Exams should be challenging and not giveaways. You should not give such simple exams that *all* students do very well and feel wonderful, but really learn very little. There is a happy middle ground. You can still have high standards and give challenging, profitable exams, if you constantly evaluate the exams you give, and determine if they are doing the job you want them to do.

HOW DO YOU HANDLE THE TEST PAPERS AND THE TEST RESULTS?

Once the examination has been administered and you have collected all the papers, your next area of concern is what to do with these papers. The disposition of the exam papers themselves can be resolved into three areas:

What to do with
a test paper

- ☐ Who grades the papers?

- ☐ What is the best way to use the graded or evaluated papers?

- ☐ How should the evaluation information be recorded?

Some teachers permit student assistants to mark short-answer exams for them. This procedure has several serious flaws. A student charged with the responsibility might be under very heavy social pressure to give a friend "a break." These pressures can sometimes be far more direct than you might imagine. Having students grade papers also cuts you off from one of the means of securing information about your students; sometimes the way a student does a math problem is far more important than whether or not he got a correct answer. Only by looking at the papers while you are grading them will you really get this kind of insight. The same idea applies to homework assignments, projects, and papers.

After you have graded the exam, and noted the final mark or grade on it, you should have an organized record book, or mark book in which to record the grades. Each time you give an exam, collect a paper, or evaluate some work by a student, you should make a record of it. Few record books are designed to provide you with sufficient space to indicate all the information you should about an exam, or paper. Some of the information you should have at your disposal regarding any evaluation includes:

Keeping a record book

Date

Type: homework, lab report, essay, quiz, examination, conference, project

Total number of credits assigned; letter grades used

Scope: area tested or treated

Explanation of symbols: ✔ = submitted
✔+ = submitted and acceptable
✔− = submitted and not acceptable

This information is most valuable to you when you are ready to make up final grades, when you discuss a student's progress with him, or with his parents or guidance counselor. If you cannot find a record book in which you can conveniently record all this information, you might use a notebook and rule off columns yourself as you gather information on each student.

You should also keep one copy of each examination or major assignment you give for reference. Daily assignments should be noted in your lesson plan, and retained for reference as well. Students who have been absent from school for extended periods can be easily updated in the assignments they missed if you have a record of what you asked the students to do in each unit.

Returning the
test papers

Each examination should be reviewed and the papers returned to the students involved. An immediate review of an exam in the few moments following the collection of the exam papers is anti-climactic. The students at that time are not concerned with why they got an answer right or wrong, but what was the right answer. Such an instantaneous review will satisfy the student's curiosity about a mark, rather than about the principles underlying the questions asked.

If a class was uniformly successful on an exam, then it need not be reviewed at length or in detail. However, if the results were poor, then perhaps extensive remedial work—supervised study, detailed homework assignments, workshops, lab experiences—may be needed. Exam results, therefore, will often determine the nature of the next one or two class sessions, if the exam is to be an effective teaching–learning device for both you and the students. When you do review the papers, you can do so before or after distributing them to the students. Reviewing areas and specific questions before returning papers helps to insure that students are giving their undivided attention to the review rather than the grade on the exam.

Students should be actively involved in the review of the exam. *They* should be supplying the answers—not you. If a particular question was missed by everyone in the class, and the question was well worded and understandable, then you might assign it as a homework question for that evening rather than immediately answering it yourself. Again the emphasis is on learning by doing—students will more readily remember what they have to "dig out" by themselves, than what you simply rattled off. After the review, and any remedial work you think desirable, you might want to schedule another exam. This is not a second chance or a makeup test. Strictly speaking, there is no such thing as a makeup test. The second exam, given later than the first, and after additional instruction and work, would not be comparable to the first one you gave.

Reviewing the exam

All exams, objective and essay, practical and oral, should be reviewed very carefully so that a student will never feel that his mark is the result of anything but a fair judgment based on standards with which he was familiar before he took the exam. However, despite all your preparation some students will always feel that their mark is unfair. One procedure that may help a disgruntled student to accept his mark is to read aloud one or two excellent answers to essays or other questions. Read the answers yourself so that test achievement and not a student's oral delivery or his personality is the focus of attention.

Usually, corrected exam papers are kept either by students or by you. A standard procedure is to have students keep their corrected quizzes for review purposes, while you keep the longer, or major exams or papers in case a guidance counselor, grade advisor, or parent wishes to consult you about the student's performance. It is also good procedure to have the student write "mark noted" and sign his name at the top of these papers so that you always have a written record of his having seen the corrected paper.

In some subjects, a display of a selected number of excellent results on a bulletin board helps to encourage other students and to give good students a chance to obtain some public recognition.

The most important thing to remember about the exams that you have given is that they represent a student's effort in a given area. They should be evaluated, returned, and discussed with the students in order to make maximum use of these instruments in your program.

CHECKLIST FOR TESTING

BEFORE THE EXAM

Yes No

1. ☐ ☐ **Is the exam ready?**

   ☐ ☐ Is it legible?

   ☐ ☐ Is there a sufficient number of copies available and ready?

   ☐ ☐ Is the stencil or ditto-master available in the event more copies are needed?

   ☐ ☐ If separate answer sheets are required, are they ready?

   ☐ ☐ Are the credit distributions clearly indicated for each question?

   ☐ ☐ Have you indicated the relative weight of the exam in your total grading scheme?

2. ☐ ☐ **Are necessary auxiliary materials available?**

   ☐ ☐ If needed are these materials at hand: graph paper, ledger paper, trig tables, log tables, reference charts?

   ☐ ☐ Are extra pencils, rulers, and compasses available?

   ☐ ☐ Is a supply of scrap paper on hand?

3. ☐ ☐ **Have you prepared a special seating plan for this exam, if one is needed?**

   ☐ ☐ Are students seated in alternate rows?

4. ☐ ☐ **Is the room properly ventilated?**

5. ☐ ☐ **Is the lighting adequate?**

DURING THE EXAM

1. ☐ ☐ **Have you instructed students as to the disposition of their books, coats, etc. so that all work areas will be free of such materials?**

2. ☐ ☐ **Have you made any prescribed preliminary announcements?**

3. ☐ ☐ **Are the students aware of the exact time limits of the exam?**

4. ☐ ☐ **If this exam is the "open-book" type where students can refer to a specific text, does each student have one?**

5. ☐ ☐ **Are you following the procedure you have previously determined for the distribution of papers?**

Yes No

☐ ☐ Have auxiliary materials been distributed in advance of the papers?

☐ ☐ Were the exam papers counted out in advance by number of seats per row?

☐ ☐ Have you placed on the desk of the first student in each row a sufficient number of papers? (These are face down.)

☐ ☐ **Is your supervision unobtrusive yet effective?** (The purpose of proctoring is to prevent cheating rather than detect it.)   **6.**

☐ ☐ **Have you provided for the periodic announcement of the remaining time?**   **7.**

☐ ☐ **Do you check ventilation and lighting periodically?**   **8.**

☐ ☐ **Do you plan to collect papers from each student as he finishes the exam?**   **9.**

☐ ☐ **Have you decided on a system for collecting the papers?**   **10.**

☐ ☐ Will you collect papers individually?

☐ ☐ Will you have each student pass his paper forward and then collect all papers at the front of the room?

☐ ☐ Will you have first or last student in each row collect papers in that row and give them to you?

☐ ☐ **Have you made provision for collection of auxiliary materials?**   **11.**

☐ ☐ **Have you made provision for some activity in the event the class completes the exam before the end of the period? (Do not go over the exam!)**   **12.**

AFTER THE EXAM

☐ ☐ **Have you made provision for a marking key?**   **1.**

☐ ☐ **Have you set aside adequate time for marking the papers so that they will be a significant teaching device when returned to the students?**   **2.**

☐ ☐ **Have you provided in your schedule of planned lessons a time for reviewing the exam with the class or with individual students, and a time for any remedial work indicated by the exam results?**   **3.**

☐ ☐ **Have you made provision for the exceptional children identified as a result of this exam?**   **4.**

☐ ☐ Have you identified the ones with a high degree of mastery?

☐ ☐ Have you identified those who seem far behind and need more individual attention?

☐ ☐ **Have you recorded the grades and all other pertinent information in your record or grading books?**   **5.**

PROBLEMS, QUESTIONS, AND ACTIVITIES

12.1 Discuss the impact and effectiveness of each of the following true–false questions.

   1. Charles Dickens wrote *David Copperfield*.

2. After the careful work of many specialists, it is now generally agreed that there was an author named Homer.

3. The formula for the area of a rectangle (W = width, L = length, A = area) is $A = LW$.

4. Ulysses Grant preceded William Taft as president of the United States.

5. *King Lear* is usually regarded as William Shakespeare's greatest tragedy.

12.2   Evaluate the effectiveness of the following matching question.

1. Match the author in Column A with one of his works in Column B by writing the corresponding number in the space provided before the name of the author.

A	B
_____ Herbert Spencer	1. Heroes and Hero Worship
_____ Adam Smith	2. The Idea of a University
_____ Charles Darwin	3. First Principles
_____ John Henry Newman	4. Origin of Species
_____ Thomas Carlyle	5. The Renaissance
	6. The Wealth of Nations
	7. Self-Reliance
	8. Pilgrim's Progress

12.3   Discuss the format of each of the following completion questions. Try to compose variant forms of the answer that you would, or would not, accept.

1. The Battle of Hastings was fought in _____.

2. In William Shakespeare's *Hamlet,* the name of the clown mentioned by the first gravedigger is _____.

3. _____ discovered the theory of evolution.

4. The chief reason for the stock market crash of 1929 was _____.

5. Robert Browning and Alfred Lord _____ are generally considered to be the principal poets of the Victorian Age.

12.4   Construct five modified true–false questions in your area. Two of them should contain a "true" underlined term. Indicate what answers you would expect to be substituted for the incorrect terms.

12.5   Evaluate the form of the multiple-choice questions that follow, giving reasons for your judgment. Reword those you feel need revision so that they will be more effective.

From among the choices offered after each statement select the answer that most correctly completes the statement. Place the number of this choice in the space provided:

1. Johann Sebastian Bach was born in:
   a. 1564   c. 1660
   b. 1588   d. 1685   1. _____

2. A compound sentence is one that contains:
   a. two or more clauses
   b. two or more independent clauses
   c. some variety
   d. two or more subjects   2. _____

3. According to the formula for the area of a triangle, the area of triangle
   ABC is:
   a. ½(BD × AC)
   b. BD × AC
   c. AB + BC + AC
   d. 2(BD × DC)

3. _____

4. Beginning with the earliest in time, the correct chronological order for
   four important events in English history is:
   a. 1564,   1588,   1607,   1620
   b. 1588,   1607,   1620,   1642
   c. 1607,   1620,   1642,   1660
   d. 1620,   1642,   1660,   1700

4. _____

5. An oblique angle is:
   a. greater than 90°
   b. less than 90°
   c. crooked
   d. a geometrical term

5. _____

12.6 Evaluate the format of the following essay questions, giving reasons to support your judgment. Rewrite any you feel would be improved by rewriting. If there is any question you would discard, construct a question with which you would replace it.

1. In one paragraph explain and illustrate the meaning of dramatic irony.

   (10 minutes)

2. Trace the westward movement in the United States.

3. Briefly describe the contribution made by men of the Renaissance of the
   fourteenth and fifteenth centuries in Italy to:
   a. science
   b. travel and cartography
   c. painting
   d. music
   e. literature

   (45 minutes — 20 credits each for a through e)

4. Explain the expression, "Thomas Huxley was the watchdog of Darwin's
   theory."

   (15 minutes)

5. Using any appropriate diagrams, trace the circulation of the blood from
   the heart and back to it again. Indicate chemical composition and changes
   in composition at different locations on the route.

   (30 minutes)

NOTES

NOTES

PART THREE

The Expanded Classroom: Increasing Student Involvement

13

Laboratory and Workshop Experiences

WHAT ARE LABORATORY AND WORKSHOP EXPERIENCES?

Effective learning requires the direct, personal involvement of the student in an activity. This is precisely why individualized student laboratory work plays so vital and dynamic a role in any instructional program. The terms *"laboratory work"* and *"workshop session,"* although most often used in connection with science and language programs, are not restricted to these areas alone. Individualized student work in home economics, shop, art, business education, and English can also be considered in this category. These activities emphasize the role of learning by doing and provide students with real opportunities to gain experience in working with materials, verifying ideas, illustrating principles, and conducting investigations into new fields.

Just as with all the other aspects of your teaching program, student laboratory experiences need definition and require careful planning in order to make them an effective, meaningful part of your total instructional program. Any teaching–learning interaction in which students, working independently or in small groups, investigate some aspect of a particular topic is defined here as a laboratory or workshop experience.

There is a wide spectrum of activities included in this type of interaction:

Conducting an experiment

Performing a task designed to gain experience using a particular technique

Learning and practicing a skill

Learning to manipulate a piece of equipment

Performing some creative activity like sculpting, playing an instrument, or writing

Lab and workshop activities

Laboratory experiences, as distinguished from demonstrations, audio-visual aids and the like, necessitate a high degree of student involvement. They are direct, firsthand learning experiences which place the student face-to-face with the problem he is exploring or the task he is performing. This principle of direct involvement applies to all levels of achievement—advanced, average, and slower learners. Laboratory or workshop experiences if well planned and properly motivated can really get people interacting and minimize the student's role as a passive observer.

WHAT ARE THE FUNCTIONS OF LABORATORY EXPERIENCES?

In addition to providing further dimension and variety to your instructional program, laboratory experiences also serve more specific functions.

1.   *Learning a technique.* You may and should demonstrate a particular technique in order to introduce it to your students. However, the students must then have the opportunity to try out the procedure firsthand in order to make it a real part of their experience background.

Learning techniques

Making a soufflé

Grinding and mixing pigments

Titrating an acid against a base

Posting entries in a general ledger

2.   *Practicing a skill.* This type of lab experience furnishes the student with the time and place to practice some skill that he has acquired in order to develop facility in its use, and is the modern counterpart of the old adage, "Practice makes perfect."

Practicing skills

Developing reading speed

Practicing fingering technique on the violin

Improving speed and accuracy in typing and taking shorthand dictation

3.   *Illustrating a principle.* This laboratory experience adds visual and material substance to a verbal description, and students can apply what they have learned to real problems.

Illustrating principles

Identifying and studying the factors affecting an ecological system

Recognizing and using alliteration in prose and poetry

Planning and preparing a balanced meal

Examining a price support system

4.   *Gathering data and gaining experience in its interpretation.* This type of experience furnishes the student with the opportunity to gather specific data, organize it, and use it in solving a problem or formulating some conclusions about a problem or question.

Gathering and interpreting data

Compiling figures and computing an income tax

Constructing a questionnaire on student activities in a school

Interpreting graphs

5. *Learning to use equipment.* Many lab or workshop experiences are specifically tailored to instruct students in the operation and use of equipment that they will be using themselves later in their work that term or at some later date in a job situation.

> Using a lathe or pressure cooker
>
> Using an adding machine or duplicating machine
>
> Using a microscope
>
> Using a manually operated potter's wheel

Learning about equipment

6. *Performing creatively in the arts, music, and writing.* These experiences give the student a chance to try out new techniques he has learned, and to creatively express an idea in music, painting, sculpture, or poetry.

> Sculpting in clay
>
> Assemblying a collage
>
> Composing a haiku
>
> Playing a selection on the piano

Enjoying the arts

Each specific laboratory or workshop experience you design generally encompasses more than one function. Each period devoted to this type of work is well spent in that it provides many different and varied opportunities—not available anywhere else—for students to develop skills, and practice techniques. It is a way in which students can involve themselves in tasks and problems they understand and consider important and meaningful.

HOW DO YOU PLAN FOR A LABORATORY OR WORKSHOP EXPERIENCE?

As you look over a unit of work or subject area you plan to introduce, give careful consideration to those aspects of it that are best taught by laboratory or workshop experiences. You should keep the following questions in mind during your preliminary planning for a laboratory lesson:

☐ What materials, books, and equipment are available?

☐ How much time is needed for assembling materials?

☐ What is the time schedule for the day you select?

☐ What pretesting of equipment and materials is required?

☐ What size group is most practical for this specific laboratory work?

☐ Are there any special facilities needed for this lab experience?

☐ How will materials reach you and the students in the laboratory or workshop area?

Planning a lab lesson

☐ What supportive personnel will be available for the class session?

☐ What modifications of materials, equipment, or procedures will be required if the room is used for different subjects during the day?

Planning a lab lesson

☐ What resource personnel are available for information and guidelines concerning a specific lab session?

☐ What written guidesheets or procedures will be required by students?

☐ What safety features must be considered in this specific session?

These questions will help you realize the requirements—both material and procedural—of the laboratory lesson you are planning. They serve as starting points in your work, and each focuses on a different, but important, aspect of the planning required for an effective laboratory or workshop session. Each question also serves to establish a set of guidelines for laboratory work. The planning details must then be completed:

1. *Know what materials are available in the quantities you will require.* Most subject departments keep an up-to-date inventory of the materials and equipment on hand. Carefully examine the quantities you will need for all the classes that will perform the work.

Planning a lab lesson: ordering materials

For example, if a given procedure calls for a quarter-pound of sand, your calculations for sand would be:

Number of classes using procedure = 4

Number of students = 4 × 30 = 120

Students work in groups of 2—therefore 120/2 = 60 groups

Total amount of sand needed = 60 × ¼ = 15 pounds

If you find that some materials must be ordered from companies, supply houses, or sources outside your school stock, check with your chairman to see what funds are available for purchasing materials on an immediate basis.

Investigate if other substitute but adequate materials are on hand and available for you to use. Be adaptable. Recommend to the chairman, supervisor, or coordinator those materials you think should be on hand for this type of work the following semester. This will give him the opportunity to order the materials from budgetary allotments during the coming school year.

Usually materials ordered from outside the school will require a good deal of time for delivery, so plan and order them far in advance. One of the most discouraging statements a class can hear is, "We can't do the work today because the materials didn't get here yet." Keep up to date on new materials delivered to your department or school. Use part of your preparation time in investigating some of the materials already in stock, and the newly delivered equipment. A piece of equipment may not be usable at once in your program, but can be a valuable input in an upcoming lesson that you would not have at your disposal if you did not search for it ahead of time.

2. *Allow sufficient time for the assembly of equipment so that it can all be pretested before the students do any work.* In the case of a complex setup, several days or one week may be needed to prepare the materials and/or equipment. This too is another important area to consider. You must decide if the equipment is best assembled beforehand by you or whether it should be assembled by the students during the lab session. This usually depends on the nature of a specific lesson. If you want the students to assemble the equipment, then you must furnish instructions to them that are clear and concise. You must also take this into consideration in allocating time during the lesson.

Planning a lab lesson: timing

You may also plan to introduce a workshop that will require several sessions to complete. You should consider if the materials can be kept together for a week or two, or if they must be used by others during that time period. Try to design workshop experiences that use simple materials and are relatively easy to set up. Where instructions are required, be sure you have provided them.

3. *Be familiar with the time schedule for the day on which you plan to give the lesson.* Find out from the administrative assistant, or assistant principal, if an assembly or other program will decrease each subject period in length, or if there are any special scholarship exams scheduled which will take any of your students away from your class.

Planning a lab lesson: timing

Consider the events in the total school calendar when you schedule the individual laboratory work. If you find that some school activity will be draining time or students from the period in which the lab lesson is scheduled, try to rearrange your schedule to avoid that day. This may not be possible at times—for instance if the workshop session requires a special room that is only available to you on certain days of the week. If this is the case, then be sure that you have modified the lab lesson to fit the time available. Perhaps the laboratory experience is such that different groups of students can work on different aspects of a problem and then pool their information.

4. *Try out all the experimental procedures yourself.* Be sure they are workable and can be accomplished during the time (1 to 2 periods) available. If only a single (40 to 50 minute) period is available daily, can you schedule the work for two successive class periods? If a double class period is available for one day, can an entire work experience be completed in it, including preliminary discussion, the work, follow-up activities and evaluation? If flexible, modular scheduling is in effect in your school, can you arrange for the necessary number of modules to provide sufficient time for the work?

Planning a lab lesson: testing procedures

Of paramount importance is the workability of the procedures you are asking your students to follow. You should run through all the procedures or directions you are furnishing students, but remember that they will not at present have your expertise in interpreting instructions, or handling materials.

Identify all the pitfalls they may encounter. Try to modify the procedures to avoid those that you find. Remember this difference in experience when you figure the time needed for the students to do the work. They will need more than you do.

Planning a lab lesson: number of students

5. *Determine the most effective and efficient size of student group for the class work.* Each work experience is a separate entity in this regard. It may be that for one experience you decide that individual work is most effective, but on another that groups of two or three students are more productive.

Students can often exchange and discuss data and share their experiences in order to avoid repetitious work and yet develop broad generalizations.

Keep in mind the materials required for the group sizes you schedule. Individual work requires more materials and equipment than you may have available at the moment. The availability of materials may be one of the most common determinants of group size for many of your lab or workshop experiences. Keep in mind that everyone should be actively involved in the experience—there should be no passive onlookers. In large groups, four or more, there may be literally no work for several students. These students grow bored and soon lose interest in the work of others. Try to establish a group size— 2 or 3 students—where the tasks can be shared and yet all the students in the group will contribute to the total solution or investigation.

Planning a lab lesson: classroom facilities

6. *Determine the water, gas, and electrical facilities that are available in your classroom.* Is a special lab room or workshop area equipped with all these facilities available? Are wall outlets (110 volts AC) required for your work, or is DC required for a specific task? You may find that you need special facilities for a given lab session. Be sure to plan for moving your class to the area. You can, if you planned ahead, tell them the day before to report to some area different from their usual classroom. Be sure to check to see if another class will be using the room or special facility you need, thus making it unavailable to you. Determine the nature of special facilities at your school. Locate the electrical outlets in your classrooms, the gas supply, the water supply, and special storage areas. An experienced colleague or your supervisor can introduce you to the different resources available.

7. *Predetermine if students know how to use any heating, electrical, or audio-visual equipment required in the work.* If students are not familiar with pieces of equipment, you will have to incorporate a time period for demonstrating the use and handling of these materials. This may be done at the start of a lab session or during class on the previous day.

8. *Determine how the materials you will need for a class session reach the students.* Are the materials put on rolling carts and brought to the work area in bulk or in preorganized trays? Are materials all readily available in the workshop area at work stations or lab benches? Do students have to go to a supply area to secure materials? Are instruments to be used stored in the room, or must they be secured and brought to the room? Who does the transporting of materials and equipment—you, the students, a laboratory assistant, or aide?

Planning a lab lesson: obtaining materials

Consider the type of room best suited for the work experience you are planning. Do you need formica tables, lab benches, or work benches? Will projection screens be needed? If such equipment is required, and not present in your usual work area, find out how you will have to secure it. Investigate the procedure used in your school. Determine if there is an audio-visual aids coordinator who can furnish you with the necessary equipment.

Experiment with the different methods of securing and transporting materials; but first see what system is in use at present and try it out.

9. *Determine the number and type of supportive personnel working with you on the preparation of materials, and those needed to assist you in the direct supervision of the work experience itself.* Is there an assistant in your department, one of whose functions is the preparation of the needed materials at your request? Do you gather and prepare your own materials? Talk over the specific laboratory experience with other teachers who have used it in their programs; benefit from their experience with it, and identify problem areas not apparent at first. On the basis of your conversations with them, you may want to modify segments of the procedures that have caused difficulties in the past, or those that have not been workable because of time limitations. Audio-visual specialists and laboratory and shop specialists can usually offer some profitable advice. Talk to as many of these teaching and supportive personnel as possible to enrich your own experience background on a specific work session you are planning. It is true that you should benefit from the experience of others. However, in the last analysis, you are the one responsible for the success or failure of any lab or workshop session. The broader and more diversified your experience background, the better will be your position in determining the most important and most effective activities for your program.

Planning a lab lesson: supportive personnel

10. *Determine how materials are handled between classes.* Can needed equipment be left out in the work area, undisturbed, and safe, for your class to use on the following day, or must the same setup of materials be used by other classes during a subsequent period on the same day as your work session?

Planning a lab lesson: maintaining materials

Consider if the room in which the work is to be done is used by classes other than the ones in your subject area. Can materials be safely left out, or will they interfere with the activities of other classes using that area? Laboratory lessons which require several days to complete should be looked at in this light. They may be feasible experiences in terms of materials, equipment, and time, but may have to be modified because of space limitations. Space is always a problem: space in which to work; space to store materials; space to keep materials from session to session. You must explore the schedule in effect in your school, and use it when you plan these work sessions.

Planning a lab lesson: maintaining materials

Remember to consider the other teachers and students using the workshop area. A piece of equipment may seem a small thing to you, but it may materially interfere with the use of the work area or visibility of the chalkboard in another class. Explore this space problem with the other teachers in your area, and those using these classrooms. Work out some mutually satisfactory schedule for maximum usage of the area.

Planning a lab lesson: working with colleagues

11. *Work with your colleagues in planning and scheduling work experiences for your students.* Often several classes can utilize the same materials and equipment and teachers can share in their preparation. It may not be possible to prepare individualized experiences for each class because of a lack of sufficient stocks of a given material or too crowded a school calendar.

In the case of a large department, you may find that one work experience is planned for all lab classes during one week, and that materials and setups cannot be kept over for any one class from period to period or day to day. In this event, you may have to set up as a demonstration an experiment that requires a long time period. For example, the phototropic effect exhibited by plants requires a significant time period in which plants must be observed daily and their direction of growth noted. One or two students can record such information on daily readings and report to the class on the progress of the work.

Planning a lab lesson: designing a guide

12. *Decide whether to use a standard manual of procedures, or to design your own laboratory or workshop guide.* Work with your colleagues on designing an experimental procedure and its related guide sheet tailored to your specific program, time schedule, and available materials. Secure copies of many current work manuals in your field, read them carefully, and assess their applicability to your program. You may find that the textbook you are using in class has an associated manual of activities or exercises designed to complement the text. You and your colleagues may decide to use such a manual in order to achieve a measure of continuity in style and flow of subject matter. This prepared material is quite a time saver but is usually not tailored to your needs. On the other hand you may decide, after discussion, to invest the time in developing a set of guide sheets for those laboratory experiences you use in your program.

Both these procedures have advantages and limitations. Though the standard workbook or manual may not be usable in its entirety, it is readily available. It frees you to devote your energies to the development of an audio-visual program, demonstration work, or creative homework assignments. The self-designed manual provides you with the procedures you want to include, the format you think best to use, the length of procedure tailored to your time schedule, and the materials you have available. However, it does require several years to design, test, revise, and retest any set of guidelines before you have one that is best suited to your program. Perhaps the investment of time and energy in such a project is a profitable enterprise, and this is what you will do. If you decide to write up your own guide sheets, consider having them printed or stenciled on 8½- by 11-inch paper and printed on one side of the paper only, so pages can be punched for a loose-leaf binder. The directions could be arranged for the left hand page and the blank side of the page on the right for recording comments and data.

Planning a lab lesson: designing a guide

FIGURE 13.1
Guide sheets

The multiplicity of these alternatives will help you determine which procedure you adopt in regard to these direction sheets: using one manual; designing your own; or using several manuals and your own guide sheets in concert. Using all these alternatives during the school year promotes the development of a rich program of work experiences for your students.

Remember to pretest each lab experience you design or plan to introduce into your program to see if the procedure will provide the students with the experience you want him to have. You may find that a procedure might be modified in order to make the entire activity more pertinent and profitable for the students. Order a trial setup well in advance of the time you schedule the class session. This gives you time to work out any snags, determine any necessary modifications, work up a guide sheet, or find a suitable one and have the materials assembled for the class session.

You may find that a number of experiences would be very appropriate for your program, but time and materials limitations prevent you from using them immediately. Keep an eye to the future. Suggest the new materials to your chairman for inclusion in his ordering during the coming year. You might find a local supplier, and furnish him his information as well to help expedite the processing of the order.

No meaningful, pertinent student laboratory or workshop experience can be worked up in an instant. The good, challenging, stimulating, thought-provoking ones require time for pretesting, evaluation, and careful examination. Provide time for students to read over the directions and gain familiarity with the procedures.

Planning a lab lesson:
safety precautions

13. *Be sure that you have considered safety precautions and the safe disposal of materials in regard to each laboratory procedure you use.* Have you provided time for demonstrating potentially hazardous or difficult techniques? Have you planned on providing instructions and facilities for safely disposing of waste materials, unused materials, and products?

Have you demonstrated to students how pieces of equipment and machinery are to be properly and safely handled and operated? Have you reviewed the skills and techniques required?

New procedures and techniques, found workable and safe, should be added continually to your program to keep it up to date and challenging for your students, and to keep the lab work relevant to the other work you are doing in class sessions. However, introduction of new activities, just as with anything new, requires the attention and careful planning that you show in all other facets of your instructional program.

☐ Develop a guide sheet of instructions for students. (Be sure to include safety precautions.)

☐ List the materials and equipment you will need and estimate their amounts. Detail how the material is to be prepared for use in class.

The proof of the pudding is the student laboratory or workshop experience itself. No matter how much pretesting and careful planning you employ, the students must really grasp the purpose of the lab work if it is to be truly successful for them, for this is, of course, the key. Students must really be involved in the work.

Ideally the need for some specific laboratory experience or work sessions should grow out of a facet of your current class work. It should serve as a means for securing information to solve a problem, or point the way to new areas of study or work. The aim of a laboratory experience—the principal purpose of that activity—must be clearly delineated and understood by the students engaged in the work. The lesson must not be a time filler or an exercise in which all of the answers and outcomes are known in advance. It should be a real learning experience.

You should have the time and the facilities so arranged that you might move into a work session at any moment that seems pertinent. However, realistically, that is not usually possible. In larger schools classes are scheduled for laboratory sessions on a specific day, and often the lab experience does not immediately "fit" into the developing program in your other class sessions. In this event the work experience must be more carefully motivated, and its aim more clearly defined. The data gathered can be introduced later in your program at the appropriate moment. However, some of the stimulus and zest is lost over a period of time, and the "flavor" of the experience may suffer. No matter when a specific lab lesson is held relative to the other segments of your program, the data gathered or the outcomes of the work must be used. Without the use of such information, the activity becomes meaningless. The same applies to any activity in which students participate — it must be meaningful and it must be useful.

WHAT IS YOUR ROLE DURING
THE LABORATORY EXPERIENCE?

In addition to all the important preliminary work you put into the lab or workshop experience, you play a key role in the lesson itself. You will motivate the work experience and elicit the aim of the lesson. You will demonstrate some of the new techniques and discuss procedures and safety precautions to be observed. You must point the way to the means for using the data gathered in the course of the work session.

Teacher's role in lab work

Once the students have begun their own work, you will function as a guide and consultant. You move about the class, questioning procedures, offering suggestions, observing progress in an experimental procedure, checking on safety, and answering some questions that arise. However, you are not there to answer all the questions or give all the answers. Students must be encouraged to think for themselves, to work out problems they encounter during their work and thus develop a measure of independence and self-confidence. You can offer suggestions or guidelines when necessary, but of prime concern in this type of activity is letting the students begin to experience the spirit of self-motivation and involvement. If you have planned and prepared work experiences that are clear as to their purpose, and meaningful and workable in character, the students will be able to reason-through many minor problems, and modify their procedures to overcome the difficulties they meet. It is relatively easy to give students all the answers, and it certainly is a time saver. However, by giving all the answers, you are really doing the students a great disservice. Your main job is to have your students learn how to learn, not just achieve the specific aim of that lesson. You want them to think and use their reasoning abilities, not to accept easy answers. It is sometimes difficult, but have the assurance and patience to let them do these things.

You may have time for brief, individual, impromptu conferences with some of your students as they finish their individual work and wait for a discussion period. These chats can help clear up minor difficulties they have encountered in other facets of their work, not only in your subject area, but also in their performance in general. Often one small point is holding up the student's comprehension of an entire principle. Sometimes you can pinpoint an area that is troubling him from a question he asks, or the way in which he works with his fellow students. You can follow up on these matters in full-scale conferences with him at a later date. Sometimes a few words of encouragement or several direct, challenging questions can help to start him thinking and help him correlate information already at his disposal in the solution of a specific problem.

*Teacher's role
in lab work*

The individualized work experience gives you the opportunity to get a different perspective on the student. In other class sessions, where his degree of involvement in discussions or other activities may be somewhat limited, you see only one facet of the total student. In his written exam papers, essays, compositions, themes, poems, and reports you see still another. In conferences you see another aspect. In the manner he approaches his work experience, the way in which he works with other students, you get insight into yet another aspect of his personality. All these activities help you form a more complete picture of each of your students.

In some departments you may have the services of a laboratory specialist or assistant to help you in supervising the work experience. The more hands, eyes, and ears, the better. Students may be just starting out in your field and may not yet have the skill or background to help them avoid pitfalls and mistakes that you might consider elementary. Supportive personnel present in the work area help facilitate movement of materials, insure a higher degree of safety, and assist in the "rough spots" that arise in any experimental procedure.

You must carefully watch the time during the work session in order to provide time for two more facets of the work experience: the clean-up and the follow-up discussion and evaluation. Clean-up activity really depends on the specific work experience. It may involve cleaning paint brushes, or storing easels and putting paints away. It may involve dismantling a complex arrangement of glassware used in a chemistry lab or washing dishes and putting food away. It may involve taking a number of business machines, or musical instruments back to a storage area. These all involve straightening up the work area and leaving it in order and ready for the next group to use. A lesson on the preparation of a Grams stain and its use on E. coli bacteria is one in which the students gain experience in the preparation of stains, and fixing and staining a microorganism. However, *cleaning up the work area and disinfecting the bench top and apparatus used in the work is as much a part of the work as the preparation of a slide of the organism.* Students should be guided in the establishment of clean-up routines in their own work so that they learn to finish their work and clean up on time. This also helps insure that the follow-up discussion period can be as complete as possible.

Once the materials and equipment are put away or back on the delivery wagon on which they were transported to the work area, the students have cleaned up and had an opportunity to look over the results of their own work, the class should meet for a discussion and evaluation of the work experience. The student should consider:

☐ **The procedures used**

☐ Where were the materials they required?

☐ Were any indicated steps in the procedure unclear, or unnecessary?

☐ Were any procedures particularly difficult or hazardous?

☐ Were the instructions clear?

☐ **The problems encountered**

☐ Were there any unworkable pieces of equipment?

☐ Did any portion of the experience require more time than others?

☐ Was adequate time available for the work?

☐ **The data gathered**

☐ Was the nature of the information they were to gather clear?

☐ How was the data to be organized?

☐ What are some possible sources of error in the work just performed?

☐ Should any procedures be modified?

The students, guided by you, can begin to correlate the data gathered during the work session in order to determine the solution to a problem, or draw generalizations about the work they have done. Data gathered by many groups of workers can be shared and correlated during this discussion period. The results of some experimental procedure can be tabulated on the chalkboard and then shared by all the students present. Experimental data can be graphically represented then, or construction of a graph can be part of the follow-up assignment for the next meeting. Direct, inverse, or other mathematical relationships between variables in an experimental procedure can be discussed immediately after the work experience, and then further explored in the class session where they will apply. If you use some of this information in the homework assignment, it should help students to formulate generalizations, focus on concepts, and evaluate the importance and relevancy of the work they have done.

Follow-up discussions, both during the work session and at subsequent class meetings, should underscore the utilization of the data or information or skills developed by a student during the work experience. Unless used, the results of the work experience will represent just a wasted time period or a period of play that a student will soon come to resent.

WHAT DO YOU CONSIDER FOLLOWING
A STUDENT WORK EXPERIENCE?

Following the student laboratory work session or workshop session, you should critically analyze and evaluate its effectiveness and ask yourself these additional questions.

Teacher's evaluation
of the lab lesson

☐   Was it a workable experience for the students?

☐   Were the procedures clear?

☐   Could the data be gathered or problems be done by students?

☐   What modifications of procedure would have made the session more effective and challenging?

☐   Was the equipment ready to use and simple to set up?

☐   Were adequate reserves of supplies available?

☐   Was time provided for preliminary discussion?

☐   Was there time for performance of all the tasks indicated, and for clean-up and follow-up discussion?

☐   Did the homework assignment grow out of the day's work?

☐   Was the grouping of students efficient in terms of materials and time?

☐   Should some other work experience have been scheduled before the present one to better prepare students?

☐   What further work experiences are indicated by this work session?

You must evaluate the effectiveness of each specific work session in terms of what you designed it to do. You must decide if the procedures were clear enough and need no further revision; if substitute materials and equipment should be used. In short, you must evaluate the current work experience immediately after it is over to assess the value of including it in your next year's program, as well as determining what further activities would be most profitable for your current students.

PROBLEMS, QUESTIONS, AND ACTIVITIES

13.1   Select a particular aspect of your subject area that lends itself to the lab or workshop type of activity. Prepare a plan for it.

13.2   For the work experience you planned in the previous problem, design a follow-up homework assignment you would give your students in which they can utilize the new skills learned or the new information uncovered.

13.3   What class activity would you plan for the school day following this individualized student work experience you have developed?

13.4   How would you modify the work experience you planned in order for it to be used

   1. For a slower (modified) class?

   2. For an honor (advanced) class?

NOTES

NOTES

14

Discussions

WHAT IS A DISCUSSION?

How many words per minute are being spoken in a school building at any particular time? If it were possible to make this measurement, two significant facts would emerge:

Most talking is done by students, not teachers

Most talking is done during the time between classes

Who talks and when?

When a bell rings ending a class period, the word output increases dramatically. This tremendous outpouring of talk is quite natural in young people especially when they are among others of their own age level. Discussion as a teaching–learning technique tries to harness that urge to talk.

Discussion is organized talk. It is not purposeless conversation; it is not casual. It is skillfully structured. Discussion to develop and share ideas is a dynamic, universal activity, not limited to any special class or group. Discussion is a means for increasing student involvement. During any lesson, the active listener is truly a participant. However, you cannot always discern who is listening actively, and who is thinking about a football game, a date, or an upcoming exam. Class discussion provides direct evidence of more active involvement in meaningful learning activities.

WHAT ARE SOME TYPES OF DISCUSSION GROUPS?

There are essentially two types of discussion groups you will frequently use:

The small-group or panel discussion

The large-group or class discussion

No matter what the small-group discussion is called—conference, colloquy, round-table—all small group discussions have the characteristics of the panel. This type of activity operates best when the group is limited to five or six. It can still function effectively with up to eight members. Having four or fewer members usually fails to provide the dynamic interaction that is the heart of this activity.

In this discussion form, only the members of the panel are involved in presenting ideas. The class or the school assembly which comprises the audience participates as active listeners, and if appropriate, notetakers. At the conclusion of the panel discussion, members of the audience may be given a chance to question, support, or refute what has been said.

Large-group discussion involves both you and the thirty or so students in your class. In this discussion form, everyone is an active listening participant and is also, at least potentially, a speaking participant. It would be ideal if every member of a class could have his say in a meaningful manner during the course of a one-period class session; however, this goal can seldom be achieved. The student who did not get a chance to speak today may be the most spirited speaker on a subsequent day. It will be up to you to see that this actually happens.

Most frequently, the large-group discussion consists of you, the teacher, drawing forth from your students their opinions, ideas, and conclusions about topics you are considering. You are the catalyst who listens, encourages, contributes, and responds when necessary.

WHY SHOULD YOU USE A DISCUSSION?

Discussions can be classified on the basis of the nature of the topic with which they deal:

Types of discussion

A practical discussion topic is one that arises directly out of the class activities, which can be discussed, and which has some prospect of action toward solution or amelioration of a problem.

A theoretical topic is one that requires extensive research before discussion, and whose outcome will be additional insight and information, but no direct action.

No matter which type of topic is considered, practical or theoretical, a discussion can serve a variety of functions including:

Identification and Refinement of Problems

Practical Problem	Theoretical Problem
Practical vs. theoretical problems Homework is a universal factor in every effective program. No matter how challenging the assignment, there is the problem of getting it done properly. You find that your students are doing the homework poorly or not at all. You pose this problem to the class, and offer information on the way homework has been done during the past few weeks.	In considering the personality of Hamlet, the question arose, "Was Hamlet mad?" Many students responded, not with facts from the play, but on the basis of their feelings or unsubstantiated opinions. You assign the rereading of the play in order to prepare the class for a discussion of this topic. During the discussion, factual information is gathered

Students are asked to consider this topic and prepare to discuss it the following day. During the discussion some of the reasons for poor homework performance are explored, including:

☐ We get too much homework.

☐ We have to work after school, and have no time.

☐ The homework is never collected or graded.

☐ The assignments are not clear; we do not know what is needed.

☐ Our questions about the homework are never answered.

☐ We have no free time if we do all the homework we are assigned.

☐ The homework has no relationship to what we do in class.

to support one or the other opinion—He was sane. He was mad.

☐ Hamlet used good judgment in swearing Horatio and Marcellus to secrecy after he had seen the ghost of the dead king.

☐ Hamlet was shrewd in tricking Rosencrantz and Guildenstern into carrying a letter which would lead them to their doom.

☐ Hamlet's suspicions of all those around him were the first signs of a severe paranoia.

☐ Hamlet's refusal to kill Claudius while he was praying lest his soul should go to heaven, betrayed a deep hatred that could only come from a demented mind.

Practical vs. theoretical problems

The discussion in both these cases of a practical and a theoretical problem helps to exchange facts, opinions, and attitudes in a dynamic, meaningful, and interesting way.

Gathering Information and Sharing Experiences

After each member of a social studies class has gathered information on a specific aspect of the Civil War, they can discuss one crucial battle and thus share the information.

Gathering information

A discussion on safety in a shop class is a valuable starting point when initiating a new project, or when using new appliances. This discussion is a real give and take of experiences and reactions in order to establish a realistic and workable code of safety.

The discussion following a field trip can be both practical and theoretical in nature. The group can discuss the data gathered and how it relates to the topic under study. The group can also discuss what modifications should be made in trail guides, instructions on dress and food, or travel arrangements.

Formulation of Hypotheses

The hypothesis is the proposed solution, yet to be tested, that the discussion group formulates as a result of the presentation of facts and views.

In the homework problem discussed earlier, several hypotheses may emerge:

Forming hypotheses

If the amount of homework is reduced, then the response would be better.

If the homework were used in some constructive manner, then students would more readily see it as a significant part of the program.

In a discussion of the gas laws in chemistry, the students explore the variables that affect gases—temperature, pressure, and volume—and propose certain relationships about them including:

Pressure varies inversely with volume

Volume varies directly with temperature

They then propose experiments to test their hypotheses.

Testing One or More Hypotheses

The most probable hypotheses advanced about the homework problem were:

Testing hypotheses

That assignments needed more clarification and specificity

That assignments needed more utilization in class

In order to test these hypotheses, you and the class set up the following schedule:

Assignments for the following school day were to be given and explained at the end of the period

Longer-range assignments were more clearly explained and discussed, and a more realistic time allowance developed for each

Longer assignments were to be collected, evaluated, and returned to students

A period was set aside daily for students to ask questions about the daily homework assignment and for specifics of it to be reviewed.

You plan for a follow-up discussion period in about four weeks in order to examine the results of this experiment.

Interpreting Information and Developing Conclusions

Interpreting information and drawing conclusions

A discussion may be used to interpret the information found in books, pamphlets, graphs, and charts. Each of these sources, as objective as they are, represents merely the raw data that the student must work with in order to make decisions and judgments, and draw conclusions. Therefore, students should practice analyzing, interpreting, and comparing information in consultation with others in class. After this kind of activity there is a built-in motivation for the type of reporting that involves discussion.

Every discussion, no matter what the topic or its specific function, will have the additional value of permitting members of the class to gain greater insight into one another, and a better understanding of each other through their developing willingness to listen. From this increased understanding among all participants, teachers and students, there can come increased respect for each other.

HOW DO YOU PREPARE FOR A DISCUSSION?

The language arts teacher has the primary responsibility for introducing students to the skills of discussion, and all other teachers can capitalize on this background. However, they should be familiar with the techniques and procedures by which this is done in order to reinforce this training in their classes.

The student must be prepared for active listening. Hearing is changed to listening, by adding the factor of conscious attention. A teacher can read a passage aloud from a book. Students can listen and identify salient points. They gain experience in recognizing facts, making judgments, and drawing inferences via hearing, rather than via looking. Becoming aware of the noise of a truck grinding its gears as it climbs up the incline outside the school is an example of hearing — a passive activity. Listening is active; it develops a frame of mind that questions what is being said, anticipates, and evaluates.

A language arts teacher can devise a series of lessons emphasizing the need for:

☐ Listening, not just hearing

☐ Considering an opinion that is diametrically opposed to your own

☐ Relating what others say to what you are going to say. This builds transitions and a free flow of ideas

☐ Using transitional phrases such as, "I want to add to what Sidney said about . . . ," to help underline the cohesiveness of the entire discussion

☐ Speaking clearly and looking directly at the people in the group

What happens in a discussion

This is the kind of background we can all count on in preparing our class for a discussion on a topic in our field.

Once you have determined that a discussion is the most effective technique to use for a given topic, you are ready to begin planning the type of discussion, the preparation needed for students, and the preparation of the setting for the discussion.

1. *Decide on which type of discussion group to use.* If all the members of the class have done some research, or have participated in the learning experience you are going to discuss, or will all be involved in the direct follow-up activity, then you should have a full class discussion. If only a few members of the class have been assigned the gathering of information, or have gone on a field trip, then they should be the major participants in the discussion — as members of a panel. The topic you are considering will be the major determinant of the type of discussion group you use.

Planning a discussion

2. *Provide sufficient time for the participants and the remainder of the class to research the problem, and to assemble all the pertinent data they will need.* Students can be instructed to use five- by eight-inch index cards for recording figures or dates they will need.

3. *Discuss the discussion guidelines with either the panelists or the entire class.* They should understand the role of the discussion leader in setting the pace, recognizing speakers, and watching the time. If you plan to use a number or series of discussions in your class, then it would be well to spend one period outlining this information with your students so that you can get into each discussion session with a minimum of time devoted to routines.

4. *Examine the physical setting in which the discussion sessions will be held.* The setting is an important factor in establishing an atmosphere most suitable for the activity. If you plan a class discussion in a large class where the furniture is stationary, you will probably have the kind of arrangement shown in Figure 14.1. One of the greatest problems in

FIGURE 14.1
Traditional discussion pattern

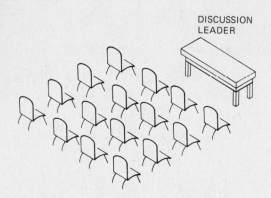

DISCUSSION LEADER

this kind of setting is that most of the students do not see the rest of the members of the class. They all see you, or the discussion leader up front, but not many of the other students. In fact the students sitting toward the rear of the room see only the backs of heads. In this case, it is well to establish certain guidelines to help insure visibility and audibility:

Guidelines for a discussion leader

Speak clearly and loud enough to be heard

Face the majority of the class and speak to them

Raise your hand to signal that a speaker cannot be heard

5. *Investigate all possibilities of the seating arrangements.* If the class is not too large, you might be able to stagger the seating arrange-

FIGURE 14.2
Variety with stationary seating

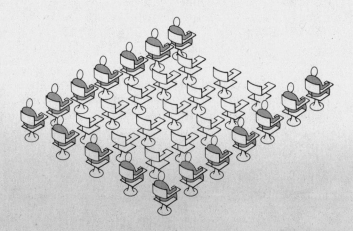

ment so that the center seats are not occupied. Opening up the center space helps to encourage more looking at one another and speaking to one another. The discussion leader also should move around the room during the session. This helps to make students look about and see the other members of the class. This problem of students not seeing one another, and yet all being in the same class, is one common to most classrooms, and can be a real stumbling block to encouraging interaction.

If you have movable seating in your classroom, then you can try a number of seating arrangements until you find the one most effective for each type of discussion in that area:

A large group discussion could be conducted using the circular pattern shown below. The moderator or discussion leader is seated in any one of the chairs.

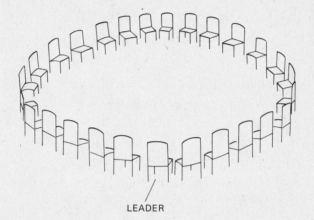

FIGURE 14.3
Discussion in the round

LEADER

The quadrangle seating arrangement is shown below. In this setting, everyone can see everyone else in the group and this facilitates the interchange of ideas and comments.

LEADER

FIGURE 14.4
Face to face discussions

If you decide that a small group or panel discussion would be best to use for a particular session, then there are again a number of alternate seating arrangements possible. The panel is assembled at the front of the room; the remainder of the class can be in their regular seats or you can group their chairs closer to the front of the room. Some of the arrangements you can use for the panel session include the three shown in Figure 14.5.

FIGURE 14.5
Three panel arrangements

6. *In planning the discussion setting, you must also consider:* lighting, need for any audio-visual equipment, and use of chalkboards.

If any audio-visual equipment is to be used, it should be in place and ready to go before the session begins. Films should be threaded to the section you want to use. Transparencies should be on the overhead projector. Be sure to try out the projector to make sure it is working. Have a spare bulb handy, as well as an extension cord and an adaptor. If a chart or map will be needed, hang it up in the appropriate, most visible spot. However, keep it rolled up until it is needed. Do not forget the chalk and erasers. Whether the boards are to be used or not they should be cleaned — washed preferably — in order to minimize distractions. Also remove charts, posters and displays that will draw attention away from the focus of the action.

If participants want to refer to information or notes, they should have the material written out on 5 by 8-inch index cards. Do not clutter the area with a great many books or pamphlets. Discussion participants, of course, should not leave the discussion to look up a date or a fact.

Your preparation and preliminary planning, then, have focused on preparation of students and the discussion setting. Before the discussion you should also consider the role of the discussion leader and your own role in this session.

WHAT IS THE ROLE OF THE DISCUSSION LEADER?

This is a job that really calls for some expertise. The leader must be able to draw from the members of the group their ideas, responses, and information. He must facilitate talk. He is the parliamentarian, as it is he who, by a nod, a word, or some transitional phrase, skillfully passes the verbal ball from person to person. It is the discussion leader who keeps the group "in the groove," when there is the potential for a heated exchange, or the group is getting sidetracked over some irrelevant point. He must know what to do and how to do it.

What to Do

☐ Elicit responses

☐ Encourage presentation of different points of view

☐ Act as parliamentarian

☐ Prevent domination by any member or small group

☐ Keep the discussion relevant

☐ Summarize the outcomes of the discussion

How to Do It

☐ Be accepting and nonjudgmental

☐ Get to know the members of the group through prediscussion conversations

☐ Know and observe the rules of order without being inflexible or rigid

☐ Set discussion guidelines as to time limits per speaker; time for summary

☐ Be well informed about the topic

☐ Elicit several statements of the central ideas presented; then present the final summary

The role of the discussion leader

The discussion leader cannot be partisan particularly if the topic considered is such that members of the group could become sharply polarized. He must prevent domination by a minority or a majority. In the prediscussion warm-up or preparation session, he should try to identify those who try to talk too much and those who do not want to offend by talking. The leader himself must never dominate the discussion for this will "turn off" all other members of both panel and audience who feel frustrated in trying to express their ideas. The leader must be alert to the signals for recognition. He can direct the discussion by using comments such as, "What do you want to add to George's statement, Frank?"

An effective discussion leader should have some idea of the maturity of the members of the group in order to be sure that he is eliciting maximum participation in quality as well as quantity. A student may be reluctant to handle controversial aspects of an issue. This reluctance may stem from his lack of experience, lack of maturity, or the fear that he will "get in bad" with the teacher or the other students if he says what is on his mind. Such inhibitions to discussion can only be removed by a long-range program in which you have emphasized:

Making a discussion work

☐ Respect for the ideas and opinions of others

☐ Protection of the right of everyone to say what he is thinking even if it is not popular

☐ Discussion as a means of seeking truth, and not a forum for forcing one idea upon all

From this consideration of the role of the discussion leader, it might appear that only a mature, experienced teacher could fill this post. Even though you may be the best equipped person available to lead a discussion, education involves the giving of responsibility to the learner. Therefore, you must use student discussion leaders, and let them learn by doing. You will have to work closely with those students selected for this sensitive position in order to introduce them to the demands of the role they are to play. As students learn to assume this responsibility, they will better understand the delicate balance that any leader must strike in order to insure the maximum benefit in a learning situation.

WHAT IS YOUR ROLE IN DISCUSSIONS?

Teacher's role in a discussion

In small-group discussions you will assist the group in setting up the presentation; prepare the audience for active listening and participation in questioning; and help to create an atmosphere in which this learning experience can be put to use. Your maturity, your greater knowledge of content, and the special insights you have developed about your students will be of great value in this preparation for a meaningful discussion.

During a large-group discussion, you may be a member of the panel, you may be the discussion leader, or you may be a member of the audience. Whatever your role in a particular discussion, stick to it. It is important to let students assume responsible positions and undertake the leadership and planning of some discussions. Your role will then be that of a consultant. You assist them in learning to express their ideas and opinions and set up guidelines and operating rules. As the students gain experience in this kind of activity, you will find that they are more willing to assume responsibility in other types of learning activities. They will be able to work more independently in laboratory or workshop sessions; they will assume more responsibility for doing their homework assignments, summarizing, reviewing, and studying. They are then really learning how to learn.

HOW CAN A DISCUSSION BE EVALUATED?

Your evaluation is continuous. You are looking, listening, and searching for signs of growth in techniques not only of discussion, but also of critical thinking, reasoning ability, and learning to understand other people. You will be asking yourself the following questions during or immediately after each discussion:

*Evaluating
a discussion*

☐ What knowledge was shared in the class?

☐ What attitudes were shared?

☐ What was the quality of students' listening to one another?

☐ Who did not participate?

☐ How did the students show respect for one another?

☐ To what extent were opinions modified?

☐ Were any issues settled, or problems solved?

☐ How could the discussion have been structured to involve more students as direct contributors?

You should set aside some time during the next lesson to evaluate the discussion with the entire class. Your primary concern then will be to determine what the class thinks about the structure, format, and outcomes of that discussion. You can use some of the content or results on future examinations. Students should be called upon to express themselves concerning facts and concepts that were part of these discussions. The inclusion of the discussion content on exams will further emphasize that discussion is a real learning experience.

There are elements of the discussion technique in almost every lesson, but the special discussion session described here involves the full utilization of a specific instrument for learning. It asserts that in the democratic classroom active listening and genuine respect for the ideas of others can lead to intellectual growth, expanded knowledge, and social maturity. Discussion vitalizes for the student essential elements of our times—the need to communicate and the ability to listen to one another.

PROBLEMS, QUESTIONS, AND ACTIVITIES

14.1 Select a lesson in your subject area that could best be taught by the discussion technique. By specific reference to composition of the discussion group, the preparation and motivation, the seating and staging, describe how you would conduct this lesson.

14.2 Assume that you have been asked by your principal to present some students from your class as a panel to appear at a junior assembly program. The topic is, "To what extent would limiting families to two children be a suitable social and scientific solution to some present environmental problems?"

1. How would you plan for this discussion?

2. What special problems would you expect to encounter in presenting this discussion to a large group of five hundred?

3. What plans would you make to try to avoid these problems?

14.3 Suppose you have invited a guest panelist to participate in a discussion which was to be held in a small amphitheater or a music room for your class and two other classes in that grade. In your preclass warm-up you notice that your students, who are usually responsive, freeze up in the presence of the visitor.

1. What immediate steps could you take to rescue this discussion?

2. What long-range steps would you consider in order to minimize the possibility of this type of reaction in the future?

14.4 Differentiate between a discussion and a debate. What are the advantages and the limitations of each? Using your own subject area, indicate two occasions where one or the other of these techniques might be used.

NOTES

NOTES

15
Review Lessons

WHAT IS A REVIEW LESSON?

A class that had finished a unit on such impressionistic writers as Thomas DeQuincey and Walter Pater went to the museum to view several of Monet's and Matisse's impressionistic paintings.

Several members of a biology class, shortly before examination time, prepared flow charts to show some of the fundamentals of an ecological succession—favorable environment, proliferation of different species, changes in food supply, and climate.

A drama class that had read Sophocles' "Oedipus Rex," Shakespeare's "King Lear," Ibsen's "Miss Julie," and O'Neill's "Desire Under the Elms," took a class trip to the theater to see a production of Robert Marasco's play "Child's Play."

A music class had learned the sonata form—the a,b,a sequence. The members of the class listened to several sonatas and parts of symphonies for practice in recognition of that sonata form they had just learned.

In each of the four situations described, the class was directly involved in an experience which illustrates the essentials of a review lesson.

A review lesson is a teaching–learning interaction that

What a review lesson does

Gives a new view

Has a strong motivational factor

Combines and interrelates different media

Projects the learner into new awareness

Intensifies and telescopes experiences

in order to resynthesize facts, skills, and attitudes in a learning experience that results in new understandings.

The review lesson involves a variety of activities, places, and people, each contributing uniquely to the atmosphere.

The class trip to the museum, or the theater, listening to the symphony, and the chart on ecology are all types of review lesson activities. In each case the teacher had determined that a review lesson was needed, and then had examined the alternatives for a meaningful review. This selecting from alternative choices means that you must be aware of the educational opportunities not only in your school, but also in the community. In planning your lessons you can capitalize on the values in community resources—people, places, and things. Although the glamour of a place or the prestige of a person are factors in vitalizing the review activity, the greatest factor is your creativity in selecting or designing the review activity to meet the needs of this particular class at this particular time.

WHAT ARE THE COMPONENTS OF A REVIEW LESSON?

Review lessons have three fundamental segments:

The aim and motivation

The development

The evaluation

Parts of a review lesson

Aim and Motivation

The *aim* of this kind of lesson is, of course, to review—to look again at a module of learning to get greater insights, reinforce skills, or develop broad generalizations. Review lesson aims, therefore, must be just as specifically worded as are the aims of your other lessons.

Motivating the review is the second major item to consider in your planning. Students will want to review a topic or question for a variety of reasons. Some may be termed extrinsic reasons:

Reasons for review

☐ Preparing for an exam

☐ Completing a homework assignment

☐ Winning a prize or medal

☐ Scoring high on College Boards

Other reasons may be termed intrinsic:

☐ His interest in a subject

☐ His personal commitment to expanding his knowledge in an area

☐ His learning for the sheer challenge or excitement of learning

Curiosity is a great motivational factor. Young children always seem to be asking why: Why is the sky blue? Why do flowers smell so good? Why do you need money to buy things?

This kind of curiosity—or intrinsic motivation if you will—is just what we must keep alive in the students as they grow older. Lessons must be so planned and developed that they will encourage this kind of questioning, searching, exploring. Lessons must not kill curiosity.

Sometimes an extrinsic motivation, if skillfully used, can become an intrinsic spur to exploration. Each motivation helps to focus the student's attention on an aspect of a problem, or a question he had not considered before, and which now is so interesting or puzzling that he wants to continue exploring that area himself. It is important for you to understand and accept the different kinds of motivation for review, and other learning as well, and start your planning from there.

There are a vast number of different techniques and instruments you can use to initiate and motivate the review lesson:

Motivating a review

1. *Start with a question.* A well-designed question can challenge students to reexamine some of the processes or ideas they have been investigating in order to develop generalizations.

> If a Greek of the Golden Age in Athens were by some miracle to be restored to life in our city this year, how would the following aspects of our theater be familiar to him: stage, dialogue, action, seating, character, theme.

Students can organize their background knowledge about these different facets of the theater. They can compare the present staging techniques to those used in earlier times, and thus begin their study of the changing and unchanging currents in the theater.

2. *Start with a statement.* Statements, like questions, also provide challenging starting points for the review. You can write these on the board when you are ready, or you can distribute copies of the statement to students at an appropriate time.

> Music says, "I'm sorry."
> Poetry says, "I'm sorry because my friend died."

This starts students in either music or English classes thinking about the interrelationships between different media of expression. This can then be expanded to other communications media and interrelationships sought out there.

3. *Start with an "If . . . then . . ." situation.* These situations open up limitless avenues for discussion, or writing. The imagination and content background of each student can come into play as the class looks back on events, people, and places.

> If Hitler had successfully invaded England, then . . .
>
> If Lucie Manette, in *A Tale of Two Cities,* had married Sydney Carton, then . . .
>
> If Copernicus had not shown that the earth revolved around the sun, then . . .
>
> If Dante had not written in the Italian of Tuscany, then . . .

4. *Start with something printed.* These materials, if distributed skillfully and at the right moment, can focus attention and get the review off to a spirited start.

Duplicate and distribute an item or article from an old newspaper, for instance, the 1890 prices of suits and eggs

Duplicate the first review of a now famous book

Clip out an item in a current issue of a school or local newspaper or magazine

Distribute a quotation from some ancient philosopher or writer, and apply it to a current question or problem

Motivating a review

5. *Start with an object.* Familiar objects, when coupled with good challenging questions, can also spark interest and serve as a starting point. They provide a touch of reality—they are real products or objects, used in real homes, by real people. They can help you initiate a review of some topic or unit by taking the learning out of the classroom to real situations.

A toy, like a miniature weaving loom

Some common household product—a detergent, a pharmaceutical, or a food item

6. *Start with a visual aid.* Use the films, filmstrips, film loops, videotapes in your school library, or those you can borrow or rent to be the focus of your review activities.

Show a film of a flower blooming (speeded-up motion)

Show a filmstrip of a trip down a river

Show the replay of a football game

7. *Start with a listening activity.* All too often we neglect the listening aspect of learning. It can play a dynamic role in engaging the attention and interest of your students.

Play a tape recording or record of an actor reading from a play or novel

Play a tape of you or one of your students reading aloud

Play an old recording of a President or some political figure speaking on an important issue

Play a record or a tape of symphony excerpts and current "top ten" records

8. *Start with a problem.*

Put a complex, "mind-bending" math problem on the board and let students start to tackle it with virtually no directions from you. When all have tried to start the problem, but virtually none can seem to get a grip on it, the review can begin with a brief summary.

Correlate the data or examine the specimens gathered on a class field trip

Use a simple device like a möbius to review spatial and surface relationships. (To make a möbius use a three-foot strip of adding machine paper and follow diagrams in Figure 15.1)

FIGURE 15.1
Making a möbius

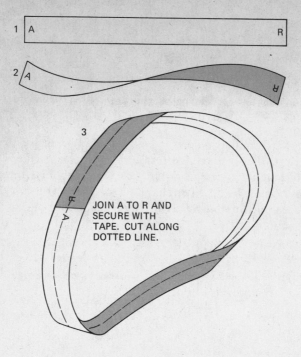

JOIN A TO R AND
SECURE WITH
TAPE. CUT ALONG
DOTTED LINE.

All of the techniques given in this segment serve to demonstrate the limitless instruments and devices for initiating a review, and getting students thinking about a problem so that they can do the reviewing themselves. Like any other teaching–learning activity, the review calls for a high degree of student involvement. It is the students, not you, who should be relooking. This does not rule out the relooking for you too. There will be many times in your career when a student asks a question, makes a statement, or phrases a generalization in a way that is slightly different. You can be introduced to new awarenesses and understandings at these times too. This is an important out-growth and asset of those lessons that are interactions, two-way streets, where learning and teaching move in two directions.

Development

Once you have established the need for a review lesson, and designed some activity or instrument to initiate this kind of interaction, you are ready to plan the type of activity most appropriate for developing the work you want to do. This might be:

Developing a review

☐ **A workshop session**

　Taping and evaluating a student's speech

　A problem-solving session in science or math

　A planning session for an assembly program

　A specific laboratory experience

☐ **A discussion**

　A panel discussion

A large-group discussion

A visiting speaker with follow-up period

☐ **A writing session**

Writing in class and then completing the assignment at home

Writing the entire theme at home and evaluating it in class

☐ **A field trip**

To a nearby location

To a more distant location

The follow-up evaluation session is part of the review too; data is shared, specimens examined, and experiences discussed

Specific guidelines for introducing each of these activities have already been discussed. Each type of activity can be used for review purposes at different times of the year. Field trips, particularly those involving extensive travel, are best included in the early fall or the late spring, when the weather is more likely to be good.

Try to vary the kind of review lesson you use. Include as many of the different types of motivations and activities as you can so that the students will not feel stifled in any one pattern of review, but instead will look forward to it as a challenging, profitable learning experience.

In review lessons, just as in all other lessons, you must provide for individual differences, and remember that not every student is capable of achieving the same degree of understanding. Recognition that some things will not be equally understood by all students permits you to teach each particular student what he has the capacity to learn. This does not mean failing to challenge each student to his utmost, or failing to use every resource at your disposal to tap the potential of each student. It does mean that you will not frustrate any of your students by attempting the impossible task of having everyone respond or participate to the same extent. Some students like one subject area more than another; some students find writing a great medium of expression while others do not. Your failure to recognize that different students acquire varying degrees of expertise in an area is a denial of the fundamental differences in individual interests, goals, talents, and needs.

In order to provide for individual differences, you should include a spectrum of activities:

Some problems that almost all students can do

Some problems to challenge the more advanced students

Laboratory or workshop experiences with additional segments for those students who want to investigate or explore further

Providing for individual differences means providing for the slower and the more talented students in a class. While everyone is moving up the scholastic ladder, some take longer on one rung; some can skip over a rung or two. Your job is to help them move up the ladder while teaching them to help themselves. Remember to utilize the valuable uniqueness of each of your students. Some may have gone to different places across the country and can lend this experience to the class; some have hobbies or after-school jobs that can be valuable resources. Capitalize on the talents, skills, and experiences of each of your students to make this interaction, like all the others, dynamic and challenging.

In your planning, provide some time in each unit for a few days of review activities. The time periods will then be there when and if you need them, and there will be no rushing or cramming to squeeze in a review.

Evaluation

Provide for some evaluation of the success of the review lesson or session. It could take the form of:

Evaluating a review

☐ A written, oral, or practical exam

☐ A written or oral report

☐ A project or model

☐ A field trip

Each of these evaluation activities is explored in detail in other segments of this book. Evaluation of the impact of the review lesson on each student is particularly important because of the unique nature of the student's participation in the review activity.

PROBLEMS, QUESTIONS, AND ACTIVITIES

15.1 In preparation for a comprehensive short-answer examination, you ask each student to prepare ten questions that might be suitable for this type of examination. The questions are all to be of the multiple-choice type.

1. What specific instructions would you give your students about the construction of these questions?

15.2 Write two essay questions—each to be worth 20 credits in a two-hour exam —that deal with a specific unit in your subject area. Indicate, not only the questions, but also the time allotments, specific instructions, marking criteria, and a "model answer" for each.

15.3 Prepare a review lesson you would use at the end of a unit.

1. Explain what skills, attitudes, and knowledge would be emphasized.

2. How would the learning activities you have planned be most likely to result in an effective review?

15.4 Assume that you have decided that a field trip to a museum located about five miles from your school is the best review activity for a unit of work. Explain what preparations you would make.

1. What are some problems you might encounter?

2. How would you solve them?

15.5 The students of your honors class have asked that you review the material in a topic you finished several days ago. They have shown great anxiety because many of them are candidates for a national honor society; they do not want their "average to go down because of low marks in this class."

Explain, with justification,

1. How you would handle the class's request for a review.

2. How you would use the students' motivation for this review.

NOTES

NOTES

16

Supervised Study

WHAT IS SUPERVISED STUDY?

Supervised study is an individualized encounter

> With a learning task
>
> In the most favorable setting
>
> Under the guidance of an expert in a subject.

This study encounter stresses the student as an individual, rather than the student as part of a group interaction. *One* student, is faced with a task which he himself must work out. Although he may be working near others, or in the midst of others, he is challenged personally to undertake and to complete this learning experience, which can take many forms:

> Exercising a skill: Developing speed in typing
>
> Mastering a body of knowledge: The conjugations of verbs in Spanish, or proving a theorem in geometry
>
> Developing creative ability: Writing a descriptive paragraph, arranging a collage, or planning the layout of the school newspaper
>
> Working in a shop or laboratory on an individual project: Wiring a lamp, setting up a terrarium, or mastering the use of a desk calculator.

Personal learning experiences

Supervised study is a learning experience in which the student is directly involved in *learning how to learn.* This is a time when the student does the work and assumes responsibility for getting a job done. You, via the vehicle of the supervised study session, can provide the setting and establish the climate in which the student can practice skills, and shape the attitudes he needs to work alone on his own initiative.

The home has become more and more a center of distraction with its jangling telephone and blaring television. You may have a quiet, comfortable, well-lighted place to read, study, and write. All your students may not have these conditions for their work at home. You may have a well-stocked library at home for reference; not all your students do. For these reasons supervised study sessions in school are all the more important today.

HOW DOES SUPERVISED STUDY HELP THE STUDENT?

Supervised study as an individualized learning encounter has several specific functions:

Advantages of supervised study

1. *Developing of the attitude of self-motivation.* Regularly setting aside a study period of forty or fifty minutes provides every student with an equal opportunity to work in a setting that approaches the ideal. The student in the overcrowded tenement who may work beneath a dim light over the kitchen table, beset with the interruptions of several brothers and sisters, now has the same favorable study conditions as every other student in the class. The same references are there for all; the same resource people are there for all.

Under these conditions, each student can determine:

The pace at which he will work

The references and resources he will use

The extent to which he will enlist your aid

These activities help to develop the idea that studying has a function; that resources are to be used; that people can help when you need it. Students can thus be introduced to the idea that they can really direct their own education in the future, if they know how to study and learn.

2. *Providing more individualized and personalized instruction.* This kind of activity gives you a great opportunity to observe the students in your class. You see them every day, but now you can really look at them and get additional insights that will help you tailor a study program to fit the particular needs of each one.

If your class is working on twenty questions, using the textbook as a reference, you can see which student is getting stuck among the first five or ten items for an excessive amount of time and can help him.

Has he bogged down because he cannot do the item, or because the language of the question is too sophisticated?

Perhaps a student's trouble is that he is overcautious in his reading. You might observe that he reads the same few lines over and over again.

The first student needs help with vocabulary, the second with his reading. Both of these problems are correctable once identified. You can design a program to help each one, but seek out the assistance of the student's English teacher and the reading counselor or expert in your school for suggestions and assistance.

In addition to calling attention to faulty reading skills, the student's difficulty with a particular question may point up some specific area of instruction with which he is having difficulty. This means that you will have to provide some information, or construct a remedial assignment for him to do and then tackle these questions again. These sessions can be used to let students learn to use special equipment on an individualized workshop basis. They can work on practicing a skill, or can with guidance perform some specific experiment as part of a project. This then is a time for the students in all parts of the talent and abilities spectrum to learn. These sessions can really let students "do their own educational thing" by providing a time period, a place, an individualized activity, and the needed guidance tailored to each student's interest or difficulties.

Advantages of supervised study

3. *Developing good study habits.* These sessions help train students to apply themselves to meaningful tasks for definite periods of time. During this session, friends cannot call them away; no interruption can make great demands on their attention. It is only through the practice of study under proper conditions that the habit of study can be strengthened.

Learning by doing is just as valid an approach for effectiveness in studying as it is for effectiveness in typing, sprinting, or painting. Through this medium of supervised study the student will learn for himself what study is all about, why he should study, and how to use resources at his disposal.

4. *Providing opportunities for enrichment.* Study, by its very nature, is enrichment. It is almost impossible for a student to use the tools of study — books, references, visits to museums — without going beyond the scope of what he has set out to learn. Knowledge leads to knowledge. The paragraphs he reads, the film he is to view, the place he has to visit are the enrichment by-products of studying. The enrichment lies not only in the task, but in the setting in which these tasks are carried out.

Supervised study increases the student's ability to engage in *unsupervised* study — in learning on his own. The attitudes and skills he develops will not only help him to complete his school work successfully, but will also sharpen his perception and awaken him to the possibilities in his environment. The advantages of supervised study, including

☐ Your opportunity to observe and help each student

☐ Your providing equal opportunities for learning

☐ Your guiding, on an individual basis, study habits and learning techniques

☐ Your providing a means for building teacher–student understanding

make this kind of activity a most valuable teaching–learning interaction.

WHAT ARE SOME GUIDELINES FOR SETTING UP A SUPERVISED STUDY SESSION?

Your initial job is to recognize the need for such a session. Some of the signs that will alert you to this need include:

When to plan supervised study

A student's limited participation in classwork

A student's inability to answer questions

Poor exam results

Poorly completed or missing homework

After you decide that such a session is really needed, you can then proceed along three lines of preparation:

☐ Preparing the location

☐ Preparing the materials

☐ Preparing the students

WHERE CAN SUPERVISED STUDY TAKE PLACE?

Where to plan supervised study

Your classroom, a museum, an art gallery, your school library, your auditorium: any one of these settings may be the most favorable for your study session. Perhaps your school has a garden where your class could go to study. Use a variety of appropriate settings for your supervised study sessions. Sometimes the nature of the task to be done will determine the best place to use. If you need reference books, special tools, chemicals, or a place to read and study, then you can use the library, the shop, the laboratory, the classroom.

If you are going to move out of your usual classroom for a study session, check to see if the location you want to use is free for that period. The library may have lessons scheduled for the day you want. Perhaps it may be tied up for a seminar, or a lecture by a visiting college professor. In these cases, it would be feasible to move the reference books you need to your regular classroom and use them there.

If you are going to use the auditorium, the stage, the greenhouse, or any other facility, explore the procedure used in your school for securing them for that day. If you can use your usual classroom for the session, you have the advantage that your students are working in an area familiar to them and to you. Probably a number of your own reference materials are handy for use.

For reading, research, and problem-solving, work space is essential. A student will be hindered if he is working too close to his classmates. Close proximity in these sessions is an invitation to small talk and distraction. In a classroom with fixed furniture, you can move students so that they are not elbow to elbow. Most of the fixed furniture classrooms have about 35 to 40 seats. Today, classes do not generally run that large. The diagram (Figure 16.1) is of a classroom with fixed desks and chairs. Changing the usual seating arrangement, and if possible securing or establishing a few study carrels in the room, provide a measure of flexibility and give students a bit of "breathing space."

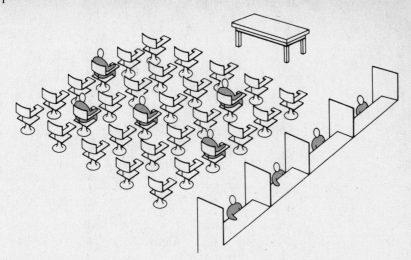

FIGURE 16.1
Patterns for supervised study

In the cases where the furniture is not bolted to the floor, you will have much more latitude in creating flexible workable seating arrangements for the study session. This will mean that you will have to move chairs or desks at the start of a class session. The students will help you; they are usually eager for a change in seating routines, and are anxious to help create a setting for productive work.

Try a variety of patterns until you find the best ones for your purpose. The pattern in Figure 16.2 involves a circle within a circle. Students in the inner circle face the center of the circle, while those in the outer

FIGURE 16.2

ring face outward. This helps to create a bit of privacy for each student. A seating arrangement that is effective in rooms with some movable, and some nonmovable, desks is that of rows and semi-circles.

FIGURE 16.3
More flexibility for
supervised study

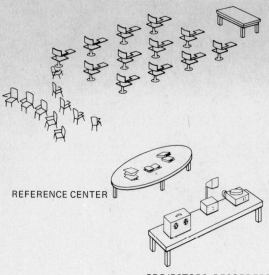

REFERENCE CENTER

PROJECTORS, RECORDERS

Another seating pattern involves a group of four desks with students facing in the direction indicated in Figure 16.4. The use of study

FIGURE 16.4

carrels can help to provide maximum privacy for each student during a study session. Basically, the carrel is a small enclosure designed to separate study areas and shut out as many distractions as possible. Some libraries have adopted this arrangement. Portable carrels can be easily made from a variety of materials. Two sheets of plywood can be hinged together as shown in Figure 16.5. Then two pairs of such sheets can be arranged on a large table to provide four individualized study areas. These sections can be folded flat for easy storage between uses. This table-size plywood divider can be built by a shop or wood-working class if you give them the specifications and a sketch of what you want.

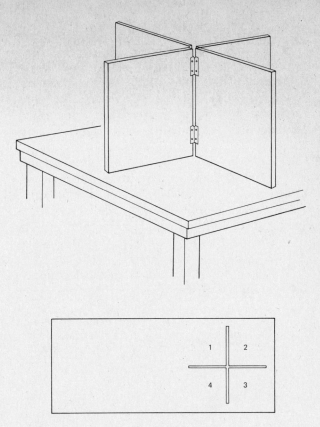

FIGURE 16.5
*An easy way to
make a carrel*

You may also find that the school has tall standing floor screens for separating study areas. These can be moved to your classroom for use in sectioning a room.

If you are good at building things or have the services of a good shop class you can build a larger version of the table-model divider and use it for other purposes, too. The large model, again built with plywood, but this time covered with cork sheets, can be used for displays of pictures, or photographs, graphs, prints, or sketches. The lumber can be cut to size at the lumber yard, and the panels then hinged and assembled.

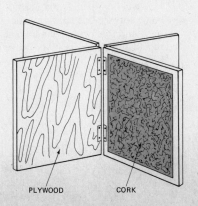

FIGURE 16.6
Space dividers

PLYWOOD   CORK

HOW DO YOU PREPARE MATERIALS
FOR USE DURING THE STUDY SESSION?

1. *Select and develop programs and materials for a supervised study session.* Your critical evaluation of the student's activities and performance in class work, on exams, and via your discussions with him, will pinpoint specifically in what areas your students need help. In algebra, for example, is it really the mathematical computation and notation that is causing a student's difficulty? Or does the difficulty lie in his inability to read well enough to set the problem up in terms of basic math skills. When you have determined the specific problems and difficulties, or the enrichments, needed for each student, your next job is selecting or preparing materials for him to use during the session.

2. *Examine programmed learning materials which may be particularly valuable in these sessions.* Programmed texts are usually organized into one of two basic approaches:

☐ The linear program, in which a student is asked a question, indicates a response, checks the accuracy of his response, and then moves on to the next question or problem whether he was right or wrong.

FIGURE 16.7
Linear programmed learning

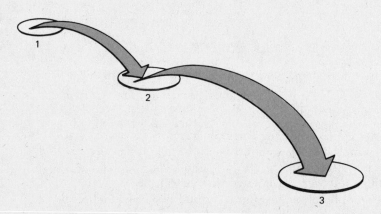

☐ The branched program, in which the student proceeds to the next question only when he makes the correct response to this one. If the student makes an incorrect response to a question, then he is directed to some remedial assistance and then to the question again. The program recycles him, with provided remedial help, so that he can select the correct response and move on in the program.

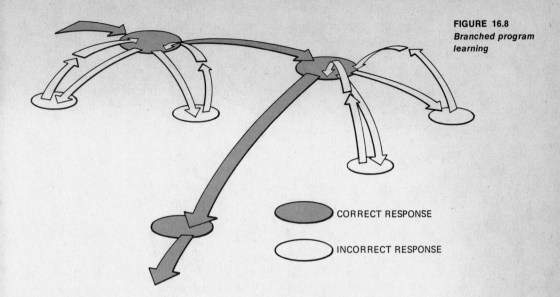

FIGURE 16.8
Branched program learning

CORRECT RESPONSE

INCORRECT RESPONSE

These programs are very adaptable. Some can be given to students for remedial work; some can be given to students for advanced work. Sometimes the same program can fill both these needs with different students. Programs, however, are not easy to develop or write. Their construction involves taking a principle or concept and breaking it down into a series of sequential statements or segments of information. These segments are introduced, questions are asked about them, and they are repeated several times in order for the reader to become familiar with terms and ideas and build them into a meaningful relationship. The presentation and sequence structure of these segments of information are the key to developing a successful program. If you are interested in exploring this technique, you should take a course in program design and construction at a college or university. Then you can develop a series of programs for both remedial and for advanced work in your area.

3. *Use prepared printed materials.* Specific questions you want to use, directions for problems you think need solving, vocabulary you want reviewed, and references you think should be consulted can be rexographed and distributed to the particular students at the appropriate time.

Supervised study materials

4. *Localize the reference materials and supplies for easy access by all the students.* Have a supply of rulers, protractors, graph paper, scissors, transparent tape, pencils, special paper, paints, or a stock of all those materials you think will be needed during the session. If you lack storage facilities for these materials, then set up a temporary resource area using large metal cans as containers for materials. Your students should grow accustomed to looking at things rather than just seeing them, and to using materials in different contexts and for different purposes than they were originally intended.

5. *Have the proper accessories available if you are using record players, or tape recorders.* Decide in advance where each instrument will be set up in your classroom to insure that one will not interfere with another, and that students can easily reach these instruments for use.

6. *Consult with the reading specialist in your school in order to utilize materials, and particular techniques he has found effective.* This expert resource person may not only be involved in your preparation and selection of materials, but may also be of assistance during the study session itself. He can work with individual students or small groups of students on specific reading problems.

HOW DO YOU PREPARE YOUR STUDENTS FOR THE SUPERVISED STUDY SESSION?

Preparing students for supervised study

The most important ingredient in this kind of interaction is, of course, the students. Each of them must understand the purpose of the total session, and the specific part he is to have in it. If poor homework caliber is the problem, discuss it with your students. Letting them begin a homework assignment in class, in this study session, is a great motivation in itself. They will have the time to fully examine an assignment, have you there to indicate how to overcome any difficulties, and thus really get a grip on the meaning of the assignment.

This may be the student's first experience with this kind of lesson. Each student must know specifically what he is to do before the class begins. A study session can quickly deteriorate into a meaningless waste of time if many students mill about waiting for you to reach them with their specific project or task. In your explanation of the session the day before, and in the homework assignment for that day, you should focus on the activities the students will be doing at the session. If you want some students to work on graphing techniques, they should bring with them two or three different types of graphs or tables of data they have taken from newspapers, or magazines. Others in a class may be practicing using a slide rule. They should bring their rules to class. If you want students to critically analyze an advertising layout in a magazine, then have them bring one or two magazines to class that day. You should have several spare magazines on hand for those students who forget to bring theirs.

At the start of the session you can quickly distribute sets of directions, or instructions, or problem sets so that work can begin immediately with no time losses. If several students want to use this time to discuss a research project or paper with you, then be sure to assign part of the time for this activity.

Your active participation as a consultant and guide is of great importance in making supervised study sessions worthwhile. This activity is more demanding on you in terms of your preparation. Students may all be working on different skills or topics and your attention must quickly shift from one area to another as they need your assistance. During each of these sessions you will be:

- ☐ Encouraging by commending efforts expended
- ☐ Reassuring by confirming that the student is proceeding correctly
- ☐ Supplying information, or indicating information sources to students
- ☐ Demonstrating special techniques or skills
- ☐ Clarifying problems

Teacher's role in supervised study

To make maximum use of this kind of study session then, you must carefully explain to your students what they are to do, prepare materials they are to use, and be there to offer any help you can. You must be alert to what the students are doing, and offer assistance to those who may need it but are too shy to ask for it. Students should know that you are alert to what is going on, available to help them, and that something concrete is being accomplished by a supervised study session.

The evaluation of this kind of interaction may not always be numerically determinable. Some of the direct, observable but really non-measurable by-products of this kind of activity include:

- ☐ More in-depth treatment of homework assignments
- ☐ Better grades on exams
- ☐ Greater participation in discussion
- ☐ More extensive reading
- ☐ Overall increase in level of participation in class activities

Evaluating supervised study

You may need a number of supervised study sessions during the semester for different purposes. Some will be used to modify study habits, some to work on research papers, and some to give practice in particular skills or techniques. In each one the students should complete some unit of work or activity, and you should look it over, either during or after the session, in order to assess the progress of each student. This does not mean that you should grade each piece of work. It does mean that you should look at the work the student has done — the writing, the problems, the diagrams, charts, pictures — in order to help him evaluate his progress. You can make comments on these materials, you can correct the problems to give him an idea of how well he is doing, or you can discuss the particular project with him. He should know that this kind of activity is a learning experience for him and for you. It helps him in some definite manner, and it helps you get a better picture of his talents, his particular difficulties, and the way he works at a task. These learning experiences for both you and the student are of tremendous value in your program's development and expansion, even though most of the time each activity cannot be analyzed or assessed mathematically.

PROBLEMS, QUESTIONS, AND ACTIVITIES

16.1   Assume that you are teaching a tenth-grade class in your subject area. After six weeks you notice a gradual slackening of effort. Very little outside effort goes into the students' preparation for your class. There is a concomitant diminishing of student interest in the daily lessons.

1. How would you find out the reasons for this slackening of interest and preparation?

2. Describe three supervised study sessions you might use to remedy this condition.

3. How would you evaluate which session was most successful?

16.2   Assume that, in your subject area, during the first five weeks of the school year, you have had a supervised study lesson once a week for four of the five weeks. After the fourth session, a group of the more advanced students in the class come to you and allege that they do not need supervised study. They indicate that they like to do their own preparation at home or in the library "on their own," and they think the class time should be spent in "regular" lessons.

1. How would you handle these complaints?

16.3   You find that many of the learning difficulties encountered by the students in one of your classes can be attributed to their inability to read the prescribed text.

1. What steps would you take to help them during a supervised study session?

16.4   You find that a few of the students in one of your classes tend to regard a supervised study period as "time out for socialization."

1. How would you get them to cooperate in the learning activities you have scheduled?

NOTES

NOTES

17
Field Trips

WHAT IS A FIELD TRIP?

At times during the school year, your regular classroom may not be the best area available to you for a particular activity or study. You and the class must move outside the confines of that room, to the school grounds, the immediate community, or some other reachable place, and do your investigations at this site. This extra-class session is known as a *field trip*, and is a most valuable activity to consider for your program.

The variety in the extent of field trips can be compared to the varying lengths of today's hemlines. A class moved to a location on the school grounds, or to another wing of your school can be termed a *Mini-Trip*. Those trips which take you out into the immediate community to places within walking distance of the school can be called *Midi-Trips*. Those excursions which require transportation, and at least one full school day, can be called *Maxi-Trips*. Although the field trips—the mini, the midi, and the maxi—differ in scope and duration, they all share many functions and features in common.

FIGURE 17.1
Mini-Midi-Maxi

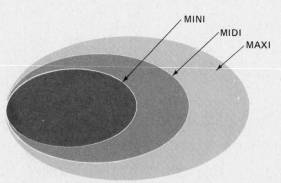

WHAT ARE THE FUNCTIONS OF FIELD TRIPS?

Field trips fall into three major classes:

Those tied directly to work you have already done

Those associated with work you plan to do

Those of cultural, vocational, or avocational interest

These three categories are not mutually exclusive; each trip may serve several different functions for any one student depending on his background and experiences.

Those field trips associated with work you have already done in class can be summary or review experiences. After discussing a water treatment system, what better way is there of reviewing the chemical, physical, and biological aspects of the system, than seeing it in operation. This kind of activity takes the student out of the textbook environment into the real world and helps to link the two together into a cohesive unity.

Functions of a field trip

After a detailed study of how an issue of a newspaper comes into being, a trip to a newsroom of the local newspaper lets students get a feeling for the magnitude of the task. They also get to see some of the operations and the people associated with them at work on a real product.

A visit to a piano factory by physics and music students really serves to tie the two seemingly different subjects together in a firsthand exploration of how these magnificent instruments are created. This is a good example of how the sciences and the arts are blended and interrelated.

With the textbook and classroom experiences in an area at their disposal, the students can, via a field trip, actively make the material come alive and take on new meaning. They can see the practical application of a theoretical concept, and more fully grasp the relevancy of what they have learned.

Another function of the field trip is to motivate and stimulate interest in some topic or subject about to be studied at length. A visit to the local zoo or botanical garden to get an overview of some of the many different phyla of living organisms on earth can certainly make the usually dull unit on classification take on new flavor and meaning.

After the preliminary study of the classification system, a revisit to the same or a suitable alternate location permits students to apply what they have learned to real plants and animals.

These field trips are sometimes data-gathering in orientation. Students are looking for certain specifics to be used later as data in laboratory or workshop lessons, or in discussions. A class trip to a performance of a Shakespearean comedy can fall into several categories too. If the trip is scheduled before the class reads the play, the students get an audio-visual orientation. The effects of the spoken word, the environment created by the scenery, and the actors help shape the total impression of the particular play. Then when the students read the play, explore the plot and the characters, it is against this frame of reference. After a thorough classroom treatment, the class can visit yet another play to compare it to the first one seen. This time they can appreciate more than they did during their first experience; they have, through their class, and field trip activities, broadened their experiential background.

Functions of a field trip

The third category of field trips, which usually includes the first two, deals with those trips of cultural, vocational, or avocational interest. Some of your students may never have visited the local art gallery, museum, opera house, or zoo. Not all of your students have been exposed to the same variety of learning experiences in their pre-school or early school days. You should recognize this factor in all the field trips you plan. To some of your students, the local botanical garden is as familiar as their backyard. To other students, it is an exciting, totally new place filled with plants they have never seen before. It is a place that you introduce to them for the first time.

Therefore, your job in selecting the field trip sites is more complex than it might appear at first if you are to utilize all its inherent possibilities. In addition to opening new community resources to your students, many of these excursions offer vocational guidance. Your students see people at work in different occupations. These experiences serve to further expand the horizons of the students and enrich their picture of the world about them.

Each field trip usually goes far beyond the specific function for which you introduce it. Aside from the scholastic, vocational, and cultural functions it serves, a field trip helps bring you and your students together in a common nonclassroom situation. They see you as a person and not only as a teacher. You get a different perspective of each of them too. You see them in a more relaxed, less structured environment as they work with and react to other students. These new views of teacher and students can serve to build up a fine class spirit. The traditionally used word here is *rapport*—a feeling of mutual understanding, acceptance, respect, and cooperation. This spirit must not be underestimated; without it, a class is simply a collection of individuals who happen to meet for forty minutes per day. With this spirit, the class and teacher are literally one unit, all working together.

HOW DO YOU PLAN A FIELD TRIP?

Of prime importance in planning for a field trip is knowing the potential local or nearby sites. Aside from those already known to you and your colleagues, several other sources of ideas are:

Ideas for field trip locations

☐ The "yellow pages" of your telephone directory for museums, pharmaceutical houses, manufacturers, laboratories, etc.

☐ The art, drama, and theater section of the daily newspaper

☐ The advertisements in magazines, and newspapers on exhibits, collections, and galleries

☐ Locations recommended by local museums, professional organizations, garden clubs, and the like

Write to the specific place you are considering to determine:

Picking a location

☐   If they permit student tours through their facility

☐   What hours or time schedules they maintain

☐   How many students they admit per tour

You can address your letter of inquiry to the Educational Division, or the Public Relations Department of the company or institution involved. Remember that some companies do not permit student tours through their industrial facility because they are concerned about hazards and possible injury to visitors. Some companies require that the students stay on the tour bus and they will provide a guide for the tour through or inside their plant.

When the company, museum, gallery, or specific location you have in mind indicates that they permit (and usually they welcome) class field trips you can begin your planning and preparations in earnest. Your planning can be organized along four parallel tracks:

Four aspects of a field trip

☐   Orientation of students

☐   Transportation, food, and supervision

☐   School clearance and scheduling

☐   Field trip guides and follow-up activities

On the pages that follow, each of these categories is explored and the items that you should consider in your preparation for the field trips you schedule are outlined.

CHECKLIST FOR FIELD TRIPS

ORIENTATION OF STUDENTS

All the students who are to participate in the field trip should know the following facts:

The specific location to be visited: 1.

    ☐   Where is the location?

    ☐   Why was it selected?

The type of facility: 2.

    ☐   What are its unique features? (art gallery, museum, industrial plant)

    ☐   Are there other facilities like it nearby?

The transportation arrangements: 3.

    ☐   What kind of transportation will be required?

    ☐   What will be the cost to the student?

4. **The role of the field trip in the class program of activities:**

    ☐ What does this field trip do that a film or class discussion would not?

    ☐ Is the trip for review or to initiate a study?

5. **The specifics of what each student is to do once he gets to the field trip site:**

    ☐ Is he to take pictures, sketch, measure, just observe, or gather specimens?

    ☐ What are his responsibilities before, during, and after the field trip?

6. **The preparation for the trip:**

    ☐ What reading assignment is suggested?

    ☐ What descriptive brochures are provided by the specific facility?

7. **The nature of any follow-up activities:**

    ☐ Will a classroom discussion follow?

    ☐ Will a laboratory lesson be scheduled for examination of specimens gathered?

TRANSPORTATION, FOOD, AND SUPERVISION

The items for your consideration include:

1. **The number of students participating:**

    ☐ How does information regarding the field trip reach the students?

    ☐ How do students indicate they want to participate in the field trip?

2. **The transportation required:**

    ☐ Will students meet you at the facility or do you arrange transportation?

    ☐ Is bus or subway transportation required?

    ☐ How many students per bus?

    ☐ How are students assigned to buses?

3. **The collection of monies involved:**

    ☐ What is the procedure for collecting money for bus fare and admission fee if any?

    ☐ What is the school policy regarding collection and deposit of this money?

    ☐ How does the transportation company request payment? Is an advance payment required?

    ☐ Are reserved tickets required? What is the deadline for cancellation of transportation or reservations?

    ☐ Is it necessary to sign any contracts?

    ☐ What is the school policy in this regard?

4. **The parental consent form:**

    ☐ Is a standard consent form provided by the school?

□   Is it necessary for you to design a consent form and have it approved by the principal?

□   What is the school policy on filing completed forms with the principal?

The supervision required: 5.

□   How many teachers are required per bus?

□   What is the student's accountability at the field trip site?

□   Do all the students remain together in a tour or do they move about individually?

The directions: 6.

Will you prepare a direction sheet that specifies:

□   The time and place of departure for the field trip site?

□   The directions to the location?

□   The assembly point and time of departure from the facility?

□   A tour map showing key points of interest, rest rooms, and food facilities?

□   Whether cameras are permitted at the facility?

The safety factors: 7.

□   Have you provided for first aid?

□   Is the school nurse one of the adult supervisors?

□   Have you briefed students on the need for comfortable walking shoes, warm clothing, or other specific dressing suggestions?

□   Have you personally toured the facility and identified any potential hazards or bottlenecks?

The provision for food: 8.

□   Do students bring their own lunch, and buy something to drink?

□   Can students purchase lunch at the location?

□   Will you schedule any stops on the trip to and from the location?

SCHOOL CLEARANCE AND SCHEDULING

There are three major factors to consider in this area:

The school procedure on field trips: 1.

Yes   No

□   □   Have the date and location of the field trip been cleared with your supervisor or principal?

□   □   Have all required parental consent forms been completed and filed with the appropriate person?

□   □   Have all monies collected been deposited with the school treasurer, and arrangements made for payments to transportation company and for admission tickets if any?

□   □   Has the insurance coverage requirement been satisfied?

2. **The trip in the total school program:**

☐ ☐ Are any other school events or field trips scheduled for the same day?

☐ ☐ Will any students participating in the field trip miss important work or exams in other subject areas?

☐ ☐ Will all other subject teachers be notified about the date of the field trip at least four school days in advance of the trip in order to adjust their plans for class work on that day?

☐ ☐ What provision has been made for students to secure homework assignments and class notes for those classes they miss on the day of the field trip?

☐ ☐ What teacher coverage has been designated for those of your other classes not participating in the field trip experience?

☐ ☐ What specific activities have you provided for those of your classes not going on the trip? (lab experience, supervised study)

☐ ☐ Have you discussed this work with the teacher who will take over your classes on that day?

☐ ☐ Is it possible to arrange for the field trip on a weekend or school holiday?

☐ ☐ What real function does the field trip serve in your program so that you can justify devoting a block of school time to it?

3. **The public relations aspect of the field trip:**

☐ ☐ Have you discussed with the students their role as representatives of the school and of all students as they move out of the school area?

☐ ☐ If you are traveling by public transportation, have you discussed with the students how to courteously share the facility with the other members of the public?

☐ ☐ Have you notified the school newspaper and local newspapers of the nature and extent of the field trip?

☐ ☐ Can you provide the newspaper with a picture of the students at the field trip site?

☐ ☐ Have you provided time following the field trip for discussing the social amenities such as writing thank-you notes to the people in the school and at the field trip site who made the trip possible and a valuable and enjoyable learning experience?

FIELD TRIP GUIDES AND FOLLOW-UP ACTIVITIES

In this area it is best to keep in mind the following items:

1. **The directions to the location:**

Yes No

☐ ☐ Have you prepared a sheet of instructions on the specifics of the trip to and from the location for distribution to students?

☐ ☐ What provision have you made for the distribution of this material to students before the trip?

2. **The tour map or guide:**

☐ ☐ Have you visited the facility to identify all the locations you want to include in your field trip itinerary?

☐ ☐ Have you prepared or has the facility provided a tour map of the location showing location of exhibits, rest rooms, cafeteria, and assembly points?

☐ ☐ Have you prepared a set of questions, or notes with accompanying questions, on the exhibits to draw the students' attention to items of major significance?

What provision have you made for the distribution of this material sometime before the day of the field trip?

☐ ☐ Have you decided and indicated to students how they will move about the location? (large groups, small groups, as individuals)

The morning of the trip: 3.

☐ ☐ Have you prepared attendance lists for each bus to check students on and off and thereby overlook no one?

☐ ☐ Have you taken all admission tickets with you?

Do you hand them in at the starting point or will students need them during the trip?

The follow-up activities: 4.

☐ ☐ Have you discussed with the students how the field trip experiences, data, and specimens will be used in class work? (laboratory lesson, workshop, discussion, bulletin board, major display)

☐ ☐ Have you made notes on your own findings about the procedures you used, the difficulties you encountered, and utilization of the field trip experience in your program to assist you in planning your next field trip?

Do not try to plan a field trip without consulting your supervisor or assistant principal. They can usually give you some valuable tips on handling all the details of the trip. This activity, like all others in teaching, requires careful, realistic planning in order to have it come off smoothly. It is wise to participate as an assistant on several field trips before trying one of your own.

You might want to start small with a mini-trip to some site on or near your school grounds. In biology, you might have a field trip through the school garden to identify the different trees and shrubs there. With this small-scale field trip, your class can go during your regular class meeting period for several days. This is as much a field trip as one to a major industrial plant three hundred miles away because all the ingredients for a field trip are still present. These mini-trips also help you to identify potential student leaders—those students who adapt quickly to the atmosphere of independence and self-reliance, and those students who may require special attention and assistance in learning to adapt to this new type of learning experience.

This kind of teaching–learning activity is a most valuable one for enrichment of your program. It will serve to further expand the horizons of your students, and to add variety and challenge to the lessons you plan and present.

PROBLEMS, QUESTIONS, AND ACTIVITIES

17.1 Select a locality within walking distance of your school. Briefly describe some institutions, buildings, points of interest, or other community resource that might be the subject of a field trip by your class. Justify your choice from an educational and administrative point of view.

17.2 Several of your colleagues object to your taking your class on a field trip because they are then called upon to cover the remainder of your school program of classes and assignments. How would you answer their complaints?

17.3 Select a midi-trip location you want to use for a field trip site. Prepare a checklist that you would use to insure your not overlooking any detail necessary for the successful initiation, conduct, and completion of this field trip.

17.4 Some parents object to your taking your classes on so many field trips. Some of them have said that their children are in school to learn "the essentials." Your principal has asked you to explain to a meeting of parents the values of field trips. Describe in detail a class trip you are going to take or have taken. Document the values that this trip has for the students in your classes.

NOTES

NOTES

PART FOUR

Beyond the Classroom: The Total Teaching Environment

18
Homeroom Activities

WHAT IS A HOMEROOM?

The term *homeroom* refers to a period of time, a room, and a group of students, whom you meet to officially start or record their school day. The students who constitute your homeroom may be:

Homeroom students

A class that you will teach later in the day

A group of students, some of whom may be in your class later in the day

A group of students you meet only for the homeroom period

If your school has "block" programming, that is, classes that move as a body from one subject area to another, then you might meet this entire class again during the day. In schools with departmental organization, or modular scheduling, only some of the students might be in one of your subject classes. If your homeroom is composed of ninth grade students, and your teaching program consists of courses taken only by eleventh grade students, then you will probably not meet any of your homeroom students in a subject class.

Whether or not you meet your homeroom students again in one of your subject classes, the relationship between you and your students is different in the homeroom from what it is in any of the subject classes. This difference springs from two factors:

What makes a
homeroom different

To your students what you are doing in the homeroom does not seem to them to be teaching. They will get no grades from you. They may not feel obliged to pay close attention to all you announce or say.

To your students the homeroom period is "their" period—to do homework, to see a counselor or adviser, to talk to a specific teacher, or just to sit, talk, and relax.

WHAT ARE THE RESPONSIBILITIES
OF A HOMEROOM TEACHER?

From your point of view, there are important duties that must be carried out for each homeroom class. These duties can be categorized as:

Homeroom
responsibilities

☐ Accounting for pupils and keeping records

☐ Providing a channel of communication

☐ Assisting in guidance activities

☐ Developing morale and school spirit

Accounting for Pupils and Keeping Records

In this area you are responsible for:

Attendance and records

☐ Keeping the record of attendance, absence, and lateness. The homeroom record of this information becomes a legal record for statistics that determine local, state, and federal financial aid. In the event of a student's claim of accident, or of truancy and violation of the attendance regulations, it constitutes the official school record. It is also useful for reports to parents or guardians.

☐ Sending a daily report of attendance, absence, and lateness to the school office

☐ Sending notification to parents of absence of a student

☐ Keeping cumulative records

☐ Following the school's method of processing marks for homeroom students

☐ Entering information on the student's permanent record

☐ Doing the clerical work to facilitate reorganization of classes at the end of each semester or school year

☐ Preparing reports needed in the organization and administration of your school, and for the guidance of your School Board

In your homeroom you are not only a teacher, but also a member of a large governmental organization, which has a responsibility for accountability and communication at all levels and must operate effectively so that the work of teaching—essentially the school's only valid function—can progress smoothly and with a minimum of interruption.

Providing a Channel of Communication

Generally it is in the homeroom (rather than the subject classes) that all school organizations, clubs, and extra-curricular activities communicate with your students. At various times there will be announcements from:

School communication

The Student Council

Junior Red Cross and other drives

Honor Society

Job Placement Adviser

Senior Activities Coordinator

Prom Committee

Yearbook Staff

Principal

Many of the club and activity notices will be in the form of mimeo-graphed sheets to be read aloud by you or one of your class officers. Some other notices are to be delivered directly to individual students in your class. In addition to these notices, it is during the homeroom period that the school public address system is most often used. On certain occasions, the principal will use the public address system to speak to all the students; sometimes an adviser or the assistant principal will make an important announcement that needs immediate attention and action. (Most schools recognize that the public address system will lose its effectiveness if it is too frequently used, and that it often interrupts what the teacher is saying to his class.)

Assisting in Guidance Activities

As the homeroom teacher you will have to provide the receptive class atmosphere for visits by the guidance counselor and grade adviser when they come to talk to your class. You will also have to guide each student so that he will know what school channels he must use to take care of such problems or business as:

☐ Getting a bus pass   *Guidance assistance*

☐ Applying for orchestra

☐ Getting on a school team

☐ Joining a club

☐ Getting a medical exam

☐ Applying for working papers

☐ Looking for a summer job

Therefore, you must know the location of the resource people to be contacted by the student. At the start of each semester, an orientation session for teachers new to the school is generally scheduled. At this time teachers are introduced to the school resource people, and in-structed in school procedures and regulations. Be sure you participate in this kind of session and that you determine the name, room loca-tion, and specific office hours of the following resource people:

☐ Assistant principal

☐ Dean

☐ School nurse and doctor

☐ Coaches and orchestra directors

☐ Subject supervisors

☐ Grade advisers

□   Guidance counselors

□   Attendance coordinator

Guidance assistance   □   Working paper coordinator

□   Job placement coordinator

Also secure a copy of the school calendar of events for that school year, so you can be alert to those times you will be called upon to give some special assistance, or particular attention to an event conducted through the homeroom sections.

Remember that you are the student's first recourse in answering questions about his program, his plans for the future, and his difficulties in any of his subject classes. Your thoughtful reaction may soothe and assist anxious or rebellious students who feel threatened by a system that they may not yet understand. You may be able to allay their fears and soothe their anger while you put them in contact with their guidance counselor, grade adviser, the dean, or any other person who may be better equipped to answer their specific questions.

As a homeroom teacher, you may also have to assist in the school's safety program of fire and shelter drills, or its program to prevent or reduce narcotics use by your students.

In guidance, you—the homeroom teacher—are the first line of action. By your skill, thoughtfulness, and sincerity, you can help students to profit from the vast system of services which most schools now have.

Developing Morale and School Spirit

Schools which have departmental or modular scheduling usually find that the homeroom is the best unit to work with for schoolwide activities. If, for example, the entire school were to go on a field trip—to an exposition, a school field day—it is most likely that the school administration would organize the activity through the homerooms. Every student, despite the uniqueness of his program, has a homeroom. He "belongs" to some homeroom teacher who is accountable for him. Thus the homerooms are the arteries through which school spirit and morale are developed. There are many activities that reflect this utilization of the homeroom:

School spirit   □   Students may participate in schoolwide assembly programs during an extended homeroom period.

□   Officers such as class president, vice-president, secretary, and treasurer are nominated.

□   The homeroom is usually the operating unit for schoolwide elections and balloting.

You, the teacher, are crucial in setting the tone of all homeroom activities. Your enthusiasm for school activities will extend itself to your students. Your pride in the achievements of homeroom students will help them develop a sense of self-esteem.

Students today often feel depersonalized because in our increasingly impersonal world they come and go without any recognition of their individuality. Young people, whether they are very quiet or very noisy, whether they are very bright or very slow, are "crying out" to be noticed. They are in effect saying, "I'm here, World; won't someone recognize me?" Busy as you may be with all the details associated with the job of homeroom teacher, your greeting, the "Hello" or "Good morning," will be the recognition that can help your students relate to their school and the people in it. Your pleasant and skillful handling of their concerns will make everything else they do that day more relevant than it might otherwise have been. This without question is an important function of the homeroom teacher. If you can make the homeroom a place where the student feels he belongs, you will involve him in the work of the homeroom and the school. This spirit will help the school further the student's intellectual growth, and personal adjustment, and will help him on the road to social and emotional maturity.

Developing morale

PROBLEMS, QUESTIONS, AND ACTIVITIES

18.1 You find that the students in your homeroom are generally courteous and cooperative in class under your supervision, but that they tend to exhibit poor manners when they go to assembly.

1. What steps would you take to improve their general conduct outside of homeroom class?

18.2 You have three alternatives for seating students in your class: alphabetically, randomly, or letting them select their own seats.

Discuss the advantages and limitations of each of these alternatives. Which would you use

1. In a homeroom?

2. In a subject class?

18.3 Your supervisor has visited your subject class on several occasions. He has commended you and the class for the fine spirit of learning that he has observed. He has commended you individually upon your careful and evidently successful planning and preparation.

Despite the success you are experiencing in your subject classes, several students in your homeroom continue to "act up," and call out in class. They show lack of interest in any activity that is taking place in the homeroom, and often call you and the students names. What action would you take?

NOTES

NOTES

19

Administrative Assignments

WHAT IS AN ADMINISTRATIVE ASSIGNMENT?

Your administrative assignment is your participation in the "overhead" of the school. It is a task that you are asked to perform *in lieu of* one or more subject classes, or for a class period *in addition to* your teaching periods, your lunch period, and your preparation period.

WHAT ARE THE DIFFERENT TYPES OF ADMINISTRATIVE ASSIGNMENTS?

The nature of these assignments, sometimes called building assignments, will vary depending on the size of your school, the grades and age levels that it includes, and the special programs that your school offers.

Administrative assignments can be divided into five general categories:

Types of administrative assignments

☐ Organization

☐ Guidance

☐ Student Activities

☐ Instructional Program

☐ Nondepartmental Activities

The most frequently encountered administrative assignments are listed on the pages that follow, together with a brief description of the duties of each position.

Organization

1. *Program Chairman, Member of Program Committee.* You devise, or continue, a system for programming students into classes, and teachers into their instructional and administrative assignments. You schedule schoolwide exams, and develop room schedules for classes and exams.

2. *School Treasurer.* You maintain monetary accounts, handle receipts and disbursements, and compile financial reports for the school.

Organization

3. *Transportation.* You organize transportation for students, setting up hours of arrival and departure, and places of pickup. You issue public transportation eligibility tickets which permit students to ride public transportation at reduced fares, and supervise processing of eligibility tickets.

4. *Yard Duty.* You supervise arrival and departure of students in the school yards or grounds, and maintain order so that students can move safely and expeditiously to and from school. You supervise and patrol during lunch periods.

5. *Security.* You are responsible for assuring that no unauthorized persons enter the school, that visitors are greeted and identified, and that students and faculty are free from harassment.

6. *Keys.* You set up and administer procedures for issuing closet and room keys to all teachers. You maintain a set of school keys and provide duplicates when necessary.

7. *Supplies.* You receive and check incoming books and supplies. You process orders submitted by authorized personnel in your school.

Guidance

1. *Grade Adviser, Part-time Counselor.* You are responsible for planning, with the student, the courses he will take. You confer with parents. You help students work out personal problems, and refer them to other resource people in school and in the community for further guidance.

Guidance

2. *College Adviser.* You contact colleges, business and trade schools to learn their current educational requirements, programs, fees, and tuition. You keep students informed via bulletins, assemblies, homeroom visits, and conferences.

3. *Placement Adviser, Cooperative Education Adviser.* You contact business firms, civil service agencies, factories, and other places of employment to provide a link between the firms seeking help, and your students seeking full- or part-time jobs.

4. *Dean, Assistant Dean.* You institute procedures to insure that students obey school regulations. You interview students regarding discipline problems, or referrals by teachers and grade advisers. You follow up interviews with letters and telephone calls to parents.

5. *Attendance Coordinator.* You supervise official attendance records of the school. With your district attendance teacher, you contact parents in regard to students' absence, cutting, or lateness.

6. *Infirmary.* You receive students in the infirmary and provide reassurance and rest but no medication. You can refer cases to the school nurse or doctor. If symptoms indicate, you contact parents to come to pick up the student from school. You handle accident reports, and keep the infirmary log up to date.

Student Activities

Student activities

1. *Coordinator of Student Affairs, Student Council Adviser.* You advise and meet regularly with the student government officers and cabinet. You develop leadership through your contacts with the students in the school. You coordinate and facilitate the activities of the faculty advisers of all school clubs. You help students to plan and conduct school activities including elections, dances, and athletic events. You are a vital channel of communication between the students and the principal of the school.

2. *Honor Society Adviser.* You implement the procedures by which students are selected and admitted into the honor society. You advise and meet regularly with these students. You assist students in carrying out all the functions of this society in the school.

3. *Club Adviser.* You advise, and meet regularly with, students to realistically plan and carry out the activities of the club. You coordinate meetings with other clubs, and arrange for a meeting place in the school.

Instructional Program

Instructional program

1. *Audio-Visual Aids Coordinator.* You maintain audio-visual equipment including the school public address system and all microphones. You supervise stage lighting. You initiate and conduct a program for supplying teachers with the audio-visual equipment they request. You arrange for the repair of equipment, using facilities indicated by the school or the school board.

2. *Publications Adviser.* You organize your student staff, negotiate a contract with a printer, and supervise preparation of school publications. You advise your staff, and assume ultimate responsibility for the finished publication.

3. *Coach.* You organize and train teams and individual students. You supervise and organize athletic events, and arrange for equipment and supplies for the teams.

4. *Music Director, Band Leader.* You organize and train musical groups and individuals. You are responsible for concerts, band performances, and other school musical activities. You are responsible for the maintenance of musical instruments.

5. *Bookroom and Supply Assistant.* Under the direction of the department supervisor, you receive, store, and issue books and supplies to teachers in your department.

Nondepartmental Activities

1. *Assemblies Coordinator.* You plan the dates for assemblies. You consult with the subject supervisors so that every subject discipline has an opportunity to present or be represented in an assembly program for the entire school. You contact outside cultural agencies and business firms which might have suitable programs for your school's assembly. You assist teachers and visiting speakers in arranging for the program and in securing needed equipment for that program.

Nondepartmental activities

2. *Study Hall Teacher.* You provide for registering, seating, and attendance-taking of students who have been programmed for a study period in an auditorium or large study hall. You provide constant surveillance so that every student has a quiet, comfortable place to study. You assist any student who is having difficulty.

3. *Cafeteria Teacher-in-Charge.* You initiate, or continue, a procedure for seating students. You are particularly vigilant at potential trouble areas, such as the food line, so that any difficulties can be avoided. You encourage students to develop good habits of socialization. You indicate how the eating area is to be maintained and cleared by the students so the area is clean for the next group to arrive.

WHAT GUIDELINES SHOULD BE FOLLOWED IN CARRYING OUT THESE ASSIGNMENTS?

1. *Know to whom you report.* As soon as you are informed of your assignment, determine the person directly in charge of that area:

☐ The principal

☐ The assistant principal

☐ A subject supervisor

☐ A teacher assigned by the principal

To whom do you report?

2. *Consult with the person in charge of your assignment.* This may be accomplished via an orientation session scheduled for you at the start of the school year. These group sessions, or individual conferences, are usually held before students arrive and classes begin for the year.

3. *At the conference be sure you determine the school procedure already established regarding the assignment.*

What are the proper procedures?

☐ What is the scope and exact nature of the assignment?

☐ Is student attendance to be taken?

☐ Do you report cutting? To whom?

☐ Does your assignment involve working with small or large groups of students?

☐ Do you work with the department supervisor or some other teacher?

☐ Do you arrange seating?

☐ Can students come and go at will, or are they supposed to remain at the location for an entire period?

☐ What procedure is used for issuing passes to students?

☐ Do you need access to student program card files?

☐ Do you have to meet with students during homeroom sessions?

☐ Are you responsible for keeping any records or preparing reports for school agencies or supervisors? When are they due? What is the format required? To whom are they submitted?

☐ What back-up personnel are available in case you need assistance?

☐ Do you have to arrange and schedule meetings periodically with students, or with other faculty members? Where are the meetings held?

☐ If you handle monies collected, have you worked out a schedule for deposit and recording of funds with the school treasurer? What are his office hours? How is money safeguarded until it is deposited?

☐ Do you have to keep inventories or supply lists? Are there standard forms available or do you have to devise your own system?

These are but a few of the considerations in your preliminary look at the administrative assignment. Once you have begun your exploration of the scope and nature of the assignment and have discussed it with the person in charge, you can more effectively and efficiently begin your assignment.

4. *Be sure that just as with each of your subject class assignments:*

What are the proper procedures?

☐ You are on time

☐ You have a plan or routine to follow

☐ Your materials are ready

☐ You are actively involved in the performance of the assignment

☐ Your alert, pleasant, and efficient manner sets the tone of the activity

☐ You seek out suggestions for improvement, advice, and assistance when needed from experienced resource people

WHAT NEW IDEAS ARE DEVELOPING
FOR ADMINISTRATIVE ASSIGNMENTS?

In recent years, in some school systems, school aides and paraprofessionals have been hired to relieve teachers of some administrative assignments. In some schools, aides are used for hall duty, building patrol, cafeteria duty, and supervising the study hall. The teachers relieved as a result of the assignment of teacher aides are expected to use this "extra" time for professional duties in connection with their teaching assignments and homeroom activities.

Administrative assignments are an important part of every school system. They must be handled well in order to complement and maximize the impact of your instructional program.

PROBLEMS, QUESTIONS, AND ACTIVITIES

19.1   Your crowded study hall tends to be rather noisy.

  1. What measures could you take to obtain a greater degree of quiet for those students who wish to do some serious studying?

  2. If your measures do not succeed, what would you do next?

19.2   Some of your colleagues and students have told you that there is talk among the students about a planned protest involving students leaving the building en masse. According to the rumor, this exodus might occur during the period in which you have been assigned to duty in the main hall. This duty includes supervision of entrances.

  1. What action would you take?

19.3   Miss X, an older teacher, who is to relieve you in your cafeteria assignment at the end of Period 4, consistently arrives late. This causes you to be late for your Period 5 class. Miss X explains to you that no matter how she rushes, the four minutes passing time does not give her enough time to get from her class to the assignment area on time.

  1. What action would you take?

NOTES

NOTES

20
Auxiliary Personnel

WHAT IS MEANT BY "AUXILIARY PERSONNEL"?

One of the most important educational developments in the past decade has been the increased use of auxiliary personnel in the schools. The term *auxiliary personnel* refers to members of an educational staff who, working with children under the direction of teachers and supervisors, are active participants in the development of viable teaching–learning interactions. The teacher and the auxiliary, also called a paraprofessional, work together as an educational team to create a unique link between the community and the school environment.

Although community members have always been in the schools as volunteers, more recently they have been introduced in the capacity of school aides and teacher assistants. In these roles the community members offer valuable reinforcement for the work of the teacher by helping the students and relieving the teacher of certain non-teaching chores. For example, school aides, working under the direct supervision of the principal or of a teacher, perform duties that do not involve classroom teaching. They are assigned to such duties as assisting with study hall, lunch room, hall patrol, and keeping order as students are entering or leaving the school. This relieves the teacher and permits him more time for helping individual students, preparing plans and materials, and performing other professional duties.

More recently, the need for incorporating members of the community into teaching–learning teams has been widely recognized by school boards. In many school districts necessary appropriations and programs have been provided so that auxiliary personnel could become an integral part of school faculties.

The auxiliary team member, coming from segments of the community not traditionally included in educational teams, represents new and different insights into the learning process. "Career Ladder" programs for auxiliary personnel provide the community member with a means of upward mobility not previously open to him. An auxiliary can enter this program and remain at any level or, if he wishes, advance to the top of the career ladder and become a fully certified teacher.

285

WHAT ARE THE CAREER LEVELS AND
FUNCTIONS OF AUXILIARY PERSONNEL?

There are a number of positions grouped under the heading of auxiliary personnel, and the field is so rapidly expanding, as the impetus for the involvement of community people increases, that a complete list of auxiliary-personnel functions is not possible. However, some of the major steps in the "Career Ladder" program are listed below.

Career levels for auxiliary personnel

1. *The educational trainee* is starting a career in the educational profession. He is assigned to work in the school on routine monitorial and clerical tasks.

2. *The teacher aide* is more directly involved in the teaching–learning interaction. The teacher under whose supervision he is working determines the limits and scope of this involvement. The introduction of a teacher aide provides opportunities for more individualized or small group instruction in the classroom.

3. *The educational assistant* is assigned directly to a classroom to work with a teacher. Under the guidance of that teacher he can perform such duties as helping students use library facilities, tutoring children who are not natively English speaking, and assisting children in the use of teaching machines. This type of auxiliary has a greater degree of competency as a result of courses he has taken, and experience he has gained in the classroom.

4. *The educational associate* has more training and additional classroom experience and can assume greater instructional responsibility. Under the teacher's guidance, the educational associate will prepare and teach lessons, and then join the teacher and perhaps the assistant principal in an evaluation of his teaching. The educational associate can work with small or large groups of students, provide enrichment activities, and develop and implement routines in class operation.

5. *The apprentice or assistant teacher* represents the most experienced and highly trained of the auxiliary personnel. With increasing independence he prepares and teaches lessons and works in long-range planning of class activities.

In summary, these various auxiliary personnel differ in their degree of formal training and in the length and scope of their classroom experience. As their proficiency as members of the teaching–learning team increases, they are given greater responsibility and perform their duties with less active supervision.

Auxiliary personnel also perform the duties of family worker, family assistant, and family associate. These school positions are used to reach out to the home when some home or community problem is preventing the student from effectively participating in the teaching–learning interaction.

WHAT ARE TEACHER–AUXILIARY–STUDENT–COMMUNITY INTERACTIONS?

From the moment that he enters the classroom, the auxiliary is changing the traditional concept of one class–one teacher. Here, in the eyes of the children, the teacher and the community is an additional authority figure and resource person to further vitalize and make more relevant the teaching–learning interaction.

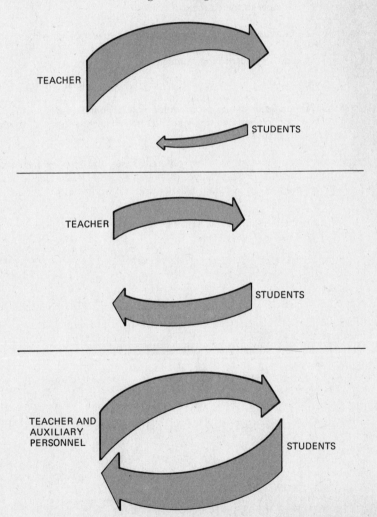

FIGURE 20.1
The dynamics of auxiliary personnel

TEACHER

STUDENTS

TEACHER

STUDENTS

TEACHER AND AUXILIARY PERSONNEL

STUDENTS

To take advantage of the talents and skills of the teacher and auxiliary personnel, an in-depth orientation program is needed. Both the teacher and the auxiliary can learn from each other and about each other so that both will appreciate the unique and significant contributions they can make by working together as an educational team. The auxiliary with his special community insights will bring added strength to the crucial teaching–learning processes which will help to develop an effective relationship and mutual trust between all school personnel and the community they serve.

PROBLEMS, QUESTIONS, AND ACTIVITIES

20.1 Assume that your principal has told you in June that beginning with the new school year in September you will be assigned an educational trainee from your local community.

   1. What would you like to know about this person so that he can be an effective member of the educational team?

20.2 An educational assistant has been assigned to work with you in one of your classes. You have ascertained that he has completed two years of college and has a rich background in music.

   1. How would you plan to use him in your instructional program?

20.3 What training or career program for auxiliary personnel is being developed in your school district, or in some neighboring school district, or in a nearby university teacher-training center?

20.4 Auxiliary personnel of many different types are used extensively in your school district. Because of your training, experience, and interest, you have been assigned an assistant teacher who will work with you for a full school year.

   1. What are some of the activities for which the assistant teacher will be responsible in your class?

NOTES

NOTES

21
Coda: Further Increasing Teacher Effectiveness

In addition to the jobs of planning lessons, teaching classes, meeting your administrative and homeroom activities, and doing all those other things that make up the daily rounds of a teacher, you will be interested, like all professional people, in your further growth and development—professional, personal, social, and intellectual. Specific and practical suggestions for helping you increase the significance of your role in a teaching–learning interaction have been the major emphases throughout all the chapters of this book. There are, in addition, a number of techniques and instruments of diagnosis and evaluation which you, you and your supervisor, or you and a teacher colleague working in cooperation, may use to further increase your effectiveness.

All of these techniques and instruments permit self-analysis of your classroom performance in terms of a number of predetermined activities or behaviors. For example, you may be interested in determining and then analyzing the proportion of class time you devote to questioning students, building on student responses, or giving directions and instructions.

To gather data, you will first have to construct a checklist that defines these categories of activities. Then you should videotape or audiotape a lesson, or have a colleague or supervisor observe the lesson and then record periodically (at brief three- to four-second intervals) each of the activities as they occur. This will give some objective data upon which you can establish a profile of your practices in these areas.

Developing your own sets of categories for analyzing your behavior or activities might appear to be highly desirable in terms of individualizing this evaluation instrument. However, before undertaking this challenge, experiment with some of the schemes that have been developed out of extensive research studies that have been done in an attempt to determine the critical variables of teacher behavior that can affect a teaching–learning interaction. For example, the Flanders Interaction Analysis involves ten items grouped under four major headings:

1. Direct teacher influence

   Lecturing

   Giving directions

   Criticizing or justifying authority

2. Indirect teacher influence

   Accepting feelings

   Praising or encouraging

   Accepting or using ideas of students

   Asking questions

3. Student talk

   Student-talk responses

   Student-talk initiation

4. Silence

   Silence or confusion

Flanders Interaction Analysis

The profile is developed here by the teacher examining and listenin. to tapes of one of his lessons and then recording the specific activity occurring every three to four seconds. An observer can record this data at a "live" class session, and the teacher will get some feedback on the percentage of time devoted to any of these specific activities. You can thus relate your use of these various activities to the extent to which you control or influence the interaction, or to which you permit student involvement in the interaction.

This scheme of analysis provides some quantitative measurement of the use of different activities or techniques but does not permit any evaluation of the quality of the questions or responses.

Another technique developed for self-analysis is the Parson's Guided Self-Analysis (GSA). Here the teacher can work from a series of programmed booklets and a videotape of one of his lessons. The videotape permits him to view the lesson repeatedly, wholly or partially, to evaluate it from a number of perspectives. At present there are four programmed booklets to be used:

A. Questioning Techniques

B. Teacher Response Patterns

C. Type of Teacher Talk

D. Teacher–Student Talk Patterns

Parson's Guided Self-Analysis

The teacher begins by reading the first program, Questioning Techniques, and becoming familiar with the categories of questions developed for the analysis. Then he looks at the videotaped lesson and categorizes each question asked. The categories of questions include:

Parson's Guided
Self-Analysis

☐ Rhetorical question

☐ Information question

☐ Leading question

☐ Probing question

He can thus determine the percentage of probing questions, the percentage of information questions, and so forth that he used in a given situation. Then the second program is used and the lesson viewed again. This time the analysis is done in terms of the teacher's response pattern and includes such categories as:

☐ Use of verbal rewards

☐ Closure

☐ Sustaining students at a given level

☐ Extending student thought

The teacher learns to relate the results of the first analysis to the results of the second analysis. The third and fourth parts of the program are designed to further help analyze the teacher behavior in that class.

These two techniques permit you to gain insight into your behavior patterns as a teacher—patterns that have a tremendous influence on the scope, relevancy, and meaning of any teaching–learning interaction.

In addition, your growth as a person with many cultural and social interests must, of necessity, affect your growth as a teacher. An alert, lively, knowledgeable, inspiring teacher must be an alert, lively, knowledgeable, inspiring person. You can share only that which you possess, be it

Sharing what you feel

A shudder when you read Faulkner's "A Rose for Emily"

A feeling of exhilaration when you hear Beethoven's setting of Schiller's "Ode To Joy"

The quiet satisfaction of reaching the successful conclusion of an extended, challenging problem in math

The excitement of winning or losing a closely fought tennis match

All the vividness of these and similar activities can be shared with your students only after you yourself have experienced them. You should, therefore, keep trying to broaden your experiential background by reaching out for new challenges: Learning new skills; developing new interests; visiting new places; working with a variety of programs and people.

Among the most frequently mentioned characteristics of a professional is that "he knows his stuff." Becoming a "pro" in the teaching field means

☐ Constant reading of current books, periodicals, pamphlets, papers, and relevant newspaper articles not only in your area of specialization but in other areas as well

☐ Willingness to learn from others who may be particularly competent in a phase of teaching with which you are as yet unfamiliar; learning from those who have perfected a technique or skill that you have not yet mastered

☐ Receptivity to supervisory suggestions and a real desire to improve your teaching by seeking such help rather than resenting the assistance

☐ Frequent returns to school yourself for courses in new concepts, skills, and techniques useful in your area; for courses in different areas that you would like to explore because of a hobby or interest or just out of curiosity

☐ Using your unassigned periods during the day effectively for conferences with students, developing materials and equipment, or observing your supervisor or other experienced teachers in real teaching situations

There are a number of study programs in the summer and during the school year, including National Science Foundation programs and those sponsored by the provisions of the National Defense and Education Act, to provide you with courses on the graduate level in your own subject area.

Many school systems provide a series of in-service courses designed to introduce you to different skills, types of teaching, evaluation techniques and materials. Contact your school board, or office of in-service education to determine if such programs are given in your area and how you can apply for them.

You may wish to explore the area of professional development in your school system. This professional development can include advancement to the supervisory or administrative levels of education, or to one of the many posts in a school for which you might be eligible and particularly suited. These include attendance coordinator, grade adviser, career or guidance counselor, and dean. Be sure to consult with your supervisors and get their appraisals of your particular strengths and your weaknesses. The teacher whose homeroom records are always in a mess would not be likely to be considered for chairman of the program committee; the teacher whose study hall is always in an uproar would not be a front runner for the position of dean. Determine where in your school you might best serve with maximum profit to the school as a whole and to yourself as an individual. Your diligence and interest in what you are doing, be it classroom teaching, homeroom, or study hall, are important ingredients in helping you advance professionally.

In some areas the teacher is expected to be active in the affairs of the community served by his school. In urban situations he frequently does not live in the inner city where his school is located, and is often removed from active participation in community affairs. However, there is an urgent need today for the teacher to understand the students as part of the environment in which they live and work. Teachers in the inner cities, therefore, must become more active in the community affairs of the area in which their school is located. Attending and participating in parent-teacher conferences and meetings, reading about and becoming involved in community affairs, and directly investigating the community resources and using them to the fullest are all important ingredients in establishing meaningful ties between school and community.

Your professional development

Developing
professionally

Your increasing knowledge about your own subject area

Your recognition of the techniques you are using in your teaching and the types of influence you have on teaching–learning interactions

Your ability to learn from others

Your willingness to look for new ways of doing things

Your involvement in other aspects of the educational environment

Your ability to extend the classroom beyond the traditional four-walls and out into the local community and larger world communities

all will be reflected in your teaching activities. New ideas you learn will be used in your lessons; new materials and techniques you master will add zest and variety to your class sessions; new interests you develop will provide you with new ideas for enrichment, assignments, and discussion topics. Your own curiosity about your field and the total environment will be communicated to your students. This in turn will help to make all interactions more meaningful for them and for you. That is what teaching is really about—helping to introduce a student to learning skills and techniques that he can use throughout his entire life.

PROBLEMS, QUESTIONS, AND ACTIVITIES

21.1 Investigate the certification or eligibility requirements for promotion in the locality in which you teach. Select one area of advancement. Indicate just what courses or other training you would need to satisfy such requirements.

21.2 Make a self-evaluation chart which may be used to evaluate the success of a lesson. Be sure that your listing includes such categories as evaluation of subject material, the different components of the interaction, the degree of student involvement, the type of influence or control you are using, and the outgrowths of the interaction.

21.3 Make some informal observations among your friends, neighbors, social organization members, etc., to get some idea of their concept of the status of a teacher—socially and professionally.

  1. If you feel that this image is unsatisfactory, what can you do, personally, to improve it?

  2. If you feel it is satisfactory, how can you try to maintain or even enhance it?

21.4 Your principal has requested you to address the PTA at its next monthly meeting. Prepare a five-minute talk to be given before this group on one of the following topics:

1. The supervised study period

2. How television can help the student

3. What books or magazines would be good to have at home

4. How your subject can help the student in life

5. How to help the student use his leisure time to advantage

6. What parents should know about the use of narcotics

21.5 Contact the division of in-service education in your locality, as well as the colleges near you. Obtain catalogues of current course offerings, and determine those in which you might be interested in order to:

1. Broaden your knowledge in your own area of specialization

2. Explore an area related to your own in which you have limited experience

3. Learn some new skill or technique or hobby activity

21.6 Survey your school and determine the different types of services and positions that are present in addition to subject class or department offerings. Some of these include: Attendance Coordinator, Dean, College Adviser, Job Placement Coordinator, Program Committee Member.

1. How would you go about securing information on these positions?

2. What program would you establish in order to prepare yourself for one of these positions?

Appendix

Write to the audio-visual-aids sources listed below for catalogues of their materials; these will indicate the spectrum of available equipment and respective purchase or rental prices. Also consult the yellow pages of your telephone directory for local listings of these offices and for other companies in the audio-visual-aids field.

Audio-Visual Library of Science Transparencies
General Aniline and Film Corporation
Binghamton, New York 13900

Bausch and Lomb, Inc.
635 St. Paul Street
Rochester, New York 14602

Charles Beseler Company
219 South Eighteenth Street
East Orange, New Jersey 08818

Stanley Bowmar, Inc.
4 Broadway
Valhalla, New York 10595

Coronet Instructional Films
65 East South Water Street
Chicago, Illinois 60601

Walt Disney
495 Route 17
Paramus, New Jersey 07652

Denoyer-Geppert Company
5235 Ravenswood Avenue
Chicago, Illinois 60640

Ealing Corporation
2225 Massachusetts Avenue
Cambridge, Massachusetts 02140

Edmund Scientific Company
Barrington, New Jersey 08007

Educational Filmstrips
Box 1031
Huntsville, Texas 77340

Encyclopaedia Britannica Corporation
425 N. Michigan Avenue
Chicago, Illinois 60611

Film Associates Educational Films
11559 Santa Monica Boulevard
Los Angeles, California 90025

Film Strip House
432 Park Avenue South
New York, New York 10016

General Education Inc.
96 Mt. Auburn Street
Cambridge, Massachusetts 02138

General Programmed Teaching Corporation
1719 Girard N.E.
Albuquerque, New Mexico 87106

Guidance Associates
Pleasantville, New York 10570

Hammond, Inc.
515 Valley Street
Maplewood, New Jersey 07040

T. N. Hubbard Science Company
P.O. Box 105
109 Pfingsten Road
Northbrook, Illinois 60062

Indiana University
Audio-Visual Center
Bloomington, Indiana 47401

Jewel Aquarium Company, Inc.
5005 West Armitage Avenue
Chicago, Illinois 60639

National Teaching Aids
386 Park Avenue South
New York, New York 10016

A. J. Nystrom and Company
3333 Elston Avenue
Chicago, Illinois 60618

Polaroid Corporation
Cambridge, Massachusetts 02139

Programmed Teaching Aids, Inc.
3810 South Four Mile Run Drive
Arlington, Virginia 22206

RCA Educational Services
Camden, New Jersey 08108

Scholastic Magazine, Inc.
900 Sylvan Avenue
Englewood Cliffs, New Jersey 07632

Science Research Associates, Inc.
259 E. Erie Street
Chicago, Illinois 60611

Society for Visual Education, Inc.
1345 Diversey Parkway
Chicago, Illinois 60614

Superintendent of Documents
Washington, D.C.

Tecnifax Education Division
Holyoke, Massachusetts 01040

3M Business Products Sales
St. Paul, Minnesota 55101

Tweedy Transparencies
208 Hollywood Avenue
East Orange, New Jersey 07018

Ward's Natural Science Establishment, Inc.
P.O. Box 1712
Rochester, New York 14603

Index